Praise for *Semantics in Business Systems: The Savvy Manager's Guide*

"It has been said that the biggest problem with communication is the illusion that it has occurred. Dave McComb hurts, then heals the world of business and technology management. He skillfully describes a world where miscommunication injures and the future is far too important to invite such injury. McComb offers semantic solutions and ideas of extraordinary value to those who wear the mantle of organizational leadership and decision-making today and tomorrow."

Charles Bacon
President and CEO, Due.Com, Inc.

"This book will help you navigate through the current batch of alphabet soup: XML, SOAP, WSDL, UDDI, and the rest. It gives a clear overview of the territory punctuated by examples. The book declines to speculate on what technologies will win out in the future, but it will make you better prepared to understand them when they arrive."

Peter Norvig
Director of Search Quality, Google

"What is the common theme behind today's hottest Internet technologies: XML, XML schemas, Web services, grid computing, integration, metadata management, ontologies, and the Semantic Web? They all strive to expand and improve how computers interoperate to solve problems, and they all challenge traditional design approaches. These technologies enable more data to be exchanged between more computers, and they increase the complexity and variability of the data your systems must respond to. Thriving in this type of business environment will require business systems to do more for us, and to do it faster and smarter. As data and behavior get more complex, we need more sophisticated techniques to understand and manage the interaction. This is where semantics fits. Semantics is understanding the relationship between data and behavior. The study of semantics provides insights into the techniques needed to manage how our systems will respond.

Great Book! *Semantics in Business Systems: The Savvy Manager's Guide* clearly explains the background and practical application of semantics that managers, architects, and software developers will need to understand how new technologies will impact the next generation of business systems."

Dave Hollander
Chief Technology Officer; Contivo, Inc
Co-chair W3C XML Schema Working Group
Co-chair W3C Web Services Architecture Working Group

D1041241

Semantics in
Business Systems

The Savvy Manager's Guides
Series Editor, Douglas K. Barry

Web Services and Service-Oriented Architectures
Douglas K. Barry

Business Intelligence
David Loshin

Semantics in Business Systems
Dave McComb

Semantics in Business Systems

THE SAVVY MANAGER'S GUIDE

➤ *The Discipline Underlying Web Services, Business Rules, and the Semantic Web*

Dave McComb

MORGAN KAUFMANN PUBLISHERS

AN IMPRINT OF ELSEVIER

AMSTERDAM   BOSTON   HEIDELBERG   LONDON
NEW YORK   OXFORD   PARIS   SAN DIEGO
SAN FRANCISCO   SINGAPORE   SYDNEY   TOKYO

Senior Editor	Lothlórien Homet
Publishing Services Manager	Simon Crump
Editorial Coordinator	Corina Derman
Design	Frances Baca Design
Project Management	Graphic World Publishing Services
Illustration	Graphic World Illustration Studio
Composition	SNP Best-set Typesetter Ltd., Hong Kong
Printer	The Maple-Vail Book Manufacturing Book Group

Morgan Kaufmann Publishers
An imprint of Elsevier
500 Sansome Street, Suite 400
San Francisco, CA 94111
www.mkp.com

Library of Congress Control Number: 2003107038
ISBN: 1-55860-917-2

This book is printed on acid-free paper.

Contents

CHAPTER 11

Extensible Markup Language (XML) 205

CHAPTER 12

Semantic-Based Enterprise Application Integration and Systems Integration 223

CHAPTER 13

Web Services 241

Foreword

For my entire professional life (and I'm getting old enough not to want to admit how long that has been), I've been working in the area of semantics in one form or another. For the past decade, I've focused on bringing this work to business practices and, most importantly, to the World Wide Web. Even before the term "Semantic Web" had been coined and before the World Wide Web was the global phenomenon it has become, a number of us realized that bringing semantics to the emerging web was a natural extension, necessary if we were going to create a web that went beyond simple text documents and got to the *really* good stuff. The fact that you're reading this book today demonstrates the emerging realization that there's a lot more this Web thing could and should be doing—and the technology to get it there is now within reach.

I've been very lucky to live through this transition, sometimes with the true joy of being one of the agents of change, and other times watching in bewilderment as others brought new technologies to the table that I, in my far less than infinite wisdom, predicted were still years away. In the mid 1990s, my research group created a language called SHOE, which stood for "Simple HTML Ontology Extensions." When I started presenting that work, I was often warned, "Stay away from the O-word—these folks won't get it." Two years ago, the World Wide Web Consortium announced the Web Ontology Working Group, and it rapidly became one of the consortium's largest working groups. Nowadays, I am invited primarily to talk about ontologies— quite a change in a brief time.

Similarly, not that long ago, I was warned not to scare the Web Services people by talking about semantics. Now, groups interested in "Semantic Web Services" commission a large proportion of my speaking engagements. The world is changing fast and, for better or worse, *semantics* is at the heart of it.

One of the reasons semantics is so important is that it may spawn some of the first technologies that help us deal with the Tower of Babel that human communication has become. Consider the following thought experiment: A large group of experts and specialists (let's say a thousand of them) from a wide range of fields are brought together by some unnamed billionaire. They are told they have a year to demonstrate a solution to a problem of world significance—cost is no object, and they'll all be highly paid for their time. A year later, it is almost inevitable that the group will have developed into many subgroups, each working on a different approach to demonstrating the solution and each using a jargon that is hard for the others to understand! The group will have splintered into the proverbial blind men approaching the elephant, each subgroup attacking different pieces of the puzzle and each subgroup unable to explain to the others why their approach is obviously the right one.

On reflection, the reason for this is pretty clear. As people start forming communities and attacking the problem, their approaches to the solution will vary. Some will think that a demonstration requires a theoretical proof; some that a demonstration is a proof of concept program or device; some that to demonstrate an effect you must run experiments with groups of human subjects; and others that a compelling demonstration requires "facts on the ground," where it is obvious to external observers that the approach has helped. As these groups separate, they must develop more detailed communication within each subgroup, and the language diverges. New words aren't usually invented, rather new meanings are imposed on the words and phrases already being used (for more on this phenomena, see Chapter 4).

Of course, this problem is just as bad for the many of us who've been working in the semantics area. We've created our own polyglot of tongues that are being used differently by researchers with backgrounds in artificial intelligence, database integration, information retrieval, Web services, Web design, thesaurus creation, linguistics, philosophy, engineering, and many others. Unfortunately, as semantics-based technologies and the Semantic Web become more and more prevalent, the smart manager will have to speak these new languages, and the informed decision-maker will have to understand what is real and what is the inevitable hype that follows "the next big thing." A book explaining the terms used in this new set of worlds, defining them in a plain-speaking way, and clearly making the business case for their use, was clearly needed.

So, join me in thanking Dave McComb for creating such a book. He will explain the ideolect (see Chapter 4) of the semantic practitioner, make the case for the practice, and prescribe the first steps for getting started in this strange new world—and not a minute too soon, because your competitors are also learning about the edge it can give them over you.

So, thanks, Dave. And to you, the reader, welcome to the world we invite you to help us create.

Jim Hendler
Director, Semantic Web and Agent Technologies
Maryland Information and Networks Dynamic Labs
University of Maryland
and Co-chair, W3C Web Ontology Working Group

Preface

This book is intended for people involved with computer software in businesses or other enterprises. I've aimed it at decision makers who are interested in staying on the leading edge as trends develop, but I think there is something here for just about anyone who deals with business software.

Perhaps you picked this book up because, like me, you have been hearing the term *semantics* more and more often in the context of computer systems. You may have noticed that, in most cases, as soon as the term comes up the speaker or author changes the subject: "The rest of the issues are all semantic. Moving on then to . . ."

From the tone and the context it seems as if the speaker is implying one of two things: either "I'm here to talk about a technical problem, and once we get down to the semantics, it's someone else's problem" or "I don't want to get into this, because this is where it really gets complicated." Or both.

I've been applying the study of semantics to software applications for 10 years. In 1992, unsatisfied with the prevailing wisdom regarding object-oriented design, I set off to find something that would be more helpful in guiding our project efforts. What I found initially were a couple of inspiring articles on semantic modeling: one by Richard Hull and Roger King,[1] the other by Michael Hammer and Dennis McLeod.[2] We adopted their philosophies, their approaches, and some of their diagramming techniques, and we applied them to our design work for the rest of the 1990s. We had many

---

1. Richard Hull, Roger King, "A Tutorial on Semantic Database Modeling," *ACM Computer Surveys,* Sept 1987, pp 201–260.

2. Michael Hammer, Dennis McLeod, "Database Description with SDM: A Semantic Database Model," *ACM Transactions on Database Systems,* Sept 1981, pp 351–386.

enlightened breakthroughs pursuing these methods, culminating in the development of what we believe to be the first purely model-driven application architecture.[3]

We had enjoyed a reasonable degree of success applying the insights that we gleaned from looking at the problems from a semantic point of view. However, the truth is that any success we had was quite haphazard. We had no methodology, no school of thought, no framework to guide our way. So in mid-2000, when venture money for product development vanished, we became consultants.

Our aim was, and is, to take what we'd learned by doing, and convert it into approaches, methods, and frameworks that our clients could use to discover and exploit the rich semantic bounty to which they are heirs. This book is one of the products of that change in emphasis. Four of the hottest areas in information systems have a semantic core: business rules, enterprise application integration, Web Services, and of course the Semantic Web.

We believe that semantics is going to become a core competency for information systems professionals in the not too distant future. We also believe that it is not primarily a technology issue, even though there are some complex technologies involved. It is a philosophy layered on top of domain knowledge, applied via technology.

This book was written for managers and advisors who have a high degree of technical aptitude. It does not require much prior knowledge in any of the specific disciplines that we examine, but a general understanding and appreciation of the nature of systems problems in medium- to large-scale enterprises would be helpful. Although the intended audience is at least partially managerial, you'll notice that I did not "dumb it down." I've tried to make things as simple as I can, but at some point we have to connect the dots between the conceptual complexity of the problems to be solved and the implementation complexity of the tools we have at our disposal. I hope I have found a balance that works for a majority of this audience.

In the year since I began this book project I have read dozens of books and nearly a thousand articles and Web sites on topics related to the theme of this book. There is a problem with this type of research. Rather than becoming enlightened, I've merely discovered whole disciplines in which I'm just a beginner. The breadth of my ignorance has expanded manifold. This subject is vast. Perhaps it cannot be mastered in its entirety. What I hope I do here is lay out a framework, where we can see which aspects of the disci-

---

3. See *www.velocity.com* and *www.instancia.com* and U.S. patent numbers 6,006,224 and 6,049,673 for further information.

plines related to semantics come to bear on what topics in the realm of information systems. I think it helps to see how things fit in the bigger picture. For those who wish to pursue some aspect of this further, the appendixes provide a jumping off point for your continued study.

Conventions

When I use the word "we" in this book I usually mean the team I was working with at the time, or currently, because very little of this is solely the product of my efforts.

The code examples in the book are simplified versions of actual code. In most cases the extra syntax or statements that would be needed to make the code executable would distract from the readability and the point I was trying to make, so I omitted them.

Acknowledgments

I have had a great deal of help with the early drafts of this manuscript. A number of people have contributed mightily with voluminous notes, clarifications, and comments on passages that were unclear. You have them to thank, as much as me, that this volume is readable at all. I can't thank them enough for generously giving of their time and expertise. I have listed them in approximately the order of the substantiveness of their contributions. I don't want to diminish anyone's contributions, because every contribution improved the book, but I do want to recognize those who provided measured improvements to the work:

Joram Borenstein
Bob Smith
Simon Robe
Mike Uschold
Kent Swanson
David Hollander
Janice Lawrence
Uche Ogbuji
R. Todd Stephens

Also much thanks to Sean Keaney, Jim Long, Scott Goode, Peter Weinstein, Peter Brown, Simon Hoare, and Lindsay Faussone.

And of course I'd like to thank my editors and publishers at Morgan Kaufman, specifically Lothlórien Homet, and at Graphic World Publishing Services, Beth Callaway.

Future Acknowledgments

I hope to have the opportunity to do a second edition of this book. I would be honored to have your comments, criticisms, or areas of confusion. I would like to have a section for acknowledgment of the major contributors to the second edition.

If you have any comments that would improve the quality of this book for future readers, please contact me at the following email address: SiBS@sementicarts.com
I would appreciate it if you would point out errors, places where you think I may be misleading, or areas that were confusing. If you know of companies that embody any of the concepts I speak of here, please let me know about them.

Finally, thank you for giving me the opportunity to contribute to your professional development.

Dave McComb
Semantic Arts, Inc.
Fort Collins, CO
February 26, 2003

Dedicated to Heidi, Addie, and Eli

For their generous support during the long hours this project kept me away from them

CHAPTER 1

Semantics: A Trillion-Dollar Cottage Industry

The U.S. economy is perched precariously on top of some 200 billion lines of aging legacy mainframe code[1] and a comparable amount of newer, but no less endangered, code on various flavors of servers and PCs. This represents a $3 trillion investment,[2] most of which will need to be replaced over the next decade, at a price more likely to hit $10 trillion.

This is pretty much business a usual, except for two things:

- A large percentage of this cost, perhaps as much as half, is avoidable.

- The approach we take to this next round of replacement will determine how much of this investment really will be an "investment" that will carry forward to subsequent generations of technology.

And the technology on which the realization of these benefits hinges is not really a technology at all. It is a 2500-year-old branch of philosophy, made suddenly relevant by a confluence of developments: semantics.

Consider the following:

- The Mars Climate Observer crashed into the surface of Mars, a victim not of a technical problem, but of a semantic misunderstanding concerning the units of measure used to calculate the thrust.

- Between half and three quarters of the $300 billion spent annually on systems integration is spent resolving semantic issues.

---

1. Rekha Balu, "(Re)Writing Code," *Fast Company*, April 2001, pp. 181–189.

2. Paul Strassman, "End Build-and-Junk," *Computerworld*, July 5, 1999. Available at *www.strassmann.com/pubs/cw/end-junk.shtml*.

- The entire Y2K adventure was two semantic problems piled on top of each other, the first being the simple problem of determining whether "01" meant "1901" or "2001," the second being that the stewards of many of the affected systems had no way to understand the applications in enough fidelity to predict what would happen to them if they were altered.

- The most promising technologies currently offered up to solve our application development and implementation problems—Enterprise Application Integration (EAI), XML, Business Rules, Web Services, Collaboration, and of course the Semantic Web—all share a foundational reliance on semantics.

Perhaps this is enough to whet your appetite, and maybe about now you are wondering: "Where can I buy some semantics?" or "How do I 'do' semantics?" or "Can I implement semantics in my organization?" But that's not the nature of semantics. Semantics is a discipline you apply, not a technology you buy.

Monsieur Jourdain, in Jean Baptiste Molière's play *The Bourgeois Gentleman:*

"And when one speaks, what is that?"

"That is prose, Monsieur."

"What! When I say, 'Nicole, bring me my slippers, and give me my nightcap'; is that prose?"

"Yes, Monsieur."

"Well, well, well! To think that for more than forty years I have been speaking prose, and didn't know a thing about it. I am very much obliged to you for having taught me this."

Like Monsieur Jourdain in the accompanying sidebar, I trust most software developers will be quite pleased to find they have been applying semantics their entire career. Maybe you haven't been intentional or rigorous about it, but in order to get anything at all done in the world of software you have had to deal with semantics.

In this book, we look at every aspect of business systems anew. We also put semantics under the microscope and find out what it is composed of, and how that might guide our further investigations. And we look at our applications and our development technologies from the point of view of semantics, to see how that changes our perceptions.

Before we go any further, let's get this out of the way:

Semantics   Semantics is the study of meaning.

Semantics is often defined as the study of the meaning of words, but we are going to take the broader definition here, allowing for the possibility for meaning to reside in something other than just words. Ultimately, the relevance and success of our application systems rest on what the symbols that we are manipulating inside the computer really mean in the "real world." Of importance is not only what they mean—but do the people, and other computer programs, that deal with the presented information understand and agree with the meaning as implied by the system?

The Semantic Era of Information Systems

Most of what we had thought were the hard problems of computer science and business system development have been solved. We know how to write efficient algorithms. We know the most effective ways to process and store data. We've solved the problems of getting diverse computer platforms to interoperate. We routinely store terabytes (trillions of bytes) of data in data warehouses. The average home has more processing power at its disposal than the largest corporation of just a generation ago. We've connected nearly a billion devices to a single gigantic Internet.

What we're left with, and what I believe will occupy us for most of the next decade or two, are some problems that don't lend themselves to quite as mechanical a resolution. We have to determine what systems we really want to build. We have to find a way to determine what parts of a system need to be made flexible for future change, and which are likely to be stable for a long time. We need a way to understand the systems we already have, before we attempt to change them. We need a way to communicate with trading partners without a long burn-in period. And above all else we need a way that computers can help us with some of the processes that up until now we have thought of as being in the exclusive realm of the human: interpretation, negotiation, and reasoning.

Scratch the surface on any of these issues and you're into semantics. Indeed, for many of these problems, once the semantic issues are resolved, the remaining technical problems are routine. No period of time is exclusively focused on one issue, but there are periods of time when certain issues rise to the top as the issue on which progress will be marked. In the 1980s it was application development: We had an incredible appetite to build computerized versions of all our manual processes. In the early 1990s it was user interfaces: What could we do to make these systems easier to learn and use? Later it was interconnections: If we could just overcome the barriers to getting our customers and supply chains, to say nothing of our internal systems, hooked up, we'd be able to move forward. Currently the top-of-mind issue may be security. But the ground swell is developing that suggests an impending sea change toward a semantic focus that may last a fair while.

This book is meant to be your guide for taking advantage of this shift, at a minimum to avoid overinvestment in projects, technologies, and approaches that are unlikely to stand up to the changes. But for many of you this will be the opportunity to vault ahead of your competitors, either corporately or individually. Let's spend a minute discussing how this book can help with that.

The Plan of this Book

The first third of this book (Chapters 1 through 5) is **descriptive.** It steeps you in what semantics is and explains why something so seemingly simple can be so complex. We deal briefly with the history of semantics and some of the closely related fields, to familiarize you with this rich subject. To make sure that you are clear about what aspects of our semantic conundrum were created by our systems and which were there before computers, we start the investigation of semantics in business systems before the arrival of computers. We then follow the progression through to the present, having looked at some of the areas that have used semantics the most to date: data modeling and metadata development.

The second third of the book (Chapters 6 through 10) is **prescriptive** and covers approaches and methodologies to uncover and make more explicit the semantics that are already implicit in your business and your business systems. This section is built for practitioners who wish to suffuse what they currently do with techniques and approaches that will raise the level of semantic awareness in all their system-related activities. As such we will cover the role of interpretation in semantics, as well as ways to elicit, record, and convey a more complete semantic understanding of the systems and processes.

The last third of the book (Chapters 11 through 15) is **subscriptive** in that it deals with relatively new technologies and approaches, some or all of which you are likely to be subscribing to in the future and each of which has a semantic twist to it. The chapter on XML deals with getting maximum value out of the tags, which have the potential to carry semantic information. The EAI chapter deals with using the study of semantics to overcome the single largest cause of integration difficulty: late discovery of semantic incongruities. To prevent Web Services from re-creating the tangle of point-to-point connections that characterize so many integration efforts, we describe a semantically inspired approach to their adoption. Chapter 14 discusses the Semantic Web, the follow-on project to the World Wide Web. Fortunately, we don't need to explain the semantic aspect of it, but we do cover some of the less obvious technologies that are being promoted along with the Semantic Web, as well as a scenario that should be helpful in visualizing how the Semantic Web will be used.

The book wraps up with a short chapter on getting started in your semantic endeavors, and two appendices: one a set of annotated resources for those who would like to pursue this further, and the other a glossary of the many arcane terms that this subject involves.

A Brief History of Semantics

I'll make this brief, but I do believe there are some developments in the long history of semantics that will still be relevant in the twenty-first century. There are some philosophical arguments that we must be aware of, or we can waste considerable time.

Figure 1.1 outlines some of the key developments in the history of semantics. For our purposes, some of the key developments included the following:

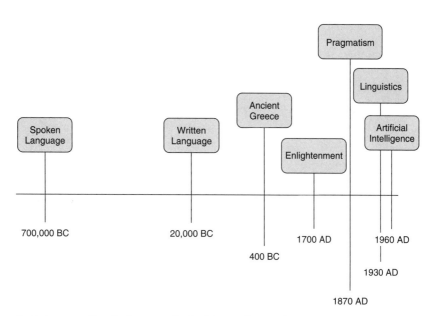

FIGURE 1.1 Key developments in the history of semantics.

- **Spoken language**—Most people rank the use of a spoken language with the development of tools as the defining event that separated our ancestors from the rest of the primate family. Semantically, early man had to make a giant leap from screaming and pointing to the use of abstract sounds to represent things that were not in the immediate environment.

- **Written language**—The advent of writing raised the bar considerably. Tone and gestures were no longer available as adjuncts to aid with the communication of meaning. Perhaps the most important development was the ability to communicate with people who were not present. Syntax and grammar gradually developed as writing became more formalized.

- **Ancient Greece**—The self-reflective knowledge of meaning with which our language was dealing had to wait until the Golden Age of Greece to be articulated. We don't know much about Socrates' formal position on semantics, other than that his famous Socratic method was mostly aimed at finding deeper meaning in thoughts, words, and deeds. Plato's forms are a good representation of his take on semantics. He believed that we infer knowledge of the perfect forms (for example, a circle) from the less than perfect examples we come in contact with (round things). His metaphor of the cave concerns how we can make inferences only indirectly about the essence of things. Aristotle's wide-ranging contributions included a great deal on classification and the establishment of identity, both central concerns for semantics. His syllogisms form the basis of how we can infer knowledge of a particular item, once we ascribe it to a type.

- **The Enlightenment**—The semantic embers burned dimly through the Middle Ages, and even the Renaissance, with its advances in many areas, saw little new work on semantics. Sir Francis Bacon, Sir Isaac Newton, and René Descartes shifted the semantic debate to focus on what could be observed and verified experimentally. A series of later Enlightenment thinkers—Empiricists such as David Hume, Thomas Reed, John Locke, and George "If a tree falls in a forest" Berkeley—debated the role of the human observer as establishing context in a world otherwise devoid of meaning.

- **Pragmatism**—Charles Pierce was responsible for several early and thought-provoking, high-level conceptual ontologies and for a formal approach to logic applied to semantics. William James, another pragmatist, brought us some of the concepts of verification and the belief that nature is to be understood deductively.

- **Linguistics**—By comparatively investigating human languages, and especially anthropologically studying the languages of cultures that have not been exposed to mainstream languages, we have learned a great deal about what aspects of language are likely innate and what aspects are a product of culture. Some of the notable contributors included Alfred Korzybski, Noam Chomsky, Ludwig Wittgenstein, Eleanor Rosch, and George Lakoff, who, although they were not all purely in the linguistic field, all contributed greatly to the twentieth century's advances in this field. In particular, Rosch and Lakoff have contributed some of the seminal work on what constitutes a category or a type, a topic that those of us in the business of information systems use constantly with little understanding of what we are describing.

- **Artificial intelligence (AI)**—The AI community has contributed many subfields to this pursuit, including the formalization of *ontologies* (organization of meaning of terms), *inferences* (how we deduce new information from presented information), and *interpretations* (for example, how a computer system can be built to interpret spoken English).

This brings us more or less up to the present. Yes, I've slighted some groups or individuals, but I wanted to get as much of the flavor for the long history of the subject as possible without becoming tedious. Throughout this rich history, people have been refining fields of knowledge, primarily within the domain of philosophy, specialized to study various aspects of the way we understand our place in the cosmos. In the next section we introduce some of these fields of study as they relate to semantics.

Putting Semantics in its Place

Semantics is not a stand-alone discipline; it is interlocked with various other areas of study that borrow from it, and it from them. If you decide to pursue this study further, Figure 1.2 should be a helpful roadmap or at least provide some idea of where the major boundaries are.

Semantics is about meaning, and about distinguishing things that are close in meaning from each other. As such, we should spend a moment clarifying semantics by distinguishing it from several other terms that are related.

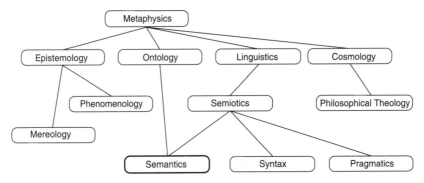

FIGURE 1.2 Semantics in relationship to other branches of metaphysics.

- **Metaphysics**—Metaphysics attempts to explain the fundamental nature of everything, in particular the relationship of mind to matter. This is the more traditional definition and is not to be confused with many popular definitions that deal with occultism and mysticism.

- **Epistemology**—Epistemology is the branch of philosophy that studies the nature of knowledge. This is more concerned with how we know things than with what things mean.

- **Mereology**—You may not think there could be a branch of study devoted to the relationship of parts to wholes, but there is and this is it. The relationship to semantics is a bit complex. At one level mereology informs us whether we are attempting to understand the meaning of something in its entirety or whether understanding its constituent parts is sufficient. On the other hand we need to apply semantics to the many mereological distinctions to understand what it means to include something, be part of something, or contain something.

- **Phenomenology**—Phenomenology is a philosophy based on the belief that reality is composed of objects and events as they are perceived by a human mind. The sophists believe that "man is the measure of all things" and that reality is as we perceive it to be. "Idealism," the belief that the only real world is the "ideal" world and that the physical world is constantly changing, is a form of phenomenology.

- **Linguistics**—Linguistics is the study of language, and generally is a broader concept and includes semiotics. Linguistics also covers many other disciplines not related here, such as the study of sounds.

- **Ontology**—Ontology is a branch of metaphysics that deals with struc-tures of systems. Currently, it is associated with organization and classification of knowledge. It is closely related to semantics, the primary distinction being that ontology concerns itself with the organization of knowledge once you know what it means. Semantics concerns itself more directly with what something means.

- **Semiotics**—Semiotics is the study of signs and symbols as used in language. It is a broader study than just the study of meaning in that it incorporates syntax, semantics, and pragmatics.

- **Syntax**—Syntax as a philosophical study is concerned with first-order logic, or how to construct very basic grammars. It forms the basis for formal semantics.

- **Pragmatics**—Pragmatics is a branch of semiotics concerned with the relationship between language (or signs) and the people using them. How does social context interact with meaning? The word *pragmatic* is often used to mean *practical.* This is an important body of work relative to semantics, especially as we come to apply semantics in a predominantly social context (business).

- **Cosmology**—Cosmology is a subdiscipline of metaphysics that concerns itself with the nature of being. It is concerned with how the universe works, not with what our terms mean. It has come to be associated more with astronomy of late. Relative to semantics, it asks "Why?," whereas semantics asks "What?"

- **Philosophical theology**—Philosophical theology is the branch of metaphysics that deals with the relationship of a deity relative to the phenomenology of the world. It has historically been a trump card in the discussion of semantics, in that the meaning of things we deal with in semantics could be construed to have a meaning not available to us but only to a divine creator.

I hope that this overview is useful in describing a few of the other fields that have been closely related to semantics over its long history.

A Semantic Solution to a Semantic Problem

To get us started, I've outlined a sketch that says, in effect: We have trillions of dollars worth of business software installed and in use. It is obsolete, or soon to become obsolete, and we are going to have to replace it. I make the claim that much of the complexity of these systems has its roots in semantics, as do most of the newer technologies with which we are now presented.

And I further claim that a systematic study of the application of semantics to business systems is our best hope for the future.

But I haven't really made an airtight case for these claims. That's what the rest of the book is about.

I could have opened with the George Jetson-style world of the future where your refrigerator not only talks with your thermostat, but they have meaningful conversations. And your day timer understands the office politics of staff scheduling. But you're not likely to buy that "if only" technologic utopian world.

Instead, I'd rather appeal to that side of you that knows the current state of business systems is a deplorable mess, many times more complex than it needs to be, and yet is still not up to the tasks we have in store for it. You suspect that things could be much better than they are now. You're eager to find out what to do to make things better.

We'll get there, but before we do, let's take a moment to understand how we built this semantic cacophony.

CHAPTER 2

Business Semantics

The reason our business systems are as complex as they are is because we have "paved over the cowpaths."[3] We have set in stone some very arbitrary semantics that have accumulated over a long period of time. I'm not advocating that we change this, but that we understand it. To bring order and reason to the domain of business systems, we have to understand what exists, and how it got that way.

This chapter also shows the semantic basis for "restatement of earnings," which routinely eliminates billions of dollars of value from publicly traded companies. We'll see how semantics can dramatically increase a physician's income, or land him or her in prison. And we'll see where billions of dollars are wasted interpreting things that shouldn't need to be interpreted.

Widespread Abuse of Language

The basic problem with semantics in business, in a nutshell:

> *We put words on everything.*
> *Then we put meaning on the words.*
> *Then we disagree.*

And then of course we computerize it. In this chapter we examine where the semantic disagreements originate. We wrap up by examining contracts, because this is one of the areas where semantics is most troubling for business.

---

3. Sam Walter Foss, "The Calf-Path." Available at *www.xenodochy.org/ex/calfpath.html.*

Business is only possible when there is an expectation of shared meaning between parties. As long as the expectations are congruent, and the eventuality agrees with the expectation, business continues.

Let's begin our exploration of semantics in business by seeing if it is possible to have business without semantics. Perhaps the simplest form of business would be straight barter. Imagine face-to-face barter, based on pointing at the items to be traded. On the surface there is no language exchanged, and therefore no opportunity for semantics.

Even in this transaction some semantics are lurking in the background. Somehow these traders have agreed to a common meaning of personal property, without which the trades wouldn't make any sense. Let this barter example stand as the minimal semantic business.

Replacing barter with buying and selling in a currency adds a layer of semantics. A seller of wheat who wanted pigs no longer had to find a pig farmer who wanted wheat; he or she merely had to find someone who would pay currency for the wheat. But only if the currency "meant" something.

The money, not being useful in and of itself, has another set of expectations associated with it: "What is it worth?" "Is this money genuine?" and so on. The currency has semantics associated with it.

Naming Things Creates the Chance for Misunderstanding

The next important semantic step is replacing physical product identification with product identification by name or description. It doesn't sound like such a big deal, but as long as the buyer is picking out the item he or she wants, there is no opportunity for the two traders to differ in meaning. However, once we begin identifying items by their names we have the opportunity for a disagreement in meaning. Someone buying firewood from another by just pointing at the wood is not going to have a semantic issue with the seller. However, if the seller sells a cord of hardwood, the buyer may have some issues if the buyer thinks that it is less than a cord, or that the wood is not hardwood (or even wood for that matter).

Why It Matters Whether We Call that Mitsubishi Expo a Car or a Truck

Does naming something change it? According to Lincoln's story in the accompanying sidebar, no, naming something doesn't change it. But for all of us some of the time, and some of us all of the time, naming something changes it. You might call a Mitsubishi Expo a car, or a station wagon, or an SUV. You probably wouldn't call it a truck. It wouldn't matter much to Lincoln what you called it. But it does matter to Mitsubishi, and by extension to you. Trucks, in the United States, are exempted from many of the emission and fuel economy restrictions that are placed on passenger cars. This may seem reasonable when you consider that commercial trucks (semitrailers and the like) represent a small proportion of the U.S. fleet and to require them to comply would be a hardship that would hurt the economy.

> Abraham Lincoln once asked a visitor: "If you call the tail a leg, how many legs does a dog have?"
> Visitor: "Five, I suppose."
> Lincoln: "Nope, four. Calling the tail a leg doesn't make it a leg."

The definition of *truck* has been established to include pickup trucks, even if they were used entirely for personal transport. And by building a passenger car with a few extra characteristics, it could be classified as an SUV, which in turn put it in the "small truck" category, and more generally "truck." You change the name of something, and suddenly it has properties and behaviors it wouldn't have otherwise had.

Does an Imaginary Line Affect You?

One of the primary buying criteria for houses, among families with children, is the local school district. The difference between a highly desirable school and an undesirable school can be quite significant. As a result, if there are a limited number of houses (which of course there always are) in a desirable school district, the demand for the houses will drive their value up. The difference in value is often as much as $50,000 to $100,000, and it applies to the owners who have no children as much as to those who do.

> A survey team visits a farm in the very south of Manitoba, and addresses the older woman who answers the door: "Ma'am, we've just completed a survey, and according to our calculations your farm is not in Manitoba as had been recorded, but is entirely within the boundaries of the United States."
> "Oh, thank goodness. I don't think I could have taken another one of those Canadian winters."

The school boundary is an arbitrary definition. It was made up at some point to define a convenient catchment area for the school. Once defined, it creates and ascribes its own meaning. The "Cherry Hills School District" is an arbitrarily defined term, but once established, a change could cost you a large sum of money.

The Semantics of the Past Are about Categorization

Everything other than the immediate present has a semantic component to it, and the possibility of semantic misunderstanding. It is not the time itself (although on reflection the passage and marking of time is a semantic issue in itself) but the fact that anything not at hand must be described using words. This includes description of things (as previously described), as well as actions. The recording of transactions is a semantic issue.

Why Your Physician Is So Concerned about What He or She Calls Your Operation

When a physician takes out your appendix, he or she fills in some paperwork where the physician names the procedures that were performed. The physician has hundreds of thousands to choose from, but luckily most specialists have a few hundred that they regularly perform.

The problem is that there are many different ways to describe the procedure that was performed. Some descriptions have a lot of individual activities ("make abdominal incision," "cauterize appendix artery," etc.); others are "groups" that include all the activities normally encountered in an appendectomy. Still others describe various complications.

What difference does it make, after you've been sewn up and are recovering, what the physician called the procedure? Depending on how physicians code a procedure, their reimbursement can change by as much as 20% to 30%. If they happen to use terms that Medicare or others have deemed inconsistent (for example, coded for a routine appendectomy and also coded for the abdominal incision), this could result in steep fines, or even prison time.

Restating Earnings

Restatement of earnings would be an academic issue if it weren't for the fact that billions of dollars of equity are routinely made or unmade when companies restate earnings, which is nothing more than the reclassification of transactions that occurred in the past, giving them new meaning.

Let's take just a moment and look at the semantics of "restating earnings." These days it is not uncommon for a firm or a firm's auditors to announce that they are "restating their earnings." Wall Street reacts swiftly and unilaterally: The stock price is pummeled. But let's take a look at what really happened.

First, unlike in a very small business, there is no shoe box full of transactions that were suddenly discovered that would change the financial health of a company. (If you were running a bed-and-breakfast that was humming along making a nice little profit, and all of a sudden you discovered your manager had racked up tens of thousands of dollars on your credit card and split, that would be a case of new transactions being discovered.) But in no case that I know of, with publicly traded companies restating earnings, have there been any "new" transactions.

There were sales. There were contracts. There were investments. In each case they were recorded. When they are recorded they are placed into such categories as "current period revenue," "capital expenditures," "contingent liabilities," or "nonmaterial third-party transactions." At some point after the fact, someone else comes along and says, "Hang on, you misclassified these transactions; according to these criteria (from GAAP or elsewhere), these transactions should be reclassified." In many cases these were not miscategorized by mistake. In many cases they involved intentional distortion. However, we should note that in each case the act of restating was the act of recategorizing preexisting events, using criteria that existed at the time.

At some level, we might think that this is purely pedantic hairsplitting. But huge amounts of wealth are being made and lost around semantic distinctions. It may behoove us to find out a bit more about how this really works. It may be possible in the future to bring semantic discipline to this categorization process at the source.

The Semantics of the Future Are about Commitment

Everything we've described up to now concerns the present or the past. But business is about the future. The future adds the dimension of committing to some described action. Most business is the making and executing of agreements and contracts. To realize that contracts are at their center steeped in semantics, we need go no further than the observation that most contracts require expensive legal talent to interpret.

You may feel that you are better served to leave your agreements semantically ambiguous and trust that your lawyers will allow you to interpret them the way you would like them to be interpreted later. But that is a game for people who would rather make their money reinterpreting what they believe was intended when an agreement was entered into, rather than for business people who really had an intention.

Contracts Are the Last Bastion of Intentional Obfuscation

There are 880,000 lawyers in the United States, representing at least a $100 billion industry.[4] One of the most lucrative things they do is draft, interpret, and litigate contracts. If contracts were easy to draft and easy to interpret, they would also be easy to litigate in those fewer cases when they would go to court.

There are tens of billions of dollars at stake to make sure the contracts remain complex. Contracts are not only so complex that a computer couldn't interpret them, but so complex that a layperson also couldn't interpret them.

> "It's difficult to get a man to understand something when his salary depends on his not understanding it."
> —Upton Sinclair

It Is Possible to Have Unambiguous Contracts

It is possible to have unambiguous contracts, even about fairly complex topics. We were involved with a pharmaceutical company once on a deal that would have been worth nearly a million dollars to us. They were quite interested in our intellectual property, and had their team of lawyers draft a contract. (Pharmaceutical companies have many highly paid intellectual property lawyers.) They drafted a 30-page document that was structured like a COBOL program before structured programming was invented: Any paragraph in the document could, and did, override provisions or change definitions elsewhere in the contract. Despite 30 pages of text, most of the essential elements of the agreement were still vague.

---

4. *2000 Statistical Abstract of the United States*, Section 12, "Labor Force, Employment and Earnings," p. 18.

We did a semantic analysis on the contract. The discussion that follows is based largely on that review. It is presented here for two reasons:

1. To show that even the most complex areas of business can be rationally and systematically understood semantically, to great benefit to the participants (assuming they want to understand the agreements into which they are entering).

2. To begin a discussion, which is taken up later in the book, about the potential for having software agents create, negotiate, and abide by contracts without having to involve humans (let alone lawyers).

What Is a Contract?

The classic definition of a contract requires that to be enforceable, a contract must have four things:

1. *Mutual assent*—There is evidence that both parties agreed to the contract. Usually this is accomplished by reducing the contract to writing, but it's not always necessary.

2. *Legality*—The subject matter is legal (you can't make a contract to kill someone).

3. *Capacity*—The parties are of age of majority, not insane, and so on.

4. *Consideration*—Each party had some sort of economic incentive to participate in the contract (this is why there are often contracts where the consideration is a few dollars).

If you dig a bit deeper, you'll find some semantics behind these considerations, and if you look at particular types of contracts, you'll see more, as we discuss next. Figure 2.1 is a highly simplified semantic representation of a sales contract.

Frequently, we would label the lines between the concepts, but in this case we can discuss it without labels. Most real estate, personal property, and intellectual property contracts that I have examined have a structure very similar to this. At their heart they contain the following elements:

- **Parties**—All contracts have parties (most have two parties), and the first part of most contracts identifies the parties. Semantically we're interested in what a party is (there are several types, including individuals, married couples, and corporations, as well as ad hoc groups that come together just for the contract) This is generally pretty straightforward, but there are some complexities regarding whether the maker of the contract can bind the parties, and whether the parties have the

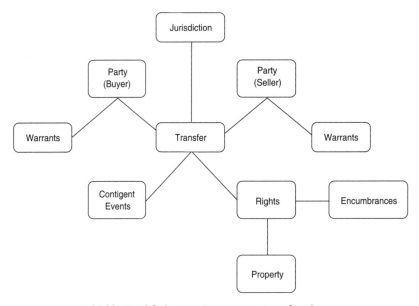

FIGURE 2.1 A highly simplified semantic representation of a sales contract.

capacity to contract. There may be an agent contracting on behalf of a party, and this must be spelled out. (There are some three-party contracts, but typically not in property transfer.)

- **Jurisdiction**—Contracts have jurisdictions, either explicit or implicit. Jurisdictions are legal contrivances that establish some of the semantics of the contract, as well as set up procedures for dealing with disagreements or violations of the terms of the contract. This also establishes whether the transfer is taxable, and if so, the contract must specify who bears this.

- **Property/subject**—Most contracts deal with something, and in most cases that something, the subject, concerns products or services. Sometimes the subject is the item to be exchanged, but sometimes the description of product or service is a contingency regarding the entire contract. As mentioned previously, the subject must be legal. But we are more concerned with what the subject is. Is it a piece of real estate, a widget to be purchased, or what? Usually the subject is property, which might be personal property, real property (land and buildings), or intellectual property (songs, movies, software, trade secrets, etc.).

- **Rights**—It's apparent that intellectual property contracts deal with what rights in the intellectual property are conveyed with the contract. For instance, a recording contract may indicate that the rights to the songs in the subject have been transferred to one of the parties to the contract. We talk about taking possession in real estate contracts, but really you just acquire rights to the property in question—perhaps the right to occupy or the right to drill for oil.

- **Transfer**—The lawyers call it *conversion*, but it basically means some physical good or right was transferred from one party to another.

- **Encumbrances**—If a right has restrictions, we call these *encumbrances on the right*. For instance, your land may have encumbrances for easements. Your employment contract may restrict what you can do while working for your employer and for a period of time afterward (called *noncompetes* and the like, but they are really encumbrances on you).

- **Warranties and obligations**—Most contracts deal with the future, and some obligation that is placed on each party. For instance, in a purchase contract the seller is obligated to deliver the goods and the purchaser is obligated to pay.

- **Contingent events and remedies**—Either of the parties may fail to execute on their obligation. Contracts often specify what remedy the other party has in that case. In the absence of specific remedies, generally the jurisdiction provides default remedies.

Other types of contracts (service contracts for consulting or employment, etc.) are scarcely different in structure, except that the property is a promise to deliver a service over some time period in the future. Typically the warranties concern noncompetes, confidentiality, and so on. An insurance contract substitutes indemnity for transfer and concerns itself with which set of circumstances are recoverable and for how much.

Contracts that Even a Computer Could Understand

It may sound a bit strange, but in the not too distant future we are going to need to have contracts that can be interpreted by software programs. A product by Business Integrity shows how this type of technology can be used to generate contracts.[5] The IntelX product saves the parameters and generates a traditional text contract. It doesn't take a huge leap to imagine

---

5. IntelX—Document Assembly Software. Available at *www.business-integrity.com/IntelX.html.*

applications interpreting the contract based on the parameters in the model. It is going to be far easier if these contracts are structured in a highly regular fashion, similar to the way the contract in Figure 2.1 is structured.

How Semantic Clarity Can Overcome Even Intentional Obfuscation

Contracts are complex, at least in part because the legal industry, by its very nature, tends to create agreements that require additional interpretation. Semantics in general, and in the future, semantically inspired tools and applications, force the composer of the contract to structure the content of the contract in a way that removes ambiguity. The way this process works is primarily through forced choice selections. If a contract concerns the transfer of rights in a program, exactly what rights are being transferred (select one from a limited list of choices)? Through this process, whether you do it by hand or with a tool, you arrive at an agreement with a small fraction of the ambiguity of a normal contract.

Summary

Business has been dealing with semantic complexity for as long as there has been business. These issues are not trivial. Companies lose billions of dollars of market capitalization from the semantic exercise of reclassifying transactions that have already occurred. Lawyers earn billions of dollars creating agreements that make it difficult for the parties to understand to what they are agreeing. There are now more "trucks" sold every year than "cars" in the United States because calling a "car" a "truck" has all sorts of economic advantages.

Semantics is a big deal, whether or not we computerize our semantic notions. Until we computerize them, we still have humans at every step, performing myriad semantic interpretations and translations. However, some very strange things happen when we computerize our businesses, as we see in the next couple of chapters.

CHAPTER 3

The Process Side of Business Systems

As we saw in Chapter 2, business is virtually impossible without semantics. Everything we do involves conveying meaning at some level. However, at the same time it is the semantics—or, more precisely, near but not perfect matches in meaning—that make business so difficult. Each industry, subindustry, and market tends to create its own semantics and its own definitions of what terms mean. Of course it doesn't stop there, because we've built systems on top of these semantics.

In this chapter we explore how automating a business process "bakes in" some set of semantics. We'll see how the roles of humans and applications as semantic interpreters interact, and specifically how getting more precise about the semantics in our systems is a double-edged sword: It allows more opportunity for automation while at the same time making those systems more brittle and hard to maintain.

Semantics in Business Systems

What happens when we turn a semantic conversation into a business system? In an operative business system, "Semantics = Data + Behavior."[6] As portrayed in Figure 3.1, the semantic aspects of the behavior and the semantic aspects of the data are constantly chasing each other.

In this chapter we examine what happens to behavior (or process) as it is turned into a business system. But first a quick definition: A business system is a formalized capital investment in a business process. We will return to the capital investment aspect of this later in the chapter.

---

6. Dave Hollander, personal communication.

FIGURE 3.1 Semantics = Data + Behavior.

Business system   Business system = Business process + Capital investment.

A business process is a special type of process that deals with information. Per some of the leading standards in this area, the process may be executable (such as in a program that can be run on a computer) or it may be descriptive (such as a process not being executed directly by the process management system).[7] Let's examine this in more detail, because the nature of the flows and the interaction of humans and computer programs is where the richness of business process lives.

A Business System Deals with Humans and Applications

When an application designer/developer builds an application, he or she "bakes in" a certain amount of semantic knowledge. When the designer/developer decides to have a field in the inventory system to maintain average cost per item, we say that the application now has this semantic. Users of this system don't get the opportunity to redefine this. They communicate with other users through the application at this level of granularity.

This is self-evident. However, there are four distinct arrangements that each have different implications for semantics. The key distinction is whether (really to what degree) the semantics are maintained or interpreted by which player (the human or the application).

---

7. BPEL4WS business process execution language for Web services. Available at *www.106.ibm.com/developerworks/webservices/library/ws-bpel/*.

Semantic origination refers to the case in which either the human or an application system is aware of the semantics of messages it produces.

Semantic interpretation means that the recipient human or application is semantically interpreting the message being sent (Figure 3.2).

Primary Semantic Flow

This gives us four primary semantic flows: human to human (H2H), human to application (H2A), application to human (A2H), and application to application (A2A).

Consider the case where, as in Figure 3.3, the message and the semantic meaning of the message are not traveling together. This occurs whenever context or some form of agreed and implied labeling of the message is needed to understand what the message means. When someone says "200 at 22" we don't know whether this means 200 shares of a particular stock at $22 per share, 200 people in room 22, or any of hundreds of other potential explanations.

Substituting either end of the communication illustrated in Figure 3.3 with humans and applications gives us the four types of interaction shown in Figure 3.2.

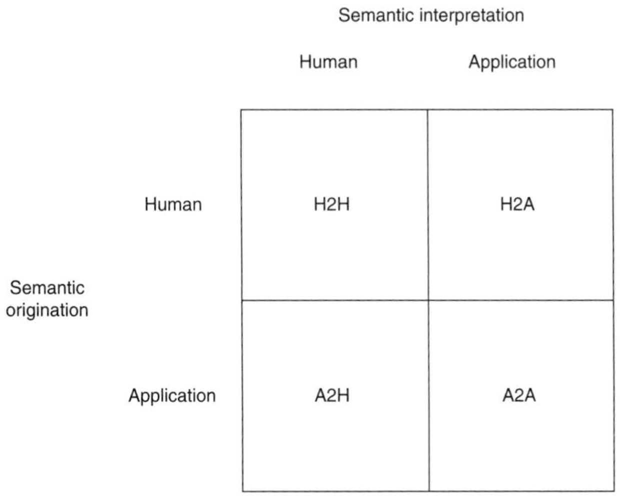

Semantic interpretation

	Human	Application
Human	H2H	H2A
Application	A2H	A2A

Semantic origination

FIGURE 3.2 Semantic interpretation and origination.

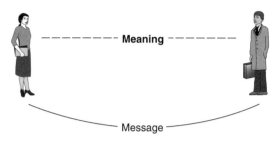

FIGURE 3.3 Message and meaning.

H2H

Our most flexible business systems involve human semantic interpretation at both ends. We won't refer to normal face-to-face communication here because there is no capital investment in the transmission of the message or the semantics.

- **Telephone**—A telephone is a classic and extreme example of this. The telephone system does not interpret any of the conversation being held on it. It is simple to deploy because it relies on the humans working out what they mean to complete a transaction.

- **Email**—Email is another classic H2H system. The email system knows nothing of the messages passing back and forth.

- **Office productivity**—The same is true of word processing and spread-sheets. It should be apparent by now that word processing is widely used in part because it has left the issue of semantic interpretation to the users. Although spreadsheets appear to have more rigor, very few enforce a semantic on the user. (This, by the way, is part of the reason why a study found that approximately 30% of the spreadsheets [in a sample] that were being used in business contained errors.) The align-ment of data into columns and the choice of which cells to total and which factor to use in multiplying are strictly determined by the author of the spreadsheet; the spreadsheet itself has no semantic knowledge beyond knowing the difference between a number, text, and a date.

A2H

Application to human means the application has a semantic model of the mes-sages to be communicated and that the intended recipient is a human who will interpret them.

- **Flight monitors**—Airline arrival and departure monitors at airports are a good example of an A2H system. The application has a strict semantic to the information contained in its database. The semantic is well enforced (you never see data in the wrong column, or invalid data where it could have been prevented). The application knows if a flight is late (it has a semantic definition of "late"—basically a revised estimated time of arrival later than the planned arrival time, or an estimated arrival time earlier than the current time, and no notification of arrival) and will mark it appropriately.

- **Reports**—A report of the state of a database, whether it is graphic or not, is an application, usually with a precise semantic meaning, that moves from the application to the human, for a human's interpretation.

- **Imaging**—Computer-aided design (CAD) systems and systems to create images for entertainment, such as Pixar, are A2H systems, because there is no real interaction on the human's part.

- **Content Web sites**—A Web site that is primarily structured content (e.g., a stock portfolio tracker) has a semantic meaning that it displays for the user (20-minute delayed stock price in the second column, annualized gain in the third column, etc.). However, it imposes nothing on the user's interpretation and interaction with it.

The airline monitor is an extreme example. What makes it extreme is that its placement and the current time are sufficient to imply what you would normally enter as parameters.

The more normal case (Web sites, reporting systems, etc.) is that you enter data or navigate to get to some subset of a vast database to find information.

One of the many implications is that the data you enter as parameters to your query are not meant to be saved. These data are not like transaction data, which you typically expect to be saved to a database; the data you enter are meant to advance you from one point to another or to narrow down the data you are viewing. This is true even if the data are entered on a form, which by its appearance might normally be used to make data persistent. (Interestingly, the current explosion in data storage volume is largely coming from capturing navigational data that was previously not captured—click stream analysis, for instance).

H2A

Human-to-application systems take potentially unstructured data from the world of the human and "massage" it to comply with the semantics of an application that is on the receiving end.

- **Card punch**—The clearest and most extreme example is card punching. In the early days of data processing the primary input mechanism was punched cards. But you couldn't put just anything on the punched card; you had to enter information in exactly the columns the system expected, using the coding scheme the system used. Typically this was a two- to three-person job. One person might interpret what had happened in the world (what the customer ordered, or how many hours the employee worked on a given day). This person typically had the job of converting this information into a rigid format and converting it to the appropriate codes (1 for straight time, 2 for overtime, 3 for shift differential, 4 for holiday double overtime, etc.). The second person had the job of punching (typing) this information onto the cards (one transaction per card). Often a third person was involved to do the second person's job a second time to make sure the errors introduced at this stage were minimal. The cards were then submitted to the computer, which interpreted each one based on a program. The computer determined which cards were valid and would be allowed to be processed and which cards were invalid and would be rejected. It should be apparent that the program is the final arbitrator of semantics of this system, and it will impose itself on the inbound side of the transaction.

- **Data entry**—The system needn't rely on off-line data entry to be an H2A system. Any system that is predominated by human data entry is primarily an H2A system.

- **Form-oriented systems**—Most applications that have been deployed over the last 20 years have been dominated by their form-based data entry screens. This has been such a popular interface metaphor that it is used even when the system is displaying information that it already has stored. The aspect that makes it most obvious that the system is imposing semantics on the human is in the area of "constrained choice"—for example, when a drop-down list requires you to select from one of the system's choices, the system has imposed its semantics on your interpretation of whatever you are recording.

The implication of H2A systems is that what you have entered is stored and may later be retrieved. Further, some validation is done when information is entered, so there must be an error detection and correction procedure. The stricter and more consistent the validation, the more you can rely on the integrity of the system.

H2A2H

Most traditional applications (e.g., client/server) are a combination of H2A (the data entry part) and A2H (the information that comes back on queries or reports or the display of entity information that is already stored). I call this an H2A2H application, as shown in Figure 3.4.

- **"Green screens"**—Green screens were the original H2A2H applications. For most of the last 30 years we've been overlaying H2A and A2H systems in the same user interface. Starting with most of the mainframe on-line terminals (3270 and the like), there was typically an input form on the screen. If you wanted information about a record that was already there, the system brought up a similar (often identical) form with the data already populated.

- **Client/server**—When interactive graphic systems became available, most of them continued the form-oriented interface, similar to the 3270, but with nicer graphics and mouse control.

- **Model/view/controller (MVC)**—With the advent of object-oriented development came a new slate of patterns and paradigms. The MVC paradigm recognized the separation of the model (the semantic content of the system) from the view (the A2H presentation) from the controller

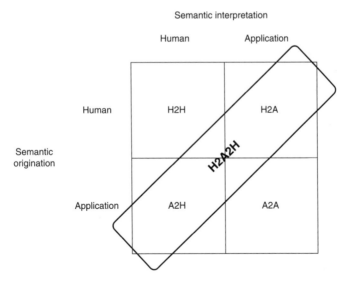

FIGURE 3.4 Application types based on their interactions.

(the H2A portion where the user could change the state of the model). However, the generally accepted practice was to overlay the view and the controller to give the user the illusion of direct manipulation of the model.

A2A

In an application-to-application system, the semantics are known by each of the applications and little or no human intervention is needed to get them to communicate.

Of course, humans set up the semantic structure so that the applications can communicate, but at run time there is generally little or no need for humans to semantically interpret the messages. The four main A2A strategies are shared databases, systems integration, electronic data interchange, and messaging.

- **Shared databases**—One of the most popular ways to have two applications communicate is to have them share all or part of a database. Rather than have explicit messages traveling between the applications, each application waits until it needs information and reads the appropriate database record. This is perhaps the simplest way for two applications to communicate and has led to ever larger combinations of applications, to the point where they become unwieldy to implement or maintain.

- **Systems integration**—Systems integration is a general category and in some respects is an industry in itself. For our purposes it is the art of interfacing two applications by constructing custom programs that read data from one system, reformat it, and write it to another. There are many technologies for this, but they all share the problem of linking the interface program with the semantics of both systems with which it communicates. As a result, any change to either system not only potentially affects the interface, it may invalidate the message transmission entirely.

- **Electronic data interchange (EDI)**—In many industries electronic data interchange (EDI) has become a common way for two applications to communicate. (Generally EDI is used only for applications that are not owned by the same organization, because the overhead is usually greater than the effort to do something else, such as shared databases or systems integration.) With EDI the message is unintelligible without the spec. The message is typically a string of characters and numeric fields separated by delimiters or of fixed length. The spec supplies all the semantics for the message. The specs go through a long review period and are published for conforming members. In effect, the semantics are defined by a consortium and are generally rigid.

- **Message-based systems**—In message-based systems, some of the semantics are carried in the content of the message body. XML is the best known and most popular example of this. Each field in an XML message is enclosed in a pair of tagged delimiters. The tags in turn are defined in a reachable location (either in the header of the message or at a reachable site on the Internet). Currently most of the XML standard messages are defined by consortia and are relatively rigid, but recent developments have created the potential for semantic discovery and bootstrapping (discussed later in this book).

Combining A2A with H2A and A2H

Until now the world of A2A communication has been completely separate from the H2A2H world. Developers built user interfaces for their applications and systems integrators built interfaces between applications, and never the twain shall meet.

With the advent of XML it is now potentially feasible for humans and applications to begin sharing message definition. A well-crafted A2A message can be wrapped for human consumption.

Some Applications Are More Semantic than Others

An application is the automation of a business process or processes in software. Applications range in size from the very large to the very small. An example of a very small application is a Web Services system that performs only a single function, such as currency conversion or freight rating.

Semantic Precision

Semantic precision refers to the resolution or precision of the terms in the definition of the system. For example, a business system that has a field for "date package arrived at sorting station" has a higher degree of semantic precision than one labeled "date." In the latter case it is often possible to derive an equivalent degree of semantic precision from the context; whether this is something that the application can do or whether it is up to a human interpreter is discussed later in this chapter.

Figure 3.5 shows a spreadsheet field with weak semantic precision. All that is known about field B3 is that it is currency, which could be U.S., Canadian, or Australian dollars. We infer that this number represents some form of income by its alignment and proximity to the label on A3, but we have no idea what kind of income this is (gross income, net income, etc.), nor do we know whose income it is (this is information you might glean from the file name, or worse, from the directory you found this spreadsheet in). We don't know which year this concerns, or when fiscal March starts and ends.

Figure 3.6 shows a section of a tax return that contains high semantic precision. The form identifies itself, the individual to whom it refers, and each category of income.

Semantic Referent

A *referent* is a person or thing to which a linguistic expression refers. An *extensional referent* is one where the exact physical instance is referred to directly. So "Joe Jones" is an extensional referent, as is the person with Social Security number 123-45-6789 whose tax return is excerpted in Figure 3.6.

An *intensional referent* is one where the final referent is not known until some rule or other indirection is resolved. Examples of intensional referents are "the president of the United States" and "the claim adjudicator for back injuries." In each case the expression must be evaluated at some time after it was originally written, with some new context (in the case of the president, with the current date). Generally, we construct these things such that they will be resolvable at the time they need to be evaluated, but that is part of the design skill.

	A	B	C
1		March	
2			
3	Income	$5,500.00	
4			
5			
6			
7			

FIGURE 3.5 Spreadsheet.

FIGURE 3.6 A small portion of a tax return.

Semantic Precision—Range

Semantic precision typically ranges from low to high along a gradient:

- General type (text, number, date, etc.)

- Type with contextual qualifier (invoice date, return reason, etc.)

- Type with context and subcontext qualifier (invoice prepared date, package cleared customs date, etc.)

- Intensional referent (admitting physician, user default location, etc.)

- Extensional referent (Dept 47, St. Anthony's Hospital, etc.)

Semantic Veracity

Semantic veracity refers to how closely represented data agree with their referents. Although they might coincide, veracity is not the same as precision. Generally, you cannot determine the veracity of data from only the data; you must also examine the system that collected and verified the data and determine how the data are used (context).

A news Web site that provides a field for address when subscribing to its mailing list has very low veracity. The site does not verify the address data, and there are no obviously negative or positive implications for providing correct information. On the other hand, a pharmaceutical Web form has higher veracity because medications must be ordered for the right person and sent to the correct address. Some effort is made to verify information, and there are obvious negative and positive consequences to providing correct information. Federal Express has a high level of veracity on address information. It delivers packages to addresses and requires a person to sign for the package, indicating validity and verification of the address.

Typical levels of semantic veracity include the following:

- None

- Syntactic validation (only numbers in a numeric field)

- Validated to controlled vocabulary (against a list of state abbreviations, American Medical Association [AMA] procedure codes, etc.)

- Validated to other internal information (part number is in our inventory, quantity on hand greater than 0)

- Corroborative validity checks (zip code is in state, procedure corresponds with diagnosis)

- Closed loop with intended originator (email verified by round trip)

- Audit—third party verified information through independent means (letters sent to creditors, transcripts verified from university, etc.)

Semanticness of Applications

The preceding was to establish what we mean by a system (or application) being "more semantically aware" than another. If a system has a high degree of semantic precision (the information in it is semantically tagged to a specific level of discernment) and the system has gone through procedures to ensure that the information is valid, the system is considered to have a high level of semantic awareness.

In Figure 3.7, a low-precision and low-veracity application is semantically unaware. This isn't necessarily bad; in fact, it is much more flexible.

Trusted documents have a high degree of veracity, but it is left to a human to interpret the data. A classic example is the county real estate recording office.

The computer industry got a lot of its bad reputation from systems that allowed garbage in and provided garbage out (GIGO). Often this was at a high degree of precision. This is where we have gathered a lot of detailed information with very little validation.

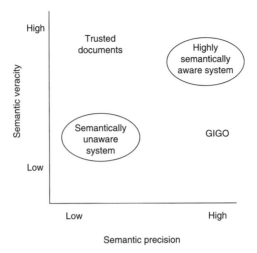

FIGURE 3.7 Semanticness of applications.

In summary, an application is semantically aware if it has high precision and high veracity.

The System Is Made Up of Processes

Pretty much all the standards concerning work flow and collaboration agree that work flow is made up of processes. However, the standards assume that all processes are information-related processes.

Because a great deal of the original work on business process management, business process engineering, and just-in-time manufacturing concerned the physical movement of goods along with the alignment of business processes, it seems necessary to bring that viewpoint back and put business process in the broader context of processes.

Business Process Is One of the Fundamental Types of Processes in a Business

Of all the processes that typically occur in a commercial enterprise, six are fundamentally distinct in the type and treatment of raw materials and human input. These are semantically valid distinctions because they allow us to ask appropriate questions and execute specific behaviors against them, depending on what their type is. For example, we might ask of a conversion process what its yield is, where it would not make sense to try to evaluate the yield of a personal service.

In an organization, these processes are taken on with an intent that each will help achieve the aim of the organization. For most commercial organizations, this includes making a profit. Most organizations engage in some constellation of activities on a fairly repetitive basis, and they have another set of activities that they do on a much more infrequent basis. Most attempts at improving a business (whether they are the old-fashioned "efficiency studies," "process reengineering," or "supply chain management") all involve attempts to eliminate, combine, or improve the efficiency of these processes.

Process

We refer to *process* as activities carried out intentionally within an organization (Figure 3.8). This is an abstract category (more on categories later), but it makes it convenient to talk about things that cover all the subcategories.[8]

Extraction

By *extraction,* I refer to activities where the raw material is in nature. These include mining, oil and gas drilling, farming, fishing, and hydroelectric and solar power generation. These processes are at the beginning of all supply chains.

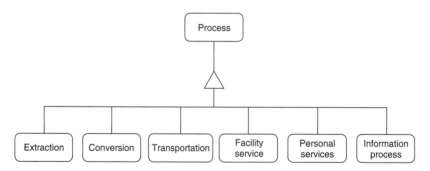

FIGURE 3.8 Primary types of business processes.

---

8. U.S. Census Bureau, "North American Industry Classification System (NAICS)." Available at *www.census.gov/epcd/www/naics.html.*

Conversion

Conversion is a generic term referring to changing a physical material from one form to another. It includes all manufacturing operations (smelting, extruding, cutting, milling, bending, welding, plating, assembling, etc.), as well as construction activity and fossil fuel power generation.

Transportation

Transportation consists of activities involved in physically moving goods, or electricity, from place to place without converting them. This includes transportation via truck, rail, ship, air freight, pipelines, and power lines, as well as intraplant movements such as conveyors and cranes. Power distribution and communication infrastructure are included in this category.

Facility Services

Facility services are services performed on a building, or occasionally other physical property, such as cleaning, guarding, landscaping, preventive maintenance, and so on.

Personal Services

Personal services are activities in which the raw material is another person, including haircutting, health care, travel, and entertainment.

Information Processes

Information processes use information or intellectual property as primary inputs and outputs. These include traditional data-processing tasks, as well as professional services such as selling, advertising, financial services, consulting, and design. Most of the internal processes in a business, such as data entry, scheduling, approving, and routing, are information processes.

The Flexibility of the Process Is a Semantic Property

Some processes are more flexible than others. That is, they can be changed more easily. There are specific semantic properties to the process and the way the process is configured that make it either flexible or rigid. We'll explore this distinction soon, but first let's return to the capital investment portion of our definition of a business process.

Formal Investment in the Process

Generally, there is an expectation that the capital investment will pay off by the repeated application of the process. The payoff may be in efficiency, quality, risk reduction, or control. The repeated application of the process comes from running similar transactions through the same process.

Capital Investment (Not the Accounting Definition)

Accountants have rules for capitalizing expenses. Per the rules and conventions, much of what is truly capital in nature does not get capitalized.

For our purposes, a capital investment in any process is a one-time investment that is expected to positively change some output variable (Figure 3.9).

To make capital investment clear, assume that your staff was carving wooden umbrella handles by hand. A capital improvement might be to introduce a spinning lathe (Figure 3.10). The lathe might be foot powered with a rest against which the worker could lean a cutting tool.

In this case, the investment in a lathe is a capital expense that is expected to improve the handle maker's productivity, as well as the consistency of the finished product.

Note: Even at this level, it is the expectation of similar transactions (in our example the need for round handles) that inspires the capital investment.

FIGURE 3.9 Cutting with more *(left)* and less *(right)* capital investment.

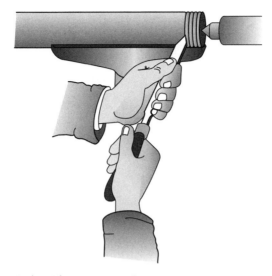

FIGURE 3.10 Lathe with some automation.

If all subsequent orders are for square handles, the investment in the lathe will be unrecovered.

"Hard" or Rigid Automation

Let's take the lathe investment to its next level. Say you've noticed that most of your orders are coming in for a particular style of beveled handle. As a result, you commission a machinist to build a rig that cuts the particular shape automatically (Figure 3.11). All the worker has to do is put the block of wood on the shaft, turn the machine on, and take the handle off when it's finished.

This capital improvement makes one shape and it makes it very well, but it is not easily modified to make another shape.

Getting Back to the Business System

Business processes are similar to the cutting process being employed by the carver and the lathe. The capital investment runs the gamut from the time invested in setting up forms and procedures and training people, to out-of-pocket capital outlays for computers and software systems to automate part or all of a process.

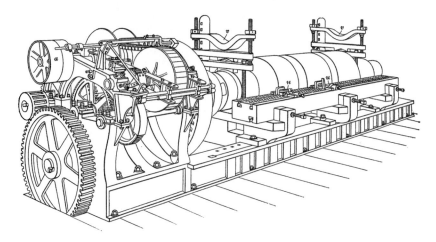

FIGURE 3.11 Hard automation lathe.

Manual or Automated

It is not necessary that a process be automated to make it a business system. Before 1950 and the advent of computers, all business systems were manual business systems. Many parts of most businesses still rely on partially or completely manual systems. A recent Hurwitz study indicated that only 10% of all enterprises have fully integrated even their mission-critical business processes.[9]

Manual Does Not Mean Ad Hoc

Although a business system can be a manual process, it is not true that any process is a business system. Ad hoc processes are not business systems. Suppose you run a small retail business and one day you spill coffee on a customer. If you offer him $5 to cover his dry cleaning bill, you have executed an ad hoc process. There was no formal procedure to handle this event; however, you acted appropriately in the best interest of the customer. Although it was a good idea, it does not make it a business system because no capital investment has been made. If you decide to formalize such cus-

---

9. "Hurwitz Group Study Finds Only 10% of Enterprises Have Fully Integrated Their Most Mission-Critical Business Processes," December 4, 2001. Available at *www.hurwitz.com/press/pressrelease_ebpiresults.htm.*

tomer service behaviors, create procedures and tracking forms, and train your staff, you have created a business system.

Semantics Determine How Hard or Soft Process Automation Is

We develop this argument more fully later in this book, but for now, take it on faith:

> *The semantic precision is what determines what is rigid and what is flexible about business process automation. The more precision, the more rigidity.*

Note that sometimes you need more precision, but it comes at a cost of increased rigidity.

Efficiency versus Flexibility

In general, just as in manufacturing, the less flexible system tends to be more efficient. But this is not always true. Much of this book is about how to have it both ways.

What Does It Mean for an Application to Be Semantically Aware?

It will probably be at least 10 to 20 years before applications are really semantically aware. By this I mean applications that could pass a variation on the Turing test and have a basis for "knowing" what they are doing.[10] At some point we will be able to program our systems with a finite number of basic concepts and allow the system to work out the meaning of new information from the clues at hand, much as a human does. In the meantime, we'll use the following definition:

Semantically aware application   An application is semantically aware to the degree to which the application designer imbued the application with semantic precision and veracity.

---

10. Alan Turing, a pioneer in computer science, proposed a test for artificial intelligence whereby if a machine could fool a sufficient number of human interrogators often enough, it would be considered sentient.

Summary on the Process Side of Business Systems

We've taken a look at the process side of business systems. We examined how humans and applications work together to create what we call a business system, and we looked at some of the issues that make a system easier or harder to change.

The reason we did this is because the business systems that we have automated are all programmed representations of processes, as described here. How flexible they are, how hard they are to change, and how resilient they are to changes in their environment are all products of how their semantics were implemented.

We introduced two concepts, semantic precision and semantic veracity, as being central, but only just touched on them. They are part of a broader issue: How do we name things, how do we form categories, and how does this affect the systems we build? This is the subject of the next chapter, which is the bridge between semantic behavior and semantic data.

CHAPTER 4

Terms: Vocabulary, Taxonomy, and Ontology

Terms and facts are semantic constructs. They are meant to have meaning that is shared by anyone who uses them. Unless the producers and consumers of information agree, the information will be meaningless.

In any large business system, we are going to be dealing with thousands to tens of thousands of discrete terms. These terms are chosen from a much larger palette of possible terms for that industry and context.

These terms have to be defined and used consistently by all the people and all the programs that access data referred to by the terms. If this is done casually or haphazardly, or, as is more often the case, with the mistaken notion that "everyone knows" what these terms mean, chaos results.

This chapter examines where that chaos comes from and the role that taxonomies and ontologies play in helping make definitions more precise and more commonly understood. The chapter concludes with a discussion on how categorization relates to behavior, and the power of dynamic categorization.

We will see that the assignment of a business occurrence to a particular concept in a vocabulary or ontology is an act of categorization, which is how knowledge is applied in business systems.

This chapter examines business vocabularies and the various ways they are organized. We then go beyond that and begin a discussion on categorization and how the mere act of categorizing something (with the aid usually of a taxonomy or an ontology) gives rise to a great deal of knowledge.

The Range of Possible Terms and Meanings Is Vast

There are so many terms in a traditional business system that few people will ever understand even a single domain in its entirety. A subtle problem this introduces is that designers often don't realize what they don't know. They interview users, learn some terms, and design their databases, but often they have only reviewed the tip of an iceberg. To acquire some insight into the size and complexity of that iceberg, we're going to review business language and vocabularies in detail.

Language

Language can be defined as a set of symbols and rules used to convey information. We tend to associate the broadest language groups with nations, either current or historical; so, for example, we have the English language and the Spanish language. We believe that two people who speak the same language will be able to communicate with each other. Human languages are often called *natural languages* to distinguish them from *computer languages*. To understand natural language, we'll take a look at vocabulary (the universe of words and how those words are typically used).

Vocabulary

Vocabulary is the set of symbols (words) to which a given language has ascribed shared meaning. There is little overlap in vocabulary between any two of the major natural languages. For example, there are very few words in traditional Chinese that mean the same thing in English.

Of course, not everyone in a language group has the same vocabulary. First there is the issue of subsetting. Virtually all people in a language group understand and use some small subset of the total vocabulary.

We're on slippery ground here, because there is (surprisingly) little agreement on what constitutes a "word" and therefore on how large a vocabulary is. I have used several sources to create Figure 4.1. An unabridged dictionary typically has 1 million or more entries. The *Oxford Unabridged* has 1.5 million entries. Abridged dictionaries typically have about 100,000 entries. Estimates vary, but the median vocabulary is thought to be around 60,000 to 70,000 words for a college graduate, and far less than half that for a student entering high school.

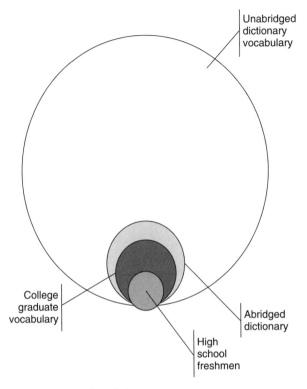

FIGURE 4.1 Relative size of vocabularies.

The first thing to note is that somehow society works despite the fact that most of us understand between 2% and 4% of the vocabulary we supposedly share. What is not shown here is an extreme skew toward the most commonly used words, which is where we do most of our communicating. I'll use the same scales as we explore specialized vocabularies in business, but for now, file this away.

Dialect

A dialect is a regional variation of a language, distinguished often by differences in pronunciation and vocabulary. For instance, we might speak of a Cockney British dialect. As we will see, businesses (more specifically their industries) create their own unique dialects.

Idiolect

No wonder there are a million words in the English language. We have words for things that at first blush don't appear to need a word, such as "idiolect." An idiolect is your own personal dialect. We are amused by Humpty Dumpty, because at least he was up front about his own personal language (see sidebar). Your idiolect is the set of words and patterns you use in your speech and writing. I assume that this is useful when trying, for example, to figure out who really wrote Shakespeare's plays, but we will find some other interesting uses for it when we look at personally developed systems.

> "When I use a word, it means just what I choose it to mean—neither more nor less."
> —Humpty Dumpty in *Through the Looking Glass*

Business Vocabularies, Professional Jargon, and Job Security

Each industry has its own vocabulary and its own dialect. Each business then typically creates its own vocabulary, which is added to its industry. Professionals in their own domain often create specific terms as a shorthand for unique procedures and to keep trade knowledge secret and thereby enhance their job security. In this section we'll look at a few of the ways in which businesses create their own vocabularies, to get an idea of the challenge we have in front of us if we hope to resolve the frequent confusion and errors that unrecognized semantic differences create for the unwary analyst. The major ways these semantic differences have developed include the following:

- Overloading of common words
- Created words
- Nonword identifiers
- Double words

Overloading of Common Words (Homonyms)

The area that has the most potential for misunderstanding is the way different industries, or different parts of the same industry, use common words differently. In the case of made-up words, or nonwords, there is little chance of misunderstanding. There is nonunderstanding, to be sure, but you generally know that you don't know what is trying to be communicated. With the case of common words, though, there is frequent opportunity for believing that you understood what was being communicated, when in fact you did not.

The lexicographer calls these *homonyms.* We'll go over a few examples to make this clearer.

Capacity, to most of us, is how much something will hold; it is a measure of volume. For educators, though, it is the ability to retain knowledge. In the legal profession it is either your role (in your corporate capacity) or whether you are of the age of majority. For electrical engineers it is the phenomenon whereby an electric charge is stored.

A **router** is a device that carves rounded edges on molding for wood-workers, a person who lays out a circuit board in the electronics industry, an electronic device that dispatches packets in the data communications industry, and a person who stocks vending machines in the snack food industry.

A **credit** is a rebate to a customer in the retail industry, a negative balance in the banking business, an acknowledgment in the entertainment industry, a free game in the arcade business, revenue to an accountant, an arrangement for deferred payment in any industry that allows payment over time, an assessment of your "loan-worthiness" in the mortgage industry, and a source of honor and distinction in plain English.

A **lot** is a batch in the pharmaceutical industry, undeveloped land in the real estate business, a place of business for the movie industry, a quantity of stocks in the stockbroking business (odd lots), a method of choosing for sports teams (drawing lots), and a large number for most of us.

I've performed several random samplings of industry lexicons, as well as industry-specific documents, and found that the number of overloaded words is about 10% of the total. That is not really a lot, except for two things: In most cases they are some of the most commonly used words, and they are the most likely to lead to confusion because there is not a direct clue that you don't know these words.

Created Words

There are a wide variety of created words. Some are brand names, some borrow from foreign languages, many are acronyms, some are technical terms, some are shortened from chemical names, and so on.

Interestingly, many technical terms borrow from dead languages (Greek and Latin are the most popular), which I think is partially to avoid the over-loading of common terms. "Microscope" is literally ancient Greek for "small see." We could call the device with two sets of lenses that allow us to enlarge the image of things less than a millimeter across a "small see," but not only does that sound somewhat childish, it opens up a great deal of confusion by overloading these common words.

Figure 4.2 is an example I pulled randomly from the middle of a defense industry contract. I boxed words that are not words in the English language and underlined words that are words (or more often phrases) in the English language, but whose use in this context is not the most common English definition. Most of the boxed words (acronyms in this case) are defined elsewhere in the document, but this still means that they must be learned and added to your own idiolect before you can understand the contract.

I'm also going to include in this category Latin words or phrases, as well as any non-English phrase that isn't in the common lexicon. *Black's Law Dictionary* has 25,000 entries. I took a random sample of 10 pages and found that one third of the entries were Latin.

Nonword Identifiers

Companies create identifiers for their products and services. Sometimes these identifiers are nonmeaningful numbers, but often the authors create identifiers that have some mnemonic intention and that often become "words" of their own within the company. Laws and statutes are also identified by "nonword words" (Figure 4.3).

The nonword words in Figure 4.3 are boxed.

A more prosaic example would be "Miller Brewing Company ordered another 6 tons of C545" as a sensible statement in a company that has a product called "C545" that might be purchased in ton increments and has enough of a relationship with a company (or person) they call "Miller" to be on a first-name basis.

```
C-9  Administrative Procedures.
C-9.1  PCR and Comment Sheet Control and Tracking:  the CTOCU AU shall
establish A PCR and Comment Sheet control/tracking log.  The control log
must include the date the PCR or Comment Sheet is forwarded to the
contractor and the date of final disposition or incorporation into the
TO.  PCR control numbers (AFTO Form 27, Block 3) shall be assigned as
specified in TO 00-5-3, and will be used to control and track the
processing/progress of the PCR
```

FIGURE 4.2 Excerpt from a contract.

D.C. Code § 16-2354(b); accord Matter of K.A., 484 A.2d 992, 997-998 (D.C. 1984).

FIGURE 4.3 Excerpt from a legal opinion.

"We'll process the return as soon as we get a 1040" is a phrase that most of us understand, but only because of the pervasiveness of the IRS.

Compounds

One of the trickiest areas is compounds, in which two or more words are combined to create a new meaning.[11] Similar to overloading of common words, these can create the illusion of understanding where there is none.

For example, knowing what the word "world" means and what the word "series" means doesn't necessarily mean we know what the World Series is. We might even think it was a sequence of planets.

"Brown shoe" is knowable if you understand the two words that make up the phrase. On the other hand, "white shoe" might mean a shoe that is colored white, or a prestigious investment banking firm.

The problem, both for humans and for systems attempting to interpret language, is determining when a phrase is really a word—or, more correctly, determining when several words together stand for one semantic thought.

Although the examples in Table 4.1 may seem contrived, I did a randomized sample in three technical dictionaries and found that over half of all the entries were compound words. On the other hand, only about 20% of my abridged dictionary consists of compound words, and nearly half of those are people and place names.

TABLE 4.1 SOME SAMPLE COMPOUND WORDS.

Phrase	Apparent Meaning	Actual Meaning
Claim check	Review of a claim	A piece of paper that lets you retrieve your property
Conduit theory	Plumbing principles	Justification for why mutual funds are not taxed on their profit
Passive exercise	Oxymoron	A physical therapist moves your muscles for you
Fill or kill	Sounds military	Stock order that must be traded immediately or it is withdrawn
Hot dog bun	Rear quarter of a warm canine	Bread roll for sausage

11. For a more complete treatment of this subject, see Barbara Rosario, "Classification of the Semantic Relations in Noun Compounds." Available at *www.sims.berkeley.edu/~rosario/projects/NC_ling181.pdf.*

This has several implications for business semantics. Most important, there is no such thing as one word/one meaning. There is so little overlap between industry and business that the key issue is establishing and maintaining context for all our communications.

An Estimate of the Amount of Overlap between Industry and Business

It is truly mind boggling how many specialized terms there are. Let's start with a few statistics and see what we can determine.

- **Retail (grocery and other)**—A grocery store has 50,000 stock-keeping unit (SKUs). (SKUs indicate the level of detail at which inventory is kept. For example, Coca-Cola in a 16-oz bottle is a different SKU than Coca-Cola in a 26-oz bottle.) Most products come in two sizes, so there are really 25,000 products. Most items have two brands that provide virtually identical products, bringing the total down to 12,500. Assume there are 5,000 distinct products in a grocery store. Clothing stores typically have 5,000 to 10,000 SKUs, but given that many of the SKUs are for size differences, there are probably fewer than 2,000 names to learn. In either environment, what this means is that new hires will have to expand their vocabulary by 10% to 20% just to go to work.

- **Any industrial manufacturer**—Most manufacturers of goods produce thousands of different products, which they of course name (usually with numbers, but the best-selling ones get "real" names). Most manufacturers also have an explosion of part numbers and names to learn about their suppliers' parts, and for all intents and purposes their customers become "words" in their vocabulary ("Is the Budweiser order ready yet?" "Will Crampton's be late?" etc). In addition, each subindustry has a vocabulary of several thousand business terms that must be relearned because they have been overloaded.

- **Legal**—As mentioned previously, *Black's Law Dictionary* has 25,000 entries. Some of these are English words with different meanings, but *Black's Law Dictionary* does not repeat English words if the legal definition is the same as the common definition. (Incidentally, for hundreds of years dictionaries included only "difficult" words; it was assumed that the reader knew the definition of common words.) My guess, from dealing with lawyers, is that most lawyers know at least a majority of the terms in such a book. Let's give them 15,000 and realize that they spent a great deal of their time at law school adding legal terms to their vocabularies.

- **Medical industry**—I believe the medical field is the winner in this sweepstakes. There are 50,000 drug names and about as many "procedure codes" (shorthand for what a physician does to a patient). SNOMED (a lexicon of pathology and disease, which has been expanded to cover procedures) covers 137,000 clinical terms. The granddaddy of them all (that I'm aware of) is the Unified Medical Language System (UMLS), weighing in at 776,940 concepts, with a total of 2.1 million concept names (UMLS indexes many foreign languages). I'm continually amazed at what a relatively high proportion of these terms many clinicians know. Let's give them 50,000 and conclude that half of their vocabulary consists of medical terms.

How Do These Vocabularies Relate?

Unlike the earlier examples we considered, which were primarily subset/superset relationships between the vocabularies, these are distinct enough that they are not subsets of each other. This creates all sorts of problems for ontologists and language interpreters. We'll discuss this situation later, but for now we'll chalk it up as part of doing business: Each industry has its own dialect, and each business has its own idiolect.

The dark circles in Figure 4.4 represent the specialized parts of each domain's respective vocabularies. They clearly share a lot of the high school freshman's vocabulary, which they don't include in their specialized dictionaries.

Definitions Are Not Enough

Occasionally a project will create a glossary to define the terms and how they will be used in a particular system. This is a useful start, but it doesn't go nearly far enough. First, the glossary may suffer from "design time" artifacts. A design time artifact is one that is used while the system is being designed, but generally is ignored by users and maintainers of the system. Second, the glossary may suffer because it is created by inexperienced workers. Third, the glossary may suffer for the same reason that more general-purpose glossaries fall short.

Glossaries and vocabularies are not designed to distinguish or group closely related concepts; they are designed to "define." As a result, most are

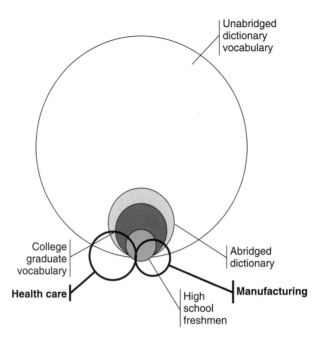

FIGURE 4.4 Two industries' vocabularies, barely overlapping.

full of ambiguity and overlap. In effect, this leaves much of the defining up to the reader.

Let's look at an example. What is a cash commodity?

Cash commodity   Commodity that is owned as the result of completed contract and must be accepted upon delivery. Contrasts with futures contracts, which are not completed until a specified future date.[12]

I took this definition completely at random. It is better than most, especially in that it makes the distinction between a closely related concept (futures contracts) and this one. However, it also points out most of the problems with relying on vocabulary alone.

First, just what is "cash commodity?" I'm guessing it is real physical stuff, such as a truckload of barley or lumber. It doesn't sound like it is cash or has anything to do with cash, except that you presumably had to pay some cash

---

12. John Downes and Jordan Elliot Goodman, *Dictionary of Finance and Investment Terms,* New York: Barron's Educational Series, Inc., 1998, p 85.

to get this stuff. If this is the case, it is only tangentially related to a futures contract, which is a contract, and, although it has a reference to a commodity, it is, strictly speaking, just a contract.

But the interesting questions come when you start asking yourself: Do either or both of these represent an obligation? Is it the same kind of obligation? With the cash commodity it is likely that the obligation is already discharged. Or is there another way to indicate whether it is or is not an obligation?

We could chalk this misunderstanding up to my personal ignorance of commodity trading lingo, except for the following:

- I'm going to guess that more than 95% of the readers of this book also do not understand what is meant by "cash commodity," even given the definition quoted earlier.

- Even experts on a given subject disagree about nuances of definitions.

- We have an expectation, or a hope, that future agent-based or Semantic Web–based systems will somehow be able to make inferences about things like this in the future, but if we can do no better than define our terms as definitions in glossaries, we won't get there.

Clearly, underpinning most of our business systems, we need some better way of defining what we mean than just vocabularies and glossaries.

Taxonomies: Ordering a Vocabulary

A taxonomy is a form of organized vocabulary. Classically the organization is hierarchic, based on some attributes of the things being classified. The most common example is the organization of living things into kingdoms, phyla, classes, orders, families, genera, and species, based on similarity of physiologic traits as shown in Figure 4.5.

Most complex vocabularies have several taxonomies that help users find unfamiliar terms. For example, SNOMED is a medical taxonomy that organizes more than 100,000 terms into a taxonomy that first distinguishes topography (concepts related to functional anatomy), morphology (changes in shape and structure of biology), function (physiology), living organisms, chemicals, and so on. Each major heading then breaks down into subheadings specific to the major head (topography breaks down into the major organs, etc.). We seem to be innately drawn to creating taxonomies. Something about the way we are wired suggests that we want to create hierarchic categories to organize things into simple maps of the world.

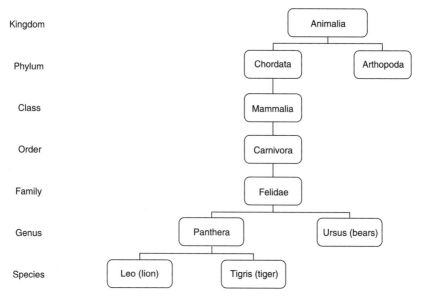

FIGURE 4.5 The biologic taxonomy showing some related species.

Although some of these taxonomies are useful, many just get in the way. Here are a few examples that will give you an idea of the useful and the dysfunctional in taxonomies:

- North American Industry Classification System (NAICS)—This taxonomy replaces Standard Industrial Codes (SIC).

- Chart of accounts—Every organization has a chart of accounts.

- Service codes—A taxonomy of types of professional services used by a procurement group.

NAICS (Formerly SIC)

NAICS is a six-digit code for categorizing kinds of business by product or process used. NAICS is a successor to SIC, which had become dysfunctional: "The present SIC, although designed as a hierarchy, in fact does not provide a hierarchical structure useful for analysis. Past revisions to the SIC seem to have focused on adding (or eliminating) 4 digit SIC's rather than reviewing the overall structure of the classification structure."[13] This underscores the fact

---

13. "Economic Classification Policy Committee Issues Paper No. 2," Feb. 8, 1993. Available at *www.census.gov/epcd/naics/issues*.

that the people who restructured the SIC codes knew what they were up against; alas, the new structure, although an improvement, still has areas where the structure is not useful for analysis. For example, "Reproduction of software" is subsumed under Sector 33, "Manufacturing," which was meant to group things that had similar use of resources and other aspects so that they could be combined.

Chart of Accounts

A chart of accounts separates business expenditures into categories of revenue, expense, asset, and liability so that managers, investors, and tax authorities can review business activity. Other than a default chart of accounts that comes with some accounting systems, there is no standard chart of accounts.

At the highest level the chart of accounts is usually meant to be a taxonomy: All of the accounts under the revenue are revenue accounts, all those under expense are expense accounts, and so on. Most large organizations have charts of accounts that are made up of five to eight independent (orthogonal) taxonomies, which gives them a coding block that is usually 60 to 150 characters long. There are potentially billions of combinations, but usually only a few hundred thousand are used.

Orthogonal The dictionary definition of orthogonal is "at right angles." In computer and taxonomy circles it has come to mean expressing two (or more) things such that they can vary independently of each other. For example, if we were going to create a car taxonomy, "make" and "model" would be part of the same taxonomy, because they are not orthogonal. "Fuel efficiency" and "safety" might be two orthogonal dimensions that could be used for taxonomies.

The problems show up three to five levels into the hierarchies (this seems to be a pattern with taxonomies). The first few levels may break expenses into a few broad categories: costs of sales, selling costs, general costs, and administrative costs. As you get deeper into the hierarchy, a tension occurs between the things that seem to be most closely related (e.g., should the printing costs for brochures be near the salary of the graphic artist who designed them?). Eventually the account structure becomes highly compromised. This is because the meaning of the subcoding relationship is not held constant as you descend the hierarchy. (It *is* held constant in the phylum/order/family hierarchy, which is probably why it is held up as a canonical example.)

Service Codes

Both the NAICS and the chart of accounts are taxonomies that people have put a lot of time and effort into making as useful as possible. However, most of the taxonomies we come across are casually assembled by one or more individuals who think that a particular hierarchy might be useful. From my observations, such taxonomies rarely take long to outgrow their original purpose. We recently came across a hierarchy that had 10 pages of documentation to group professional services into a dozen categories for the purpose of slotting vendors into the type of services they offered. The longer you studied the taxonomy, the less certain you were about what each category meant. One category was "technical architecture," but as you read the subcategories and descriptions, you noticed that they had added in specific technologies that were covered in other categories, such as project management. As a result the category headings were only vague indicators of highly overlapped categories. Most vendors tried to get in as many categories as they could, because if someone needed their services they couldn't be sure which category they would pick for the search.

A smaller but more typical example of a code set, Figure 4.6 is an example of a taxonomy of order status codes from a well-established office supply vendor.

Status Key

CAN—This item is cancelled.

CBO—This item is on backorder.

CMP—This item has been transmitted to a retail location for delivery.

DLV—This item has been delivered.

INV—This item has been received and is awaiting final in-stock verification.

OPN—This item is in stock and transmitting for fulfillment.

PIP—This item is being packaged for delivery.

STG—This item has been packed and is staged for delivery.

TCL—This item will be delivered by a local retail location.

FIGURE 4.6 Order codes.

When you first read it, it appears to be sensible. We'll return to this later in the chapter to find out why what sounds like a good taxonomy isn't always very useful. For now, just consider this as a casual taxonomy.

The Trouble with Taxonomies

We build a lot into the analogy between taxonomies and genus/species. The main reason the analogy breaks down and taxonomies don't work as well as we expect them to is that biology has two interesting characteristics not shared by other domains to which we apply taxonomies:

- **Evolution**—All biologic organisms descended from common ancestors. The closer any two species are to each other in the descent tree, the more similar they are likely to be. (Modern cladistic analysis[14] has adjusted Lineas's original categorization, but not drastically; the similarity of biologic function and morphologic structure tends to re-create their evolutionary history well.)

- **Unique location**—There is little ambiguity about where a species belongs. Both bats and birds fly, but a brown bat about the same size as a sparrow is no more closely related to it than a duck is to a dog. However, our made-up taxonomies rarely have this kind of rigor.

The biologic taxonomy is consistent in its use of the link meaning "is a kind of." A taxonomy that is consistent in this way is powerful, because the application can imbue items lower in the taxonomy with attributes higher in the taxonomy.

Often the most useful taxonomies are the simplest. My experience is that, with the exception of the biologic taxonomy, as a taxonomy grows its integrity shrinks. So one suggestion is to keep taxonomies small, single purposed, and orthogonal (see definition earlier in this chapter).

A powerful taxonomy has the following characteristics:

- An item categorized to a lower-level category is also a member of all its category parents.

- An item categorized to a category may also be treated as one of its supertypes (although it needn't be).

- There should exist some set of rules that would allow a classifier to determine whether any of the subcategories are appropriate (we call these "rule in/rule out" criteria).

---

14. Cladistic analysis is a technique for determining the relatedness of species from their DNA and other clues, rather than from their physiologic features alone.

In the linguistic study of semantics, words or concepts that are related by the "inclusion" relationship (the "isa" relationship) are called *hyponyms.* Hyponymy is a good basis for taxonomies, because all of the subsumed concepts can still be treated as the parent.

However, taxonomies do not have a rich enough semantic for most of our uses. That is where ontologies come in.

Ontology: A Web of Meaning

Tom Gruber was affiliated with Stanford University when he penned this oft-cited definition of an ontology:

Ontology　"An ontology is a specification of a conceptualization."[15]

Gruber points out that ontology has a rich history in philosophy, where it deals with the subject of existence and is often associated with epistemology. His definition, originally for the artificial intelligence community, has to do with concepts and relationships, and in particular how agents (computer programs) can commit to sharing definitional information.

Typically ontologies are "graphs" or networks, rather than hierarchies, although this isn't a requirement. More important, ontologies have a much richer set of relationships, constraints, and rules, such that we can reason about the information in the ontology, and, by extension, reason about items that have been classified by the ontology.

Medicine has been a very rich field for the development of ontologies. UMLS is a large but not extremely rigorous ontology of medical concepts. Its primary use is to help with searches, so having a large graph of interrelated concepts is helpful rather than cumbersome. The UMLS ontology has several almost orthogonal taxonomies for categories such as "anatomy" (the thigh bone's connected to the knee bone…), "system function" (circulatory, digestive, etc.), and "morphology" (shape; e.g., distended, elongated, etc.). The UMLS ontologies contain rich sets of cross-taxonomy relationships, such as "the heart valve is a part of the heart," "the heart is a member of the circulatory system," "the heart is in the thorax," and "the heart is above the diaphragm."

WordNet is a public domain lexical database. It serves as a base for many ontology projects that deal with natural language and lexical issues; however, it is not an ontology in itself.[16]

---

15. Tom Gruber, "A Translation Approach to Portable Ontologies," *Knowledge Acquisition, vol 2,* pp. 199–220, 1993.

16. The WordNet database can be downloaded at *www.cogsci.princeton.edu/~wn/.*

Ontologies are now relatively easy to build, and thousands of them are springing up. This isn't a problem, except that there is a desire to have ontologies use each other to extend their range of knowledge. One factor that will greatly accelerate this is the creation and acceptance of what has been called an "upper ontology."[17] The basic idea of an upper ontology is that it would be a base ontology that could be shared across many domains. In other words, if other ontologies were expressed in terms of the upper ontology, an agent would only need to know the upper ontology to be able to work out most if not all of a subscribing ontology.

How Categorization Informs Us

Let's consider something closely related to taxonomies and ontologies, but in practice not quite the same thing: categorization. We categorize things all the time. Sometimes we use preexisting taxonomies to categorize things, as in the previous examples, but often we just make up ad hoc categories ("That was a 'boring' movie," or "It was a 'chick flick'"). More interesting is when this happens and is codified in an application.

Application systems are littered with categories. Although a typical application system might have dozens of essential business entities, each business entity will have hundreds to thousands of data entities, many of which represent different categories. The real explosion of categories, though, is not formally documented. Almost every "if" statement in a program implies a category of some sort.

The fragment of code in Figure 4.7 states that we have two categories of purchase orders (cheap and expensive, say) and that we treat them differently (one has to be approved, the other does not). Often we have multiple tests to complete before we take some action. For example, we might test whether a task's actual start date is greater than 0 (and maybe less than today, but let's assume that validation was already in place) and whether the task's actual complete date is 0; if so, we categorize this task as "in progress" and deal with it in a particular way. We may make further tests; for example, if the estimated completion date is less than today, we may categorize it as being "late." If the

```
If (purchase_order_amt > $100,000) then hold_for_approval = "Yes"
```

FIGURE 4.7 Code that implies a category.

---

17. IEEE has a working group at *http://suo.ieee.org/*.

earliest completion time equals the latest completion time, we may categorize the task as being "critical."

Check this out yourself. Almost the only if statements that don't represent hidden categories are those that are testing whether a field is blank (in order to move it to another field) or those testing the end of an array or collection.

A complex application will have tens of thousands of such categorizations. This means that the business system has a vocabulary, if you will, of tens of thousands of distinctions, things that we treat slightly differently. This, by the way, is the main reason that large organizations have more complex systems than small organizations have. At one level, all businesses make stuff and sell it, or deliver service. You may have wondered why a large company needs a system that by any measure is one or two orders of magnitude more complex (they have more screens, more reports, more lines of code, etc.). Some of that is to handle volume, performance, and reliability, but by far the greatest percentage is due to the complexity introduced by making more and more distinctions of this sort.

Categories and Taxonomies

We can categorize things without taxonomies, as we alluded to in the previous section. However, categorizing and taxonomies are complementary because, rather than having a flat structure of terms for which we must find some sort of match, a well-constructed taxonomy allows us to categorize things a layer at a time, which compensates for our innate ability to hold only a limited number of things in our mind simultaneously.

Categories and Inheritance

One of the things that object-oriented methodologies do well is to replace "if . . . then . . . else" logic with subtypes, which is a major improvement. The categorization comes out of the code, where it is largely hidden, and into the class hierarchy, where it at least has some visibility. However, there are still some major problems with using class-based inheritance as a categorization mechanism.

Object-oriented systems do not deal well with multiple inheritance (a network hierarchy instead of a strict tree). Many of the languages don't support it, and even those that do get caught because once a class is inserted into a multiple inheritance location, it can no longer avail itself of its parents' specializations.

An even more pressing problem with object-oriented systems is that objects don't change classes. Once an object is created (instantiated), it will remain an instance of the type of class that created it until it is destroyed. As we will see in our discussion of categories, this is not how we want our categorization schemes to work.

What Categories Tell Us about Items in the System

If all we know about an "item" is that it is a "part" (a manufactured item), we can't make many assumptions about it. We can't even ask many intelligent questions. We can, for example, ask what it weighs. We can ask where it is. Maybe we can ask for its description, or its cost, but not much else.

However, if we categorize it as a "bolt" we suddenly have many more questions we can ask or values we could set. What is its length? Diameter? What material is it made of? How many threads per inch? What is its tensile strength? Head shape? And so on.

If we categorize it as a carriage bolt, we now know even more. We know it has a round head and a square shaft. We know it is at least 2 inches long. How do we know all this? We use a few properties to classify an item into a category, and then from that category we obtain additional information "for free."

Categorizing things accomplishes two fundamental purposes:

1. It allows us to infer some information (based on the category) that we didn't access directly.

2. It allows us to pose and answer new sets of questions relative to the item.

Prototype Theory

Another problem with categories is that they don't have the nice edges we wish they did. As Eleanor Rosch and George Lakoff point out, the way we typically create categories is based on what they call "prototypes" (unfortunately, this has almost nothing to do with what application developers call "prototypes.").[18]

People create categories (Rosch and Lakoff dealt extensively with what they call "folk categories"—things that almost everyone categorizes, such as

---

18. Eleanor Rosch and B. B. Lloyd, "Principles of Categorization," *Cognition and Categorization*, Hillsdale, NJ: Lawrence Erlbaum, 1976; George Lakoff, *Women, Fire and Dangerous Things*, New York: Basic Books, 1990.

birds and dogs), and each category has some members that are exemplars of the category and others that are fringe members. For example, most people have robins and sparrows as exemplars (prototypes) of their "bird" category. They accept that penguins and ostriches are members, but they do not share all the ascribed properties that have accreted to their "bird" category (fly, eat worms and insects, make nests, etc.). They deal with these fringe members using a sort of "fuzzy logic" in which members on the fringe either do not have certain properties or have unknown properties (i.e., the less central a member is, the less certain we are about the properties we ascribe to it).

One area where practitioners and systems developers have made some interesting progress is medical diagnostics.

How We Use Rule In/Rule Out to Adjust Categories

A technique that is popular with diagnostic physicians is the concept of differential diagnosis, or rule in/rule out. For example, a patient may show a certain set of symptoms that may suggest a disease assignment, such as gestational diabetes. (Disease, by the way, is a crude medical categorization of the patient's health status.) As they refine a diagnosis, doctors look for tests that would "rule in" (confirm) or "rule out" (disqualify) the diagnosis. For example, chest pain, shortness of breath, and pain in the left arm may indicate heart attack; a positive thallium stress test, however, rules out heart attack as a cause of the symptoms. As Figure 4.8 indicates, there may be contraindicating symptoms to severe acute respiratory syndrome (SARS).

I believe this is the general case, and not the special case. We see it on the business side of health care when certain combinations of diagnosis and procedure are ruled out by the insurance companies. They are, in effect, telling doctors that although they claim to have performed a qualifying operation, it was contraindicated (ruled out) by diagnosis or other tests. I am advocating that all categorizations have this characteristic. In the short term it may still be human-only interpretation of these rules, but eventually we expect that systems will be able to look through a patient's data, rule in or rule out certain categorizations, and suggest tests that would more precisely subcategorize them.

Dynamic Categorization

There are other ways to model systems using more precise taxonomies, more elaborate ontologies, or object-oriented hierarchies arranged differently. But that's not how we think. We may make more semantic progress when we

"The symptoms are consistent with SARS except for the third eye."

FIGURE 4.8 Diagnosis can be perplexing. (Original artwork created by Brian Loner, Fort Collins, CO, 2003.)

realize how people think, and any categories they are likely to make are going to be subject to the prototype effect; therefore we may want to embrace it, rather than work around it. Two design approaches embrace this style of dynamic categorizations: metapatterns and associative databases. In *Metapattern, Context and Time in Information Models*, Pieter Wisse[19] argues that the current approach of classifying items by what class they belong to (e.g., in an Object Oriented system) is far too restrictive and suggests an approach whereby instances can morph their behavior by shifting "contexts." Each "context" is like a class, except it is dynamic and additive. Simon Williams's "The Associative Model of Data"[20] suggests that all properties can be treated as "associations," which can vary by instance and are thereby not restricted to the properties set up in schemas or classes.

---

19. Pieter Wisse, *Metapattern, Context and Time in Information Models*, Boston: Addison-Wesley, 2001.

20. Simon Williams, *The Associative Model of Data*, Bucks, Great Britain: Lazy Software Ltd, 2000.

State and Status

State and *status* are terms that are used freely in business system development, often without giving a lot of thought to what they mean. As we'll see, they are a special case of categorization.

For many people, *state* means "state machine," as in "finite state machine" or "finite autonoma." The assumption with a state machine is that there are a limited number of discrete states and a countable number of transitions from one state to another. In Figure 4.9 we show a state machine for a garage door opener. In this case, because the transition between open and closed is not instantaneous, and because the interesting differences are what happens when a car or a child breaks the electric eye beam near the flow, we model "opening" and "closing" as states. This gives us some assurance that we know what is going to happen. It also lends itself to a table-driven structure—the arcs, or actions, can be entries in a state table, letting the system know what the allowable transitions are from any given point. As such, it is tempting to want to apply this to anything that appears to exhibit statelike behavior.

People like to think that things such as purchase orders move through a similar set of discrete states. However, for use in business systems, this concept suffers from two flaws:

1. Most states in business systems are not discrete; in fact, most of the things that we want to move from state to state can be in multiple states simultaneously.

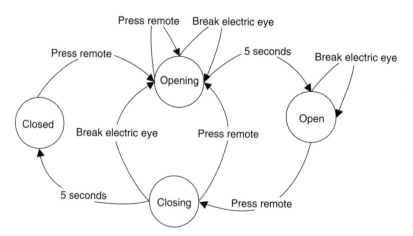

FIGURE 4.9 Garage door state machine.

2. Most business systems do not obey the rigid constraints of a state machine when moving from state to state.

So you may start with purchase orders being statelike: They are approved, issued, partially received, completely received, and closed out. At each stage, you have a set of allowed behaviors (you can change the quantities before the purchase order has been issued, but not after; you may have some ability to cancel before it is received).

But what happens if you want to use state behavior to answer questions such as the following: Have we received an invoice for the item? Does this purchase order require additional approval? If so, by whom, and how do we know this? Where will the process stop while we're waiting for approval? Do we need a letter of credit? Have there been changes to this purchase order? Somewhere along the line you find that the purchase order can be in several states at once. You find that transitions can occur at any time, because there are humans involved (unlike with the garage door opener). So although we can restrict some choices, we can't necessarily restrict the transitions. Like prototype categories, states have fuzzy edges.

Using State as a Proxy for Behavior

We need to rethink state machines in the context of categories. This will enable us to merge some interesting concepts. Let us recap what we've just discussed:

- The state (or status) of an item is really just a shortcut for the set of behaviors that can be executed on the item.
- These behaviors are not limited to the behaviors that lead to another state.
- The item is dynamically changing its "class" over time. This is not handled well in object-oriented systems.
- As we learn more about an item, or as an item goes through a state change, we can continually challenge its membership in the category (rule in/rule out) and thereby affect its potential behavior.

Status and Roles

The term *status* is often used interchangeably with *state*, as in "What is the status of that purchase order?" The main difference is that *status* tends to be associated more with permanent entities (customers and vendors) whereas *state* tends to be used more with shorter-duration transactions. This explains why medium-duration entities, such as purchase orders and contracts, tend to have either term applied to them.

A "role" is a relationship-specific way of referring to a person or an organization. For example, a person might have the role of an employee in an organization, a patient in a hospital, or the on-call doctor at a clinic. The existence of the role sets up one kind of categorization for the entity, so there are properties we would expect of an employee (hire date, salary, etc.) that we would not expect of a patient. The role itself also runs through states, mostly independent of the individual being referred to (on leave, probation, etc.).

Summary

Business systems use too many terms, and each term has too many possible meanings, for anyone to remember. We need help organizing our terms.

How we perform this organization and how we use the resulting categories will determine the quality of our systems. Mechanisms for storing and using ontologies and taxonomies exist. That isn't the hard part. The hard part is building or recognizing good ontologies.

The fact that we all categorize things naturally and automatically doesn't mean that we all do it equally well, nor that we can communicate what we mean by any given category. Therein lies our challenge.

If we expect the categories in our computer systems to be as dynamic as those in our linguistic systems, we need the following:

- The ability to refer to a category and thereby become one of that type (so a "Joe Jones" object could become "adult" and acquire new behavior)
- The ability to refer to more than one category at a time (the equivalent of dynamic multiple inheritance)
- The ability to disconnect from a type with which the object had been associated
- The ability to retain properties acquired while in a prior state/type
- The ability to have a type remove behavior as well as add to it

Once we have defined our types, taxonomies, and ontologies, we can begin to structure them for storage and sharing. This is the realm of data modeling and database design, which we take up next.

CHAPTER 5

Data and Object Modeling

In this chapter we begin the exploration of how to bring semantics into systems design. The primary mechanism for enterprise applications is in the design of databases, and the primary tool is the modeling of these databases. As mentioned in Chapter 3, semantics is a combination of data and behavior, and this chapter covers a modeling domain in which data and behavior are tightly interlinked: object-oriented modeling.

Although data modeling and object modeling are both well-established fields, the vast majority of practitioners conduct their modeling implicitly, following semantic leads, without being aware that they are doing so. To make this modeling more explicit, and thus more accessible, we begin this discussion by examining the semantic differences between documents and databases. From there we investigate where the semantics in a database application reside. We review what schemas are and how they are defined, and then discuss how semantics relate to normalization. We conclude by looking at the normalization of logic and how object-oriented modeling has shaped semantic understanding.

Semantic Differences between a Database and a Document

At one semantic level, documents and databases are alike. Both contain information, not physical objects or events. (By "document" I mean the information content and not the rendering onto paper, which, once rendered, is a physical object.) Once you get past this abstract similarity, though, databases and documents appear to be very different. Let's explore this with a thought experiment.

Imagine a simple document such as the letter in Figure 5.1.

Data   Data is intellectual property. It shares with other types of property the fact that it can be owned and ownership rights can be transferred. As intellectual property it was created by humans or by a device created by humans. It is distinct from other forms of intellectual property, such as ideas, inventions, or performances, in that it has been rendered into symbolic representation. We are primarily interested in data that has been rendered to electronic or magnetic media, because that makes it easier to process by computer. Information is a type of data made relevant through aggregation or conversion.

The letter, as data, could be stored in a database. But we typically don't think of this as the product of a database. Practitioners typically refer to this as "unstructured data." The data referred to in the definition box is data stored in a business system. The act of storing it is what elevates its status to intellectual property.

Figure 5.2 is a three-table database that has data similar to that contained in the letter in Figure 5.1.

Not Two Views of the Same Thing

First, let's dispense with the obvious. These are not (as they currently stand) two views of the same thing.

Database-centric people will look at this and say, "We can generate the letter from the tables." What they mean is that they can write a program that would read the database and insert the appropriate fields into a document, filling in the rest with boilerplate and layout information supplied by the program.

But what if the letter were not generated? What if the letter was the record of the transaction and the database was something we populated from the letter?

Both the database and the letter imply several things:

- That "we" are Ms. Jones, affiliated with House of Gum
- That we have some knowledge of a Mr. Smith (enough, we believe, to ship gum and requests for payment)
- That we offered gum for sale

```
August 1, 2002

Mr. Smith
Perpetual Inc.
1 Main ST
NYC, NY 10000

Dear Mr. Smith,

Enclosed is the gum you ordered. Please remit $9.95 to include
postage and handling.

Sincerely,

Ms Jones
House of Gum
123 Broadway
SFO, CA 99999
```

FIGURE 5.1 Business correspondence.

CustID	CustomerName	Contact	CustomerAddr	CustCity	CustSt	CustZip
001	Perpetual Inc.	Mr. Smith	1 Main St	NYC	NY	10000

VendID	VendorName	Contact	VendorAddr	VendCity	VendSt	VendZip
200	House of Gum	Ms. Jones	123 Broadway	SFO	CA	99999

VendID	CustID	OrderDt	Product	Qty	UoM	UnitPrice	Amt
200	001	8/1/2002	Trident Original	1	Box	$9.95	$9.95

FIGURE 5.2 A "structured data" version of Figure 5.1, as cast in a database.

- That Mr. Smith ordered a pack of gum
- That we shipped it to him
- That we expect to be paid

What is interestingly different is that in the letter we can tell (but only by being human and interpreting) that the gum is traveling with the notification, which is also the invoice. In the database example we can't tell where in the process we are. Has the gum been picked? Shipped? Is the database updated before or after the shipment? And so on.

If the letter were generated from the database, what is the difference between automatically generating the letter without allowing subsequent changes, versus generating the letter and then allowing someone to edit the generated letter? As we will see, this seemingly innocuous question has a profound impact on what can be inferred from the structured data we have after the fact.

Although the two versions cover approximately the same semantic scope, it is more accurate to say that these are two different ways of recording the same event. However, they are not equivalent.

Another interesting area of investigation is the hybridization of documents and databases. Before we begin to examine the hybrids between databases and documents, let's clarify their distinctness. In particular, there are two key dimensions to their distinction:

- Timing of the semantic interpretation
- Ability to be used by programs

Timing of the Semantic Interpretation

A major difference between a database and a document is the timing of semantics evaluation and enforcement. We can write whatever we want in a document. Whether it makes sense, is true, conveys meaning, or memorializes some event is up to a person or potentially a program to interpret when the document is read.

In a database (really a database application) the semantics are enforced as the data is entered. As we enter the data, the semantic rules (implemented in application code or in database constraints) ensure that the data in the database semantically conforms.

If we go back to our discussion of contracts in Chapter 2, we will note that a contract is a document. Although there is some interpretation going on while the contract is being drafted and reviewed, the fact that it typically is not reduced to a schema suggests that much of the semantics of the document are left to be interpreted much later, often in a court of law. We might then notice that the contract did not describe the property to be transferred or that no consideration was indicated. If contracts were expressed as well-defined databases, such flaws would be evident when we wrote the contract.

Ability to Be Used by Programs

The other difference of note between a document and a database is that with a database, application programs are able to use the data in a way that is not available to applications that process documents. In the previous example, a database application programmer could write a program that would sum up the gum sales for a customer, a time period, or a particular type of gum.

Without doing some semantic interpretation, the document-based application programmer really can't do much of anything.

Hybrids between Documents and Databases

Life has become more interesting since we began "tagging" data in documents. "Tagged" languages are covered in more depth in Chapter 11, but you are probably familiar enough to follow the example in Figure 5.3.

This tagging essentially creates a hybrid between a document and a database. (The evidence that it is a hybrid is that a database person will say, "The tags are really just the schema," whereas an HTML programmer will say, "It's just a document.")

As we will discuss later in much more depth, the presence of these tags creates not only an interesting hybrid between document and database, but also a hybrid between transaction and document. However, before we discuss the fuzzy boundaries of the hybrids, let's take a longer look at some of the differences between a document and a database.

Where Are the Semantics in a Database Application?

We've reached the point where database applications have more explicit semantics, their semantics are introduced earlier and more strictly, and these

```
<letter>
<Customer> Perpetual Inc
  <Contact> Mr. Smith </ Contact>
  <Address> 1 Main St NYC, NY 10000 </Address>
</Customer>

...

</letter>
```

FIGURE 5.3 A tagged form of the letter in Figure 5.1.

semantics are available for application programmers to use. But this begs an even more interesting question: Where are the semantics? These semantics exist whether the designer of the system studied semantics or not. The database designer and the application programmer must deal with semantics, yet the definition of these semantics is often informally expressed and widely dispersed.

To begin the search for where the semantics currently live, we will start with an extreme case. Figure 5.4 is data, destined for a database, that will be processed by a database application program.

An application program understands that this is data, and not noise, by reading it into an input area and then applying some rules (known to the program, and by extension to the person who wrote the program) to the data. The rules left over from the old days of punched cards tend to be based on fixed-length fields (e.g., in Figure 5.5 the price might be in columns 31

```
ISA*00*         *00*          *ZZ*0        *ZZ*1234567
*020116*1123*U*00401*1107     *0*P*:
GS*PT*0*1234567*20020116*1123*1107*X*0040101
ST*867*0001
BPT*00*1107*20020116*C1*****DP123456NoLosses
N1*8S*Independent Electricity Market Operator*ZZ*0**41
N1*SJ*PARTICIPANT*ZZ*1234567**40
REF*LU*1234567
PTD*PM***0Z*EL
REF*6W*1*
REF*LU*1234567*
REF*MG*1234567*
REF*MT*KH005*
QTY*QD*101652*KH
MEA**MU*1.0*KH***22
DTM*150****DT*200201140000
DTM*151****DT*200201140005
QTY*QD*10060*KH
QTY*QD*10436*KH
QTY*QD*10012*KH
QTY*QD*10110*KH
QTY*QD*10642*KH
QTY*QD*10538*KH
QTY*QD*10491*KH
```

FIGURE 5.4 Electronic data interchange (EDI) data.

```
          1         2         3         4         5
12345678901234567890123456789012345678901234567890
Perpetual InSmith   Trident000100099506012002
```

FIGURE 5.5 A fixed-field data record.

through 37). However, as we went beyond that we adopted many conventions for rules to help us understand the data, including the following:

- Field lengths (the first two bytes tell how long the next field is)
- Delimiters (everything up to the next "special character" is one field)
- Repeaters (the following field or fields repeat *n* times)

Once we find the fields in a chunk of data, the next challenge is interpreting them. Is "01-05-02" a date, a part number, a lock combination, or a string? If it's a date, what date is it? Is it May 1 or January 5?

The same sort of issues concern us when we write new data to the database, with the added issue of having to conform to some additional rules that writers of data need to be interested in (e.g., "This number must be not only an integer, but must be less than 25").

In a sense, the semantics of the data are applied by the mind of the programmer, enter the code, and subsequently "manage" the semantics of the data.

So far so good, but we've brushed aside several issues that end up being the crux of the problem:

- How does a subsequent programmer determine what the first programmer had in mind?
- How do we deal with these semantic issues in cases where we allow multiple programs to access the same set of data?
- How do we know that what the programmer intended was implemented consistently and completely?

The Next Programmer

The obvious nonanswer is "documentation." It is a nonanswer because of how rarely useful program documentation is written, and how rarely programmers refer to it.

What programmers do is read the code. And what they do as they read the code is attempt to extract the semantics of the code into a form that they can understand, and then modify it accordingly.

To do this, they rely on a few clues that they hope the previous programmer has left for them. Note that these conventions have become so well established that we sometimes forget that they are there entirely for the subsequent programmer (even if it is the same programmer who comes back to it later).

Clues to Understanding the Meaning in Programs

The meaning of business application programs is bound up with the meaning and description of data elements. In a typical business application program, there are as many references to data elements as there are lines in the program (the number of lines with more than one reference is about equal to the number with no reference). A great deal of the history of best practice in programming revolves around methods to make code more understandable to humans. This section reviews some of these practices from the standpoint of how they reveal the semantics that have been embedded.

Module Size

For 30 years managers, designers, methodologists, and other programmers have been exhorting programmers to keep modules (subroutines, methods, etc.) to a human scale (a page of printed text). The computer doesn't care. The semantics don't care. It's only the maintenance programmer who has to deal with this, and studies have shown that as the size of a module increases, the odds of it being correctly interpreted drop drastically.

With the help of some of the following techniques, a competent programmer can look at a page of code and can generally understand what is going on.

Data Hiding

One of the key conventions is "data hiding," or making sure that there isn't some other access to the data this module is dealing with that would create unwanted side effects to this particular module's processing. In the early days of mainframe programming, it was common to define all your variables in one common "global" area, and then let any of the subroutines access that data.

The problem with this approach is that you cannot evaluate what a module is doing if one of its subroutines is manipulating its data without providing any clue that this is occurring.

Cyclomatic Complexity

The prohibition against using "goto" commands in most programming languages is not so much that there is anything "wrong" with the "goto" command (if it were really that bad, it would have been excised from programming languages a long time ago), but what was found in practice was that the use of "goto" coincided with programs that had a high degree of cyclomatic complexity.[21]

Cyclomatic complexity is a measure of the number of possible paths a given execution can take through a module. In general, adding conditionals (if statements, case statements, etc.) to a program increases its cyclomatic complexity. The greatest increases in cyclomatic complexity are caused by nested looping structures in which the execution can conditionally exit different places in different ways.

The computer doesn't care about cyclomatic complexity; it handles it just fine. Indeed, some legacy systems continue to this day because they do what they were supposed to do, and maintenance programmers are afraid to touch them because they are so complex that programmers are unsure of the impact of any change they might make on the implemented (and tested over time) semantics.

Naming Conventions

The final convention that leads to semantic understanding is use of naming conventions. Anyone who has tried to maintain a program with poor naming conventions understands this experientially, but perhaps they haven't reflected on why this is so.

Case Study: Labowe's Program

Labowe was a programmer on one of my first projects. One day, to overcome the drudgery of cranking out yet another inventory-related program, he wrote the whole program, tested it, and then used the editor to replace all the local variable and internal subroutine names with women's names. (This code was written in DIBOL, a high-level language that Digital Computers used at the time.)

The result was a program that was hilarious to read, with lines like

---

21. Edsger W. Dijkstra, "Go to statement considered harmful," *Association for Computing Machinery Magazine*, March 1968, pp 147–148 (letter).

```
If (NOT Sally) then goto Susie
Else call Sarah(Sandy).
```

And so on. What was almost as comical as the anthropomorphized text was the fact that it processed inventory receipts exactly as the spec required. While we were testing it in the interpreter, and howling at statements like

```
Processing interrupted at Jamie 150; "Jessica" undefined,
```

we were busted by our bosses, who insisted that this was "unprofessional" and required that we clean it up.

Not being one to take defeat easily, Labowe resorted to the naming conventions that we had recently been taught in an assembler language course, which were based on some very old (and counterproductive) standards that hadn't been removed from the course. The conventions were to (1) index every line of code with the page and line number based on when it was first written (and sent off-site to be keypunched!) and then (2) to name variables based on the line and page number where they were defined.

So, Labowe's "professional" version of the program became

```
If (NOT AA110) then goto BB104
Else call BA224(AC107).
```

No more understandable, and certainly less fun.

I bring up the story in the sidebar to point out the crucial role of semantics in human understanding of programs, and how we use language for our clues to semantics. Had the programs been given semantically meaningful names—for example, If (NOT OutOfStock) then goto PickListCreation—a maintenance programmer would have had a much better chance of understanding this. But it doesn't make any difference to the computer.

Not all semantics are created equal. There are principles that lead to better (i.e., more precise, easier to understand) semantics, and we will discuss them in more depth later in this book.

Multiple Accessors = Multiple Semantic Interpretations

Database programs have an additional problem to resolve: Typically there are many programs accessing the data, each of which is relying on the fact that all the other programs are imparting an equivalent semantic on the data.

This turns out to be one of the central problems of large systems: The consistency of interpretation has historically been in the head of the analyst/designer. Methodologies and design approaches attempt to make as much of this as explicit as possible, but inevitably a large portion remains in the analyst's head.

Imagine a scenario where one program is updating an accounting file. Accounting systems typically have debits and credits, which often confuse programmers because they are arbitrary distinctions. So let's say a programmer was writing a program to process inventory adjustments. Because most of the adjustments decreased the inventory, the programmer made a local variable called "increase," which was mapped to the debit entry. (Inventory is an asset in which debits are increases.)

Another programmer comes along later, clones the program for use in accounts payable, and uses "increase," which to the second programmer means "increase the liability." However, because it is mapped to the debit field in the database, the opposite occurs.

This is just one possible scenario of the hundreds that come up in typical projects. Over the course of a project this tacit understanding evolves, and programs designed later in a project have the benefit of additional semantic richness or clarity.

There have been two responses to the problem of determining whether all the programmers (and therefore all the programs) are interpreting the model equivalently:

- **System testing**—Since we can't ensure that all the programs treat the data consistently, we test as many combinations as possible of access to the data by different programs, in different sequences with different types, in hopes of uncovering a high percentage of the semantic mismatches.

- **Shifting semantic evaluation into the database**—Another approach (and the two are often used in concert) is to take as much of the semantic interpretation as possible out of the code and put it where all programs must access it (e.g., database constraints or stored procedures).

Consistency

Assuming we can come up with a semantic description of the rules that we wish to apply to the data, how can we assure ourselves that the rules are consistent and complete?

For example, it is easy to define a rule that says that no time card can have negative hours on it, and another rule that says if time is charged to the wrong account it must be corrected by charging a credit to the incorrectly charged account. However, these rules can be implemented in many ways that would be inconsistent. If we are to have any hope of shifting the evaluation of semantics out of the individual application programs and into a shared part of the system (DMBS, middleware, etc.), we must have some way of determining whether we have a complete set of semantic constraints. We discuss this topic in more detail in Chapter 8.

How Was the Schema Defined?

People (process owners, developers, database analysts) build models of the data they would like to store. The more detailed and precise they make their model, the more possibility there is to extend the useful range of things that can be done with it. The flip side is that the more complete, complex, detailed, and explicit the model is, the more difficult it is to change. Developers are constantly faced with this tradeoff.

Explicit models come in two major varieties: descriptive and prescriptive. A descriptive model describes some aspect of the world. For example, a map is a descriptive model of a region of the world. A prescriptive model describes something that we wish to bring into existence, such as the blueprints for a house, or the model that predicts its ability to withstand wind shear.

Vocabulary, taxonomy, ontology, and categories are primarily descriptive; that is, they enable us to describe what we find in the world. The models that we will deal with in the remainder of this chapter are all prescriptive; their primary purpose is to do something.

Another aspect of models is that each model addresses some aspect of the thing to be built. In the case of the models to be described, we generally proceed from abstract and high-level models and refine them until we get to models that can be implemented. Following is a summary of some of the key models that you might encounter as you begin the process of codifying the semantics of an application into a database model.

As we examine these models, we need to keep in mind that each model is generated from a set of requirements (which themselves may be models). We take a set of requirements, add a set of constraints for the target we're trying to instantiate the requirements into, and then, through a design process, render a model that attempts to balance the needs of the requirements with the constraints of the target environment.

Semantic Model

A semantic model is a conceptual model in which the goal of the process and the resulting model is to convey unambiguously what the items being modeled mean. The main difference between a conceptual model and a semantic model is the effort spent on resolving meaning. Typically, a conceptual model would document the definition of concepts in terms that the business would understand, whereas a semantic model would attempt to resolve the concepts to semantic primitives or some other means of reducing ambiguity.

Unfortunately, you rarely see either in practice. I believe there are several reasons for this. One is that very few tools focus on conceptual or semantic modeling. Two, many practitioners saw conceptual modeling as a stepping-stone to their more refined logical and physical models, and as soon as they could figure out how to safely skip a step, they did. Three, because there is no implementation of a semantic model, all maintenance is done to the physical model, further cutting the conceptual models out of the loop. Chapters 6 through 9 go into much more detail on how and why to do semantic modeling, and Chapters 10 through 14 discuss tools that are becoming available for semantic modeling.

We'll start with a simple conceptual model such as the one in Figure 5.6, where we model that customers can order products.

In Figure 5.7 we embellish the model with some previously well-defined semantic primitives (shown in gray). In practice we would further embellish this, for example, by indicating the constraints on the parties in the role relationship that make them eligible to be customers.

Most of the semantic modeling texts use ovals rather than boxes, but there isn't any real difference at that level. There is also a mixed message in the literature on semantic modeling. Some suggest, as per this example, that semantic modeling be done at a high or conceptual level. Others seek to model all the properties, which makes for a much more complex graph at this point in the analysis.

FIGURE 5.6 Conceptual model.

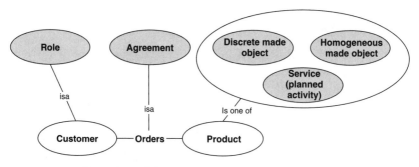

FIGURE 5.7 Semantic model.

There is nothing inherently semantic about customers, orders, and products, as drawn here. We will return to this and describe where the semantics come from in Chapters 6 through 9; for now we will focus on the evolution of a model, from conceptual modeling through logical and physical modeling.

Logical (Entity Relationship) Modeling

Entity relationship modeling can be used for conceptual and logical modeling. In the example in Figure 5.8 we use the earlier, Chen notation.[22] There are many variations, but they share the identification of entities and relationships, and especially the cardinality of relationships (in this case the I's and the M's, signifying that there must be at least one customer, but the customer can place more than one order).

Most data modelers add attributes to the model at this point and introduce the entities that will be needed to resolve the many-to-many relationships (in this case product to order will need an order line entity to be implementable in a relational model, which we show in Figure 5.9).

It is also at this point that most modelers "normalize" their data models. Normalization is a process of refining the design such that each table contains only attributes that are dependent on the key of the table. This arrangement greatly improves the integrity of the data, especially when updating or

---

22. Peter P. Chen, "The Entity-Relationship Model—Toward a Unified View of Data," *ACM Transactions on Database Systems*, March 1976, pp 9–36. Available at *http://bit.csc.lsu.edu/~chen/chen.html.*

deleting information (you don't have to traipse through all the rest of the data to see what might have been affected).

In Figure 5.9 we introduce some of the key attributes and normalize the OrderLine entity. Note that by introducing the OrderLine entity, the cardinality on the relationship to product goes from *M* to *1*. This is because the OrderLine entity acts as a junction record and removes the many-to-many relationship. It should also be noted that extended-entity relational modeling includes the concept of subtypes and inheritance, but the use of inheritance is much more widespread in object-oriented design.

Physical Modeling

The physical model is a transformation of the logical model into a form that has acceptable access and performance characteristics for the intended use, using a specific target technology.

In Figure 5.10 we have added the attributes to the entities (which now represent physical tables) on which they will reside. The inverted triangles represent indexes, which have been added for performance reasons. Several of the tables have multiple indexes, to speed access on different types of queries. At this stage we introduce calculated attributes that we expect to be used often enough to "cache." We consider QtyOnHand to be a cached value, because it could be recalculated from issues and receipts, but generally it is easier to maintain as a value that is refreshed whenever any of the factors change.

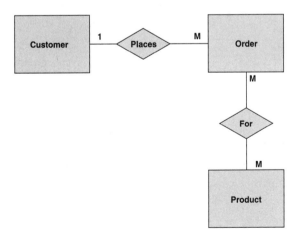

FIGURE 5.8 High-level logical model.

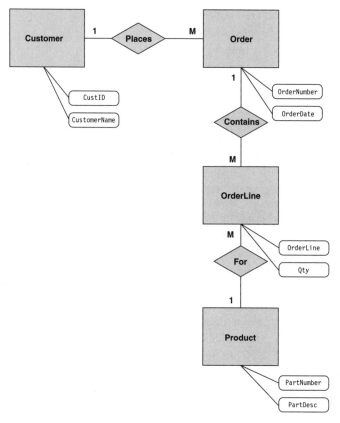

FIGURE 5.9 Logical model, normalized with some attributes.

Object Modeling: Data Models with Behavior

While data normalization was going on in a formal way, the logic of the programs was being "normalized" in a much more informal manner. Once upon a time, programs owned their data, such that there was often one big program for each sequentially organized data file. But since the advent of the database, and the ability for multiple programs to update shared data, we have been dealing with the problem of keeping those updates consistent.

Object Modeling

Object-oriented development involves designing your objects in a process called *object modeling*. The basic process is a conceptual modeling approach,

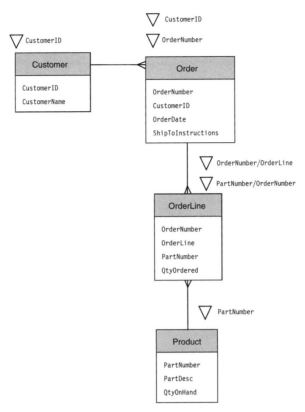

FIGURE 5.10 Physical data model.

with one difference: In object modeling you are simultaneously modeling the data and the behaviors allowed on the data (Figure 5.11).

The "class" is the basic building block of object-oriented design and is a product of the observation that good design packaging follows from modularity. Good modularity emphasizes the following:

- **High cohesion**—Attributes and the code that accesses them are packaged close together.

- **Data hiding**—Classes do not know the internals of other classes, and communicate through public methods.

- **Loose coupling**—Objects interact only through public methods, and therefore there is a known set of side effects if something is changed.

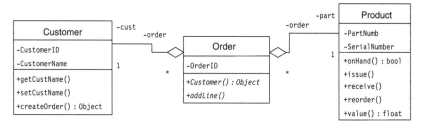

FIGURE 5.11 Object model in a unified modeling language (UML) class diagram.

In this example, the key classes are Customer, Order, and Product. In the UML class convention we show the attributes (data) in the top half of the box, and the methods (behavior) in the bottom half.

Object-Based Systems

Objects are instances of classes, created (instantiated) by making a request of a class to create a new object. So the equivalent of a row in a relational database is an object or an instance in an object-oriented implementation.

However, these features alone create only what has been called object-based systems and not object-oriented systems. It is the addition of inheritance and polymorphism that gives the approach its power and appeal, and also has led to widespread semantic abuse.

Inheritance

Inheritance is a feature that allows the developer of a class to extend the features of an already defined class. The new class inherits attributes and methods from the existing class, which can then be added to.

Figure 5.12 shows an inventory system with a class called Product, which has information about items in the warehouse. After this inventory system was created, the company began dealing in perishable items—parts that have a specific shelf life. So you look at the Parts class and realize that it has most of what you need. It has a part description, a part number, a serial number, methods to issue and receive it, methods to move it to a different location in the warehouse, methods to allow a cycle count, and so on. It has attributes to keep track of the cost of the item and a reference to pricing information.

So all you need for your perishable item is a "use by date." This implies that you will need a method to set this date at receipt time, and you may

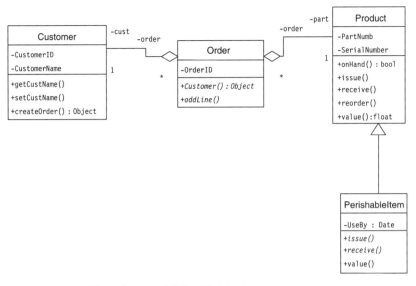

FIGURE 5.12 Object design in UML with inheritance.

want to change your picking routines to look for and pick first any items that are closest to expiring.

To accomplish this, you use "inheritance" and say "Class PerishableItem 'isa' Product." What this means to the system is that any time you ask for a "new" (new();) PerishableItem you will get all the attributes of Part plus all those of Perishable in a single object, with all the methods of both available.

Inheritance: Object-Oriented Programming versus Artificial Intelligence

Object-oriented programming languages and various artificial intelligence (AI) subdisciplines each use "inheritance." However, the two uses are distinct enough to cause considerable confusion. In each system, inheritance means that the child item is a subtype of the parent. The difference is that object-oriented languages create static subtypes. A class inherits from another class at design time, and the new class is compiled and linked as a subclass of the parent. When an instance of the subclass is created, it is an instance of the subclass and of the parent class at the same time. Instances do not change their classes or types during their lifetime.

In most AI disciplines, including ontology building, the inheritance or "isa" relationship is dynamic. As soon as we declare an instance "isa" type, it is of that type (in addition to any other types it "is").

Polymorphism

Polymorphism (literally "many shapes") allows you to treat all the descendants of a class as if they were items of that class. So any method that worked on Product should also work on PerishableItem because PerishableItem is a Product.

This allows you to extend a system without breaking it. So the "onHand();" method on Product might work exactly the same for PerishableItem, because it was inherited unchanged, whereas the "value():" function may return a value, just as in Product, but that value may be $0 if the item has passed its expiration date.

Object/Class Modeling

In summary, object modeling, or class modeling, is an exercise in trying to define a set of concepts that will work well together in your domain and be easy to extend.

In Pursuit of Reuse

Object-oriented design has been caught up in the attempt to foster code reuse. It was believed that reusing code was the Holy Grail of productivity, and that the inheritance feature of object-oriented design could be used to facilitate this reuse. As a result, class libraries became places to put code to "reuse," as opposed to letting the goal of extensibility drive the design. This didn't lead to very good designs, and paradoxically didn't deliver on the reuse. Well-designed object systems used delegation (sending a message to another object) far more than inheritance, and therefore there wasn't any measurable reuse. I use the term *measurable reuse* because in the late 1980s and early 1990s one of the metrics for object-oriented systems was the degree of reuse, and reuse was measured by inherited reuse (if you reused code from a parent class, you received "reuse" credit; if you reused code from an existing class, via delegation or any other pattern, it did not show up on the reuse metrics). The idea of code reuse through inheritance has fallen out of favor.

Limits to Inheritance

For the aforementioned reason, and several others, rookie object-oriented developers all seemed to overdo inheritance in their conceptual models.

Many of these were inspired by examples in textbooks that used biologic analogies (human is a primate, primate is a mammal, mammal is an animal, etc.). Unfortunately, good inheritance trees are rarely found outside of biology. The reason they work so well in biology is that all the classes and phyla descended from a common set of ancestors, by gradual accretion of features and adaptation. So the fact that we can "inherit" our warm-bloodedness from our mammalian ancestors, and our bipedalism from the primates, is mostly because that is how biologic organisms evolved.

Object-oriented design teams often construct large, deep inheritance graphs for the objects in their domain. In general this makes their designs brittle in precisely those places where designers had hoped it would make them flexible.

Summary

In this chapter we have introduced databases and data modeling and described some of the key data and object modeling approaches. The intent of this discussion is to provide the background for the next several chapters. The main issues for this chapter are to understand that there are many modeling techniques, and that each makes many assumptions about that which is being modeled. Models generally evolve from general, abstract, and high-level models to more detailed and implementable models.

All of the data models are based on semantic models; however, up to now the semantic model has rarely been documented. Practitioners usually jot down entities and attributes and start normalizing and making performance trade-offs. It is generally left for developers and maintenance programmers to shoehorn in the special cases and special meanings that the users of the system decide they want implemented.

Logical modeling has followed a parallel path. Object-oriented models document classes, which are analogous to entities. Object-oriented design has taken inheritance to a new level, relative to entity modeling. However, in practice it has overshot the mark. Systems with tens of thousands of classes are not uncommon, but they are unwieldy.

In the next chapter we address the following questions: How do you segue between abstraction levels as you are modeling? What does this do for the system you are modeling?

| 6

Metadata

Metadata has gone from being a documentation aid to being a central part of a development environment, and in some cases it has become the application itself. As "data about data" it is almost pure semantics; that is, it stores the meaning of the data it describes.

Metadata *Metadata* is data about data.

Unfortunately, metadata is at its most powerful in situations when it is crossing many levels of abstraction, and therefore it is sometimes hard to comprehend. In this chapter we discuss a real life example in a fair bit of detail to see how to apply metadata concepts to everyday applications. This will provide grounding for a subsequent discussion on semantically inspired systems.

The list of tasks in Figure 6.1 shows the relationship between data and metadata. In the absence of metadata, there is often little we can do with data. Before we delve into what we can do with metadata, it is important to explore the history of metadata so we can understand where it is now.

A Brief History of Metadata

The business systems industry has changed metadata from being a data dictionary (documentation about the fields used within an application) to being a style of development that recognizes that the definitions of the data are subject to change in the same way as the rest of the data in an application. We have moved from metadata being an afterthought to being an architectural principle. Let's review how this came to be.

| Date | Task | Resp | | Metadata |
| | | | | |

	Date	Task	Resp
	2/1/2002	Receive Dry Wall	JS
Data	2/2/2002	Install Dry Wall	DL
	2/4/2002	Tape and Sand	DL
	2/7/2002	Paint	MK

FIGURE 6.1 Data and metadata.

Data Dictionaries

Once upon a time, metadata was documentation for the data model (often the file and transaction layouts) of an application, as shown in Figure 6.2. Initially, the data dictionaries were used after the fact (at the end of the project or later) and were the equivalent of "as built" drawings of buildings. Arthur Andersen's (now Accenture) "Lexicon" is generally regarded as the first of these products.

The information was primarily about fields and records: which fields were on which records and which records were accessed by which programs. Moving this documentation to a central location made a world of difference as applications were becoming more and more complex.

The Data Dictionary Database

It didn't take long for people to figure out that putting this documentation into a database, as shown in Figure 6.3, would make it eminently more usable. "Where used" reports and various other analyses were now easy to create.

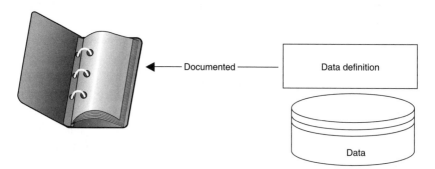

FIGURE 6.2 As built metadata.

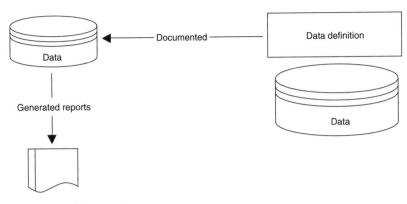

FIGURE 6.3 The data dictionary.

The "Active" Dictionary

Next was the "active" dictionary, an innovation that made it possible to
(1) create the record layouts and COBOL copybooks from the dictionary
and (2) install procedures to make sure they were updated only from this
dictionary (Figure 6.4).

Once this was done, the architects of this innovation felt a need to
distance themselves from the old "as built" approach and dubbed this the
"active" dictionary. Changes to the dictionary became changes to the system
(admittedly after some delay).

Computer-Aided Software Engineering Tools

Computer-aided software engineering (CASE) extended the concept with the
generation of application source code (or at least shells of application source
programs), as indicated in Figure 6.5. These were generally based on metadata, sometimes proprietary to the tool and sometimes using the native capability of the database management systems.

Data Definition Language

The term *data definition language (DDL)* was coined along with the implementation of relational databases. It distinguished statements that manipulated metadata (DDL statements) from those that manipulated regular or
instance data (data manipulation languages [DMLs], the most prevalent of
which was structured query language [SQL]), as shown in Figure 6.6.

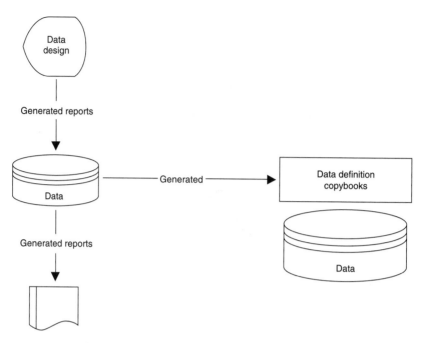

FIGURE 6.4 Active Data Dictionary.

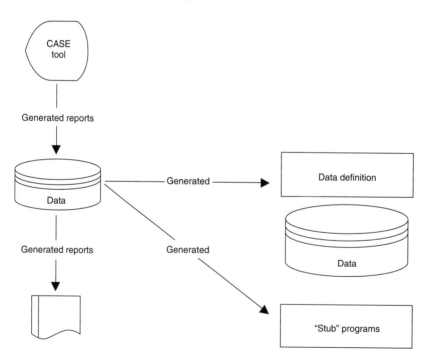

FIGURE 6.5 CASE tools generating metadata and some code.

```
DDL
    ALTER TABLE orders
        ADD orderID
DML
    SELECT orderID FROM orders
```

FIGURE 6.6 Data definition language and data manipulation language.

Schemas

The term *schema* began to be applied to database design, particularly data models, in the 1990s. However, it was primarily the rise of object databases and extensible markup language (XML) that led to the current popularity of the term.

Object-oriented database management systems introduced the concept of *schema evolution*. This can be understood as the answer to the question, "How can you update the definition of the data in a database if there is data in the database that depends on the old schema?" Until this point, little effort had been spent on trying to update the schema while the system was running, because the prevailing wisdom was "dump and restore." What would later be called "schema evolution" was "dump, reformat, change the DDL, and restore."

Standard Generalized Markup Language Document Type Definition

Standard generalized markup language (SGML; a tagged language for document-centric systems on which hypertext markup language [HTML] and XML were based) introduced its own type of DDL called the document type definition (DTD) (Figure 6.7). The DTD was both a schema (in that it constrained what could be stored in an SGML document) and a grammar (in that it defined what sequences of elements needed to be present). These DTDs were metadata for the data in the SGML documents.

Extensible Markup Language Document Type Definition

XML, created in 1997, is a derivative of SGML that is intended to bring semantic markup to the World Wide Web. Chapter 11 covers XML in more detail; for now we will outline the XML initiatives that relate to metadata. XML began life with DTDs that were expressly present to define the schema

```
DTD
  <!ELEMENT order (line*)>
  <!ELEMENT line (product, qty, price)>

SGML
  <order>
    <line>
      <product> .... </product>
      <qty> ... </qty>
      <price> ... </price>
    </line>
  </order>
```

FIGURE 6.7 DTD schema with an SGML document.

of the document or message. The XML DTDs were very similar to the SGML DTDs.

XML Schema Definition

In the last few years, the shortcomings of DTDs have become apparent. One area of shortcoming was the lack of any real ability to control, at a detailed level, the conformance of a document to the schema. The developers of XML schema definition (XSD) decided not to continue the DTD tradition of separating the grammar for the schema from the instance data, and therefore XSD is expressed in XML.

Figure 6.8 is part of an XSD that would define an equivalent structure to the DTD in Figure 6.7. We won't go into the syntax of XSD (or DTD); it is sufficient to know that there has been a progression from treating metadata as being different from regular data to treating it as being the same as regular data.

```
<xs:element name="line">
  <xs:complexType>
    <xs:sequence>
      <xs:element ref="product"/>
      <xs:element ref="qty"/>
      <xs:element ref="price"/>
    </xs:sequence>
  </xs:complexType>
</xs:element>
```

FIGURE 6.8 Part of an XSD document.

Metaobject Facility, XML Metadata Interchange, and Common Warehouse Metadata Interchange

There has been a great deal of effort recently to standardize different aspects of metadata. The unified modeling language (UML) was built on and incorporates the metaobject facility (MOF), essentially the metamodel for software architectures. XML metadata interchange (XMI) and the common warehouse metadata interchange (CWMI) are standards that allow metadata to be converted from one format to another.

Resource Definition Framework

Resource definition framework (RDF) has recently emerged, essentially as metadata for content. We'll save most of the discussion of RDF for Chapter 14, but to put it into a metadata context, consider that although XML has a schema (its metadata) we don't necessarily know what the schema means. We need metadata that would be rich enough to store an ontology, and that is where RDF comes in.

Levels and Types of Metadata

There is a certain subspecies of the population of computer scientists who, once they solve a problem, "go meta." Exactly what this means varies from situation to situation, but it generally involves looking for a more generalized or more abstract way to solve the same problem.

When successful, this leads to a solution that covers a broader domain or solves the same problem more flexibly. Often these solutions involve rethinking the way the problem has been expressed, and this is usually at the level of the metadata. The expression "going meta" is sometimes used derisively to describe those who become too abstract, but if the practitioner can abstract and then reassemble the problem at hand (unfortunately, the second step sometimes gets dropped), useful designs often emerge.

To give some idea of the richness of metadata, Figure 6.9 shows one piece of primitive data (the number 42) and more than a dozen individual bits of data about that data. Most of this data is kept in most systems. It is not always easily accessible, and it is not all repeated for each instance of primitive data. But all of this, and more, is potentially at the disposal of the metadata designer.

"Going meta" means taking any one of those pieces of data on the periphery and putting it in the center. For example, if we put "alpha time" in the

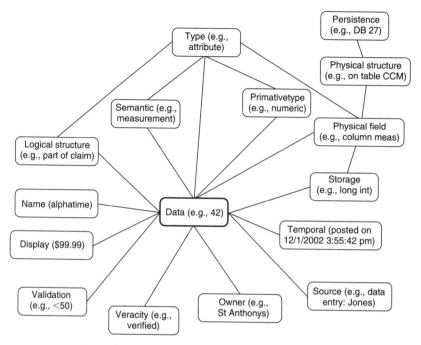

FIGURE 6.9 Types of metadata.

middle, what is the metadata that is the "name" of "alpha time"? It is probably "attribute." What is its type? It may be "entity." In one sense, the metadata for a database is the database schema. To go "up" a level, the metadata for the schema (often called the "meta-metadata") is a model in which you can store the schema (imagine a database whose tables were called things such as "table" and "column," and you'll be close). This is what the MOF described previously has done for software architectures.

It is sometimes thought that "going up" a level adds semantics. Initially, it does just the opposite; abstracting actually removes semantics. The benefit is that at this more abstract level, you now have a location in which to define semantics. Whether or not, and how well, this occurs is completely up to the implementation, but it is the opening that we have to step into to explore how semantics will be expressed in applications.

Most Semantics Live in Metadata

The evolution of formal means to describe metadata is only half the story. The other half is how people have evolved their applications designs to make better use of metadata.

Application Metadata Design Is Subtle

The shift to using more metadata in application design occurred in parallel with the evolution of the metadata expression. However, the shift in application design has been much more subtle, for two reasons:

1. It requires no new languages, acronyms, or conferences; designers just do it.
2. Many good designers do this without being aware that they are doing it. The longer they are in the field, the more likely they will see a "nonmeta" design as less appropriate, without necessarily knowing why.

Metadata in Packaged Applications

Several studies have indicated that building a packaged software application takes between 5 and 10 times as much effort as building the same functionality once on a custom basis for a single site. Much of the reason for this difference is that package vendors realize that they are going to have to tailor their system to most of the customers for whom it is installed.

Many techniques are used to aid in this process, including metadata-based design. At one level, many packaged application vendors use the active repository approach for such things as screen labels and report headings. With this approach, a single change to the metadata repository can change the system's appearance. For example, if one company wants to call parts "items," a single change to the metadata repository changes all the screens and all the reports.

More flexible, but not as widely implemented, are metadata designs in which the implementers (and by extension, theoretically, the end users) can extend the data model, rather than just create aliases for things already in the model. The most simplistic implementation occurs when vendors leave the last dozen fields on any given master record as "user1," "user2," "user3," and so on. This allows the users (i.e., the company) to redefine these fields for their own use. So if they decide that they need to store shoe size and favorite wine on their contact lists, they simply redefine "user1" to be "shoe size" and "user2" to be "favorite wine." The screens prompt and the reports display these new labels. However, these are miscellaneous fields. They are not recognized by any of the rest of the application programs. Some designs contain custom validation rules that allow you to validate shoe sizes or pick favorite wines from a list, but that is about it. In other words, there are ways for one user to communicate some semantics to another user, without the application becoming aware.

Some Developments in the Use of Metadata-Driven Architectures

The examples described so far are low on the "semantically aware" scale we introduced in Chapter 3. Now let's examine metadata in the semantically aware system.

A key hurdle has to be jumped for the metadata to be treated as semantically aware: The application code can no longer refer to the semantic definition as expressed in the database schema directly; it must refer to it indirectly. I'll describe two generalized examples and then conclude the chapter with a case study of an application that illustrates the value of the metadata-driven approach, taken to the architectural level.

Generating Code from a Metadata Model

Tenfold Corporation markets a product based on its Universal Application Platform architecture.[23] This product allows developers to define an application in metadata, including much of its validation logic. The system then generates code that corresponds to the semantic rules as set up in the dictionary. As long as the code is not modified, subsequent changes to the dictionary will allow the system to generate a new set of code, complete with new semantics.

The Crucial Role of Metadata for Non–Self-Describing Content

Velocity.com[24] created health care applications based on Organic Architecture (now marketed by Instantica[25]). Organic Architecture allowed developers to define a schema, and then build the application to that schema, without writing application code. The application execution engine understood the same semantics as the design tools, which meant that the application construction process obeyed assembly rules that prohibited most of the errors that plague traditional development.

These two examples point toward a future in which applications will be fully described and implemented in metadata. Applications fully defined in

---

23. See *www.10fold.com/* for further information.

24. See *www.velocity.com/* for further information.

25. See *www.instancia.com/* for further information.

metadata is quite a stretch for many developers to imagine. To get a sense of how this is possible, in the following case study I focus on a smaller example that requires virtually no new technology and handles many of the issues needed to scale this to a larger endeavor.

A Case Study on Metadata Application Design

Because of the subtleties of metadata design, we work through a case study in enough detail to point out where the metadata design was introduced. As we see later, this knowledge is the keystone to effective semantic design. The case is based on a real project.

The business problem involves a company that mines and processes an industrial mineral, diatomaceous earth (DE). The firm's information technology (IT) department, in conjunction with outside consultants, was asked to convert their QC lab from manual systems to a computer system (in 1992). At that time they believed (based on their largely handwritten spreadsheets) that they had about two dozen tests. A first-cut, traditional design modeled each test as a column in a test table.

A metadata-inspired design was proposed and implemented. Before the system was completed, the design had paid for itself many times over. By the time of conversion, nearly 100 tests (mostly customer-specific variations on tests) had been uncovered and implemented in the system. What would have been nearly 100 significant changes to the system were accommodated with no change. There are now (10 years later) millions of test results and more than 300 test types in the system. The system has outlived the obsolescence of its hardware, operating system, and database, as well as Y2K, with only a few maintenance changes along the way.

Diatomaceous Earth

DE is the sedimentary remains of the exoskeletons of diatoms. A diatom (Figure 6.10) is a single-celled creature. (Technically diatoms are members of the kingdom Protista and are neither plant nor animal.) Diatoms are most closely related to algae; however, they often have intricate silica-based shells or exoskeletons. Millions of years ago, they were deposited on the bottom of seas and lakes to eventually be compressed into sedimentary rock, chalklike in appearance.

Once mined and processed, DE has an amazing array of properties. Among its many applications, it is used to filter beer and wine, to make paint

FIGURE 6.10 A diatom. (Photograph by P. Roger Sweets.)

less reflective, to make Saran Wrap less sticky, and to make toothpaste more abrasive.

Quality Control

Quality control for DE is similar to that for other process manufacturing industries. When producing, say, beer-grade DE, the plant will set the process control levers at a particular setting, and then the QC department will take samples ("in process" and of packaged finished goods) to ensure that the product is staying within preset tolerances. (At this level, the process is no different than making soft drinks or synthetic blood.)

Quality Control Procedures

The QC team will have a set of procedures for taking samples (including the number, frequency, and method of obtaining them), as well as procedures for the tests to be performed. Each sample type should have a template for the tests to be done, which can then cross reference to the specific procedures. This is especially useful for infrequently performed tests.

Lots and Samples

Each lot will have many samples, as shown in Figure 6.11. One or more tests are done for each sample. The results are averaged, and often statistical tests are performed to determine the deviation from the target values.

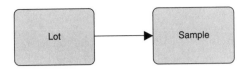

FIGURE 6.11 Any lot can have many samples.

Results and Control Limits

Typically either the average of the samples or the range of standard deviation of the samples is compared with the target values (usually an upper and lower limit, as in Figure 6.12).

Alpha Time

Alpha time is the length of time it takes a predetermined percentage of a standard volume of distilled water to pass through a standard amount of DE in a standard-size container. Low (i.e., fast) alpha times indicate large, porous diatoms, which are more suited to filtering material with more particulates.

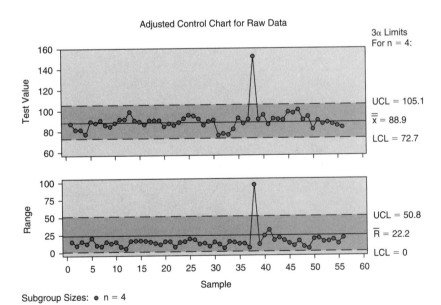

FIGURE 6.12 Control charts showing actual results compared with control limits.

Wet Density

Wet density is a measure of how heavy a given volume of DE is after being soaked in a fixed volume of distilled water. It is a measure of the smaller openings in the diatoms.

First-Cut Database Design

Let's say we decided to design our database to allow us to take alpha time and wet density samples and average them per lot.

Figure 6.13 is one of many possible designs. The "result" table is shown in dashed lines, because depending on the volume of data and inquiries, you may choose to build that table dynamically, when necessary.

The "lot" table is created by the production scheduler when we decide to make a "lot." It contains information about the lot itself (when it was made, where, what we were trying to make, etc.). There will be one row in this table for each lot that we produce.

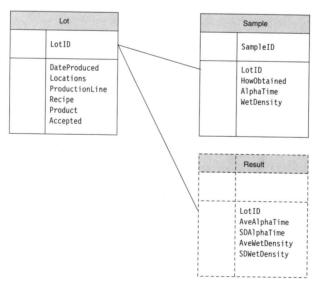

FIGURE 6.13 An early, typical relational design of the QC system.

The "sample" table will have one row for each sample we take. Each sample is cross referenced to the lot it came from, and there may be some information about the methods that were used to take the sample.

Figure 6.14 is approximately the same design, in table form, with some sample data. The test data in Figure 6.14 show six samples taken from two lots. For each sample there was a measurement of alpha time and wet density. These were then averaged, and a standard deviation was calculated in the results table.

You can imagine the use cases for this design:

- Start a new lot—This sets up a record in the lot table.

- Take a sample—This records where the sample was taken from and some information about what was to be made.

- Record measurements—If the alpha time and wet density are done at different workstations, potentially by different people, each test could have its own queue of samples to process.

LotID				
LotID	**DateP**	**Loc**	**Product**	**Accepted**
112	20-Dec	WA	DEFlo	Y
113	20-Dec	WA	DEFlo	Y

Sample				
Sample	**LotID**	**HowOb**	**AT**	**WD**
2700	112	Bag	25	101
2701	112	Bag	29	104
2702	112	Bag	24	99
2703	113	Silo	32	120
2704	113	Silo	32	121
2705	113	Silo	31	111

Result				
LotID	**AveAT**	**SDAT**	**AveWD**	**SDWD**
112	26.00	2.65	101.33	2.52
113	31.67	0.58	117.33	5.51

FIGURE 6.14 The original design, with test data. *AT*, alpha time; *SD*, standard deviation; *WD*, wet density.

- Lot closeout—Review the results, make sure there are no outstanding tests, and determine whether the lot passed or failed. (This implies that the control intervals are either in another table, not shown, or are done manually.)

Change at the Metadata Level

It's not hard to imagine what the most likely change in this type of situation is (even if the users swear it never changes, you can be pretty certain it will have changed by the time you finish the implementation). A new test is required. It may be a variation on an existing test, but one where you can't mix and match test results (there are several different alpha time tests, each with a different volume of material and water, for products of widely differing porosity).

The first impact of the change is a metadata change: We now need a new column on the sample table and the results table. But that's only the beginning, because the use cases have been affected. The screens used to enter the measurements will have to be adjusted.

At some point (after the fourth or fifth new test has been incorporated via a system change), it will become apparent that not all of the tests have to be done for all of the samples. Initially this will be handled with programming logic, but eventually the developer will realize a need to do something else.

One of two things usually happens at this point: Either the developers become skilled at making these changes (which have now become routine), or they realize that this change has become the norm, and it is time for a new design that incorporates that. This new design moves some of what was the metadata (the definition of the tests) into primitive data.

Who Gets to Mess with the Metadata?

When it comes down to it, the question is, Who gets to mess with the metadata? Historically this has been reserved for data administrators and the like. It was too dangerous for mere mortals (end users). But it turns out that, in many cases, the metadata can be expressed as ordinary data, as long as there are safeguards to prevent its misuse.

New Design

The "sample" table in Figure 6.15 now no longer has a column for each test. Instead it now has two columns, one to describe the type of test and the other

LotID				
LotID	**DateP**	**Loc**	**Product**	**Accepted**
112	20-Dec	WA	DEF1o	Y
113	20-Dec	WA	DEF1o	Y

Sample				
Sample	**LotID**	**HowOb**	**TestType**	**TestValue**
2700	112	Bag	AT	25
2701	112	Bag	AT	29
2702	112	Bag	AT	24
2703	113	Silo	AT	32
2704	113	Silo	AT	32
2705	113	Silo	AT	31
2700	112	Bag	WD	101
2701	112	Bag	WD	104
2702	112	Bag	WD	99
2703	113	Silo	WD	120
2704	113	Silo	WD	121
2705	113	Silo	WD	111

TestType		
TestType	**LoValid**	**HiValid**
AT	20	40
WD	80	150

Result			
LotID	**TT**	**Ave**	**SD**
112	WD	101.33	2.52
113	WD	117.33	5.51
112	WD	101.33	2.52
113	WD	117.33	5.51
112	AT	26.00	2.65
113	AT	31.67	0.58
112	AT	26.00	2.65
113	AT	31.67	0.58

FIGURE 6.15 A metadata-inspired design.

for its value. For the same amount of data, the table is now longer, but this turns out to be insignificant in all but the rarest circumstances.

If we did nothing else, we'd be guilty of lack of semantic precision. If we stopped the design change at this point we could type anything in the Test-Type column. (This is a common design error.) The problem is that if you use different names for a single test (e.g., alpha time, Alpha time, AT), when you go to search or summarize, one of them will be missing.

The new design introduces a new table, the TestType table. The TestType table has a row for each valid test type. Requiring that the TestType column in the sample table be validated to the TestType table is straightforward.

Note that we now have a convenient place to put valid ranges for the tests. These are not the upper and lower control intervals, which are specific to the product being produced (and potentially the process being used), but they do provide a handy place for basic validation (especially for order-of-magnitude errors, which are common in this type of system).

It doesn't take much to extend this design to add a table that asks two things: Which tests do I want to do for which products? And, on the same table, what are the upper and lower control intervals?

Columns-to-Rows Pattern

What I just described is a powerful pattern that we call the columns-to-rows pattern. As you can see in Figure 6.16, data is being shifted from column headings to rows (instances).

Is It Still Metadata?

At one level, this doesn't look like metadata any more. It was metadata when it was a column heading (and in the data dictionary, etc.). But when we shifted it, it became ordinary data.

Don't let this fool you. This is metadata, just as much as it was when it was a column head. It is metadata because the data in the TestType table are very much data about the data in the Sample and Result tables.

Sample

Sample	LotID	HowOb	AT	WD
2700	112	Bag	25	101
2701	112	Bag	29	104
2702	112	Bag	24	99
2703	113	Silo	32	120
2704	113	Silo	32	121
2705	113	Silo	31	111

TestType

TestType	LoValid	HiValid
AT	20	40
WD	80	150

FIGURE 6.16 The columns-to-rows pattern.

If the system is designed properly, it should be just as impossible to add a row to the sample table with a bogus test type as it would have been to stick a nonexistent column on the end of the old sample table. This does, however, shift some of the responsibility to the application developer.

Enforcement and Visibility Shift

Some other things have shifted in this scenario. The test types are no longer visible to a traditional metadata tool (e.g., a report writer running off a database). This doesn't mean that reporting is not possible; in fact, it is more flexible in this scenario. It just means that the application has to play a role. Where columns were selected before, now there will be query pieces. For example,

```
Select Sample.AT From Sample Where LotID = 112
```

Is now

```
Select Sample.TestValue from Sample Where LotID = 112 AND
Sample.TestType = "AT"
```

Is There More Metadata or Less in the New Solution?

This is an interesting question. In the first example we had 3 tables, each of which had 5 columns, for a total of 15 pieces of metadata. In the second design we had 4 tables with a total of 17 pieces of metadata.

Now look at what happens when we add new test types. In the original design the explicit metadata grows every time we add a new test type. Along with that, all the code that accesses the metadata is affected.

In the new design, adding a new test type does not affect the (official) metadata at all. Nor is the code affected, unless there were hard-coded SQL routines that took advantage of knowledge of a value in the TestType table.

Epilogue

The case study described here was converted from a manual system to a computer system 10 years ago. At that time they believed (based on their large, handwritten spreadsheets) that they had about two dozen tests, and the original design was the more traditional design, with two dozen columns.

The meta design paid off even before the system was converted. By the time the system was converted, nearly 100 tests and variations had been uncovered. At a recent review (10 years later), there were 336 tests in the system (some obsolete and retained only for historical purposes). Although it would have been possible to continue with the traditional design, it would have involved more than 300 system enhancements over that period. As it was, there have been few changes to the system as the users of it have extended it to meet their needs.

Metadata-Driven Systems Are More Flexible

Most people would agree that metadata-driven systems are more flexible than traditional designs, as the case study shows. Flexibility is generally a desirable trait, but there are a few issues to address.

Clearly, there can be performance penalties with this approach, and they should be considered. However, don't reject the idea on performance grounds before you've investigated it; in many cases the performance penalty is not that severe. Another consideration is knowing where you need flexibility. If you build flexibility in where it isn't needed, it won't improve the system.

Issues that come up with metadata designs include the following: Where should we be looking for abstractions? What does it mean to mix and match instances and schema? How does this work with tagged languages?

Semantic Implications

What makes this pattern possible are two semantic manipulations:
- Shifting the schema to a more abstract definition
- Allowing instance data to be used as if it were schema

Schema Abstraction

What was a specific definition of a particular test (alpha time) was replaced by a generic term (test value). Once you've looked at it this way it's hard to go back to the old way of looking at it and believe that alpha time really was metadata, but it certainly was; there could have been hundreds of thousands of rows in this database conforming to this metadata.

Instances for Schema

The other shift consisted of allowing instance data (rows) to be treated as if they were schema. This is anathema to most DBAs, largely because the separation of DDL from DML causes them to categorize schema and data differently. On the other hand, ontologists mix and match categories and instances so freely, they may not even realize they are doing it.

Additional Metadata Provides Additional Semantics

As we saw in this example, shifting the metadata from the database schema provided us a means to provide additional semantics (in this case the range checks and the inclusion of tests to sample types). Once you begin looking for these opportunities, they show up frequently.

Metadata in Tagged Languages

These techniques of applying meta thinking also apply to tagged languages such as XML. Later chapters describe how the level of definition in XML schemas has the same profound effect on the robustness of design as this example.

Summary

We've covered a lot in this chapter. We started from a historical angle, explaining how the description of data in an application has been expressed differently from the data it describes. We've described how even technologies as modern as XML started with metadata that was distinct from the data it was describing (DTDs versus XML) and then morphed to a language where the metadata (schema) is expressed in the same language as the data (XSD is expressed as XML). We've begun to discuss how we might use a "metametalanguage" to describe the meaning of the schema.

Most of the rest of the chapter is devoted to a case study of the powerful advantages that are available when you model metadata as data. Applications become both more flexible and more powerful. Although we used a narrow domain for the example, my contention is that virtually every aspect of every design is subject to these same improvements.

The resulting design may have looked obvious in retrospect. Prospectively, though, this type of design is anything but obvious. Getting from the "before" to the "after" is primarily a matter of understanding the semantics of the concepts and information being modeled. It is that semantic understanding of the details of the domain that leads to superior designs. The next several chapters outline an approach for systematically finding and exploiting the semantics in any application.

CHAPTER 7

Interpreting Meaning

In 2001 businesses captured, recorded, and stored more than an exabyte of data.[26] An exabyte (1,000,000,000,000,000,000 bytes) is a billion gigabytes. This is a million times the total textual content of the U.S. Library of Congress. Most of this data is unstructured, meaning it has little or no detailed schema to describe what it means.

The task of finding meaning in this data falls largely to humans, who are generally not keeping up; there is just too much data to interpret. This chapter is about interpretation: how people interpret the raw data in their environment, and how computers are beginning to help.

We set up a general model of how humans interpret and ascribe meaning to unstructured sensory input, as a basis for how systems and tools will aid us in this process in the future. We survey the state of the market in this area, starting with the simplistic interpretation in features such as Microsoft's Smart Tags, through a number of commercial tools that use much more sophisticated reasoning to impart meaning on unstructured documents.

Interpretation: Clues from How Humans Interpret Unstructured Information

The most common dictionary definitions of *interpret* include "to understand" or "to explain the meaning of." As with many dictionary definitions, this gets us only so far.

---

26. Peter Lyman et al, "How Much Information," University of Berkeley. Available at *www.sims.berkeley.edu/research/projects/how-much-info/summary.html.*

Interpret   To determine the intended meaning of something.

We have a good idea of what the word *interpret* means. We talk about "interpreting our dreams," "interpreting financial statements," and "interpreting the law." We also talk about an "interpreter" as someone who converts one language to another. Computer science has an alternative meaning for interpreter: an architecture that compiles and executes program code one line at a time instead of compiling an entire program at once.

A Model of Interpretation

The following is a simplified description of how humans interpret their world. As we go through the model, we will describe how human-designed business applications are doing something similar. Interpretation involves the following:

1. Perception
2. Initial, low-level classification of perception
3. Synthesis with things previously perceived and classified
4. Hypothesis of higher-level classification
5. Prediction of further perception
6. Testing to confirm or deny the perception

These six aspects fit together as shown in Figure 7.1.

Business systems do far more interpretation than we think they do. Once we are clear about what this is and how it works, we are much more likely to recognize system processes that are interpreting their environment and how this analogy could help us fine-tune this process.

Context is included in Figure 7.1 to represent that it is the act of establishing context that determines what we will initially perceive, and also what aspects of our body of knowledge we are likely to bring to bear on a perceptual situation. One possible interpretation (not shown here) is one that changes context. Within a context the process is perception.

Perception

Without perception, there is nothing to interpret. Perception is any access of information. Perception need not be of the external environment; we also can perceive internal states (a human may perceive pain or discomfort, an application may "perceive" information it has already obtained). A business system

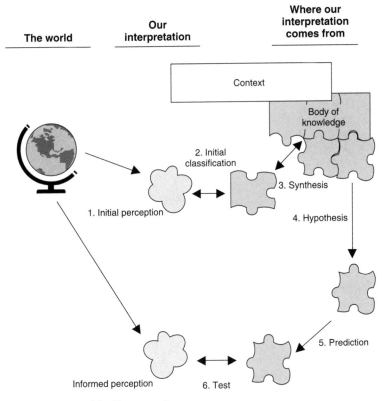

FIGURE 7.1 A model of interpretation.

begins this perception process when a customer approaches a knowledge worker at his or her desk, or a user visits a Web site.

Initial Classification

Raw perceived data is not interpreted. First, we make some sort of initial classification of the perception. With voice, for example, we classify the sounds we hear into phonemes, and combine the phonemes into words. Much has been written about this low-level classification process. Humans can discern aurally about 200 different phonemes (language sounds). In the first 2 years of life, a human is exposed to about 40 phonemes that are the building blocks of the language and culture the person was born into.

The application equivalent is the initial parsing of information. A business system separates events into transactions and then into fields within records or screens. Note that in our business process, forms and screens dictate the quanta that we perceive as business events. We make initial classifications, and we then challenge them later.

In either case, what is happening is that the "interpreter" (in this case, the person who is interpreting) is chunking (grouping it into larger units to deal with) the perceived input and making some rudimentary classifications.

Synthesis

The least understood part of this process, from a human cognition standpoint, is how each new bit of data is synthesized in with what is "already known." Our body of preexisting knowledge is available on many different levels. The perception of moving color is synthesized with other information to conclude that it is an object. We synthesize it further with additional stored information, and we conclude that it is a car.

To date the application side is far more mechanistic. A new token is acquired and "synthesized" against a grammar or a schema in order for it to fit in. Where the two seem to be greatly different is that the body of knowledge of most applications is not dynamic.

Hypothesis

Using perception, classification, and synthesis, the mind, and occasionally an application system, comes up with a hypothesis: for example, "That is a car moving toward me rapidly," or, in the case of a business application, "This patient has valid medical insurance."

At the language level, as we begin to hear or read a sentence, we form a hypothesis about the meaning of the whole sentence. If the sentence begins "Time flies like . . ." we might predict that the sentence will end with "an arrow" or some other similar analogy of time moving rapidly in a physical direction. If the sentence ends with "a banana," we first try the analogy of something "flying like a banana" but then go back and recheck our initial categorizations. We might decide that "flies" must be a noun (the insect) and "time" an adjective. There must be a new species of fly that we haven't heard of called the "time fly" that, in common with most flies, is attracted to fruit.

Once we increase our level of abstraction from the lowest-level sensory input, we begin making subjective assignments of things and events into categories. As we'll discuss later, these categories, especially when validated, can be extremely useful, but we need to keep in mind that categories aren't real things. Categories are concepts that we create to help us deal with a complex world. We must remember that they have some level of veracity (probable truth). In other words, when we classify, we might be making a wrong assignment to the category, or we might have a category that is not useful.

Prediction

The hypothesis leads to some predictions. If a car is moving toward me at high speed, I can predict that within 4 seconds it will either pass me or hit me. I can predict that over the next 4 seconds the image will grow larger and the sound louder. At the nearest point I will either feel the car strike me, or feel the wind from the car passing nearby.

In the case of an application system, we predict that certain other information will be available and meet our preconceived ideas about validity. We predict that the patient will have an insurance card with a plan name and number, and that if we call the number on the card, we will get an authorization number.

Beyond data gathering, we make many other predictions. For example, in an inventory system, we predict that we will run out of widget number 27 within 2 weeks at our current level of consumption. We predict that the project will run over its deadline by 2 weeks, based on precedence and progress to date.

Testing

After we make a prediction, we test it. Most tests are validating. As the car approaches, we take several more readings. In most cases, each confirms our hypothesis: This is in fact a car, and it is moving in our general direction at high speed.

The patient did have insurance; the insurance company did confirm it. If we get contradictory information (the insurance company is not in our system, the number does not match the patient's name, etc.), we usually start by reexamining the most recent perception; for example, "Did I type in that number correctly?"

Eventually we will challenge either the hypothesis ("Maybe this person doesn't have insurance") or the body of knowledge ("Am I logged into the right database?" "Did they process the updates to the beneficiary lists at the end of the month?" etc.).

Sometimes the test comes much later. Unfortunately, with delayed tests, we usually forget to close the loop. By the time the project completes, and either does or does not hit our predictions, we have lost track of exactly what there was about our hypotheses that led to an incorrect prediction. This is potentially valuable information that is almost completely ignored in contemporary applications.

For example, in project management applications, people routinely miss their scheduled completion dates. However, systems rarely close the loop and find out what it was about their assumptions, or perceptions, that led to the disconnect between the predicted reality and what actually occurred. Was there a difference in the amount of work? The productivity of the individual? The availability of resources? These questions, if answered, could drastically improve the effectiveness of a project management application and enable it to learn from past mistakes.

Interpreting a Foreign Language

The main difference between interpreting perception and interpreting a foreign language is that in the latter case you are actually reinterpreting something that has already been interpreted. In other words, it is not raw sensation, but someone else's perception, predigested and presented as language.

The interesting corollary to this is that it is obvious that you need to interpret a foreign language. It is evident that someone is trying to communicate with you, and you will need to do something if you hope to understand the person. Looking at a painting, after you interpret that it is a painting you may feel no need to interpret further, until someone points out that it is titled "Nude Descending a Staircase," at which point you are prodded to do some more interpretation.

How Does Translation Work?

The simplistic view of translation is that it works something like the illustration in Figure 7.2. Each word in the source language has an equivalent word in the target language and it is just a matter of looking them up and making the substitution. The existence of language-language dictionaries (French-English, English-German, etc.) implies that this is a useful strategy.

However, this strategy is useful only to a point. For example, it works for specific nouns, such as if we want to know the German word for "tiger." However, most word-for-word translations miss the contextual meaning and require some level of semantic interpretation.

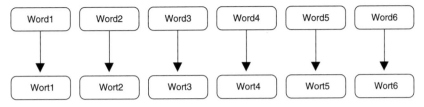

FIGURE 7.2 Naïve assumption about translation ("wort" is German for "word").

Language translation is closer to what is shown in Figure 7.3. A person (or potentially a program) interprets and understands a series of words. If the person (or program) has a sufficiently expressive vocabulary and grammar, he or she (or it) can express the concepts in another language.

In the process of translating from one language to another, does the human translator create a semantic version of the thought in his or her source language? From that, does the translator construct a semantic version in the target language, and then map that to the target language vocabulary (as shown in Figure 7.4)? Or is there just one semantic version, as in Figure 7.3? In other words, are our deep semantics expressed in a spoken language, and if so is it our native language? Or are they expressed in some other fashion?

The question for business systems is, Are we stuck with translating one schema to another for any possible pair of schemas, or is there an intermediary to which all schemas will reduce, without losing meaning? The answer to this question is unknown.

Some anthropologists believe that certain thoughts are not expressible in other languages or cultures. Sometimes a culture doesn't have a word, but

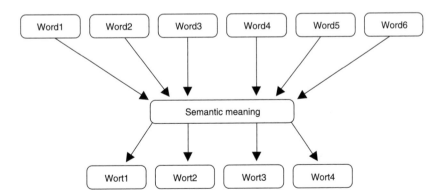

FIGURE 7.3 Translation as words to meaning to words.

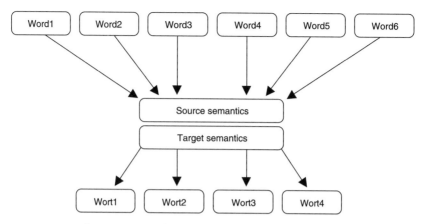

FIGURE 7.4 Semantics in two languages.

once it gets the concept it creates a word. The German word *schadenfreude* means "taking delight in the misfortune of others." English doesn't have a word for this. But clearly this is a concept we understand, and we now have the choice of expressing it as a phrase or adopting the German word into our vocabulary (which seems to be happening at a rapid rate). This line of reasoning seems to lead to a language-specific set of semantics.

The fact that, with translation, we can understand each other, and that people raised in one culture can learn another language and culture, leads me to believe that all humans share a common semantic model. I may have 40 fewer distinctions for snow than an Inuit does, but I don't think I'd have to be brought up Inuit to acquire the Inuit distinctions. There are probably a small number of concepts that have an experiential basis and that therefore have words that are not translatable, but from my experience and research these seem to be more the exception than the rule.

Work by linguistic scholars suggests that out of a large number of possible grammars, only a few are used. This gives us a few semantic templates onto which we insert a few hundred thousand verbs, nouns, adjectives, and so on, and we have all possible semantic thoughts. Indeed, a vocabulary is just a flat representation of a few deeply nested and intertwined trees of generalization and specialization.

Interpretation is far harder than expression, as hinted at by Figure 7.5. Once we have the concepts, all we need for automated expression is a small knowledge base about the domain and vocabulary. Interpretation, on the other hand, involves context, interactive involvement with the environment, and potentially a much larger knowledge set.

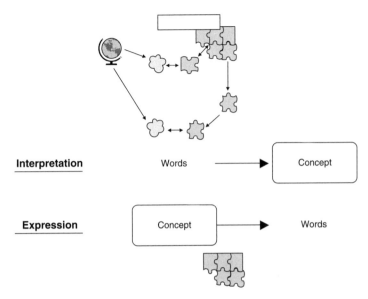

Interpretation   Words ——————▶   Concept

Expression   Concept ——————▶   Words

FIGURE 7.5 Expression is far easier than interpretation.

Why Interpret Documents?

As we discussed in Chapter 3, a document is unstructured data. Until interpreted, it might as well say "blah, blah, blah." Once we have "interpreted" a document we may:

- Know whether it applies to us
- Know what "type" of document it is
- Know what it is about
- Understand the content (potentially at many different levels)

Does It Apply?

It has been said that "information is data that changes you." A forecast of snow will change you only if it is relevant to your future plans; for example, if you're planning a ski trip and the forecast is for heavy snow, you might choose to bring your good skis instead of your "rock skis."[27,28] Until we interpret data, at least at some superficial level, it cannot possibly change us.

---

27. As pointed out by one of my reviewers, "rock skis" is not only a compound but is part idiolect (see Chapter 2). "Rock skis" are the skis with which you don't mind if you run over rocks.

28. In another reviewer's idiolect, these are "rock hoppers."

What "Type" of Document Is It?

The "type" of document is often shorthand for what it is concerns (primarily a stereotypic format and a relationship to the reader). For example, we think of an "invoice" as a different type of document than a "testimonial." We could put all our documentation in letters in the exact same format, but this would require detailed reading of everything to find what we are looking for. The "type" of document sets up an expectation of the content.

What Is It About? (Superficial Understanding)

A mortgage broker can sift through a large pile of papers and rapidly find the ones that are appraisals and income verification, passing over reams of disclosures and estimates. Mortgage brokers can do this because they have practiced this interpretation and reduced it to sets of patterns that work rapidly and generally accurately. They also have a mechanism for checking whether their initial interpretations were accurate.

Once they know what type of document it is, and that it applies to the real estate property they are working on, they quickly move to understanding the content (e.g., extracting the appraised value or the income).

What Is It Really About?
(Levels of Content Understanding)

It is possible to interpret and therefore to understand a document at many levels. Key levels include the following:

- **Traditional document metadata**—There is a set of information that is generally available as a by-product of creating or recording the document. This information is not specific to the content of the document. It includes author, date created, most recent modification date, language, document length, source, media, and format.

- **Keywords**—Many techniques exist for extracting and indexing documents based on keywords. Generally, these words are not interpreted, but are indexed because they represent unusual words on which someone may want to base a search. One of the most common techniques is to eliminate all the common English words from a document and then consolidate the duplicate words in what remains. This gives a reasonable summary of words on which to base a search, again, without any interpretation of the meaning or context of the words.

- **Key concepts**—The next level requires interpretation. As we discuss later in this chapter, several techniques exist, including human interpretation, but all share the goal of determining word meaning in context. This level of interpretation has to find meaning in phrases, as well as individual words.

- **Document type**—For most of our correspondence, knowing the type of document is the most important factor. Remember, though, that types are a form of idiolect. Although we may have partial agreement on the difference between "bills" and "junk mail," many people make little or no distinction between "invoices" and "statements." There are three main ways to deduce a document type. The first is to have a human interpreter code it. The second is to have the type identified on the form or template from which the document was produced (this is how humans do a lot of their document recognition). The third is to interpret enough of the concepts to determine the type from the content.

- **Context**—Sometimes context is easier to define than document type. There are two levels of context: a document within a broader group of documents (e.g., within a correspondence or within a compilation of related works) and the concepts within the document in the context of the document. For example, the word "frame" might be ambiguous, because it could mean the border around a picture, too rough in the walls of a house or a room, to implicate someone who is innocent, or to put in context. Context can often be derived from clues, and once derived can be used to further disambiguate other terms.

- **Relevance**—Generally, we wait until we have established a document's type and context before we determine its relevance, but some approaches take advantage of surrogate measures of relevance. As we will discuss in the section on Google,[29] there are means of approximating relevance that can be effective even in the absence of any further interpretation. However, general relevance cannot help us when we wish to determine whether a document is specifically relevant to a particular task at hand.

- **Obligation and relationship**—Finally, we interpret documents to determine if they specifically relate to us. In particular, does this document obligate us, or give us some special opportunity? Is this subpoena

---

29. See *www.google.com/* for further information.

for me, or for someone else? Is this really a subpoena? How about this notification from Publishers Clearing House—is it legitimate, have I really "won" something? When our systems can sift incoming messages as efficiently as a personal assistant can, we will have made a leap forward in having computers help with semantic tasks.

The ability to automate some of the task of interpretation will become more significant as the knowledge explosion continues. We will not be able to know everything we need to know. It may be sufficient to be aware of whole fields of knowledge, as long as you can access them when needed.

Some Current Approaches to Document Interpretation

In this section we discuss some of the approaches that are being brought to bear on the problem of interpreting unstructured information.

How Google Interprets Relevance

Google doesn't attempt to interpret the meaning of the content on the sites it indexes. It focuses on keywords and relevance. The keywords are harvested mechanically. The relevance algorithm makes use of a number of "clues" to determine the likelihood that a given page will be of interest to a searcher. Some of the main clues include its listing in DMOZ[30] (the Open Directory Project, which is a human-based indexing) and the number of other sites that refer to a given site or page.

Although this includes very little interpretation, Google has become the most popular search engine based on the breadth of its offering (over three billion pages as of the end of 2002), the speed of access (Google has local copies, called "caches," of all the pages on their own servers), and ability to rank pages in a way that most users find approximates their intentions quite well.

Microsoft Smart Tags

Microsoft has recently introduced what they call "Smart Tags" in two different products. The Microsoft Office Suite has implemented Smart Tags to automatically interpret a few words or phrases in a document. The XP Oper-

---

30. See *http://dmoz.org/* for further information.

ating System also contains a Smart Tag feature that potentially allows in-route annotating of Web pages. We'll briefly consider each, from the standpoint of its bearing on semantic interpretation.

Office Smart Tags

Microsoft has created eight Smart Tags in Microsoft Office. These are the items that it would be possible to parse out of context and get right at least enough of the time to make it worthwhile. The tags are shown in the Smart Tags dialog in Figure 7.6.

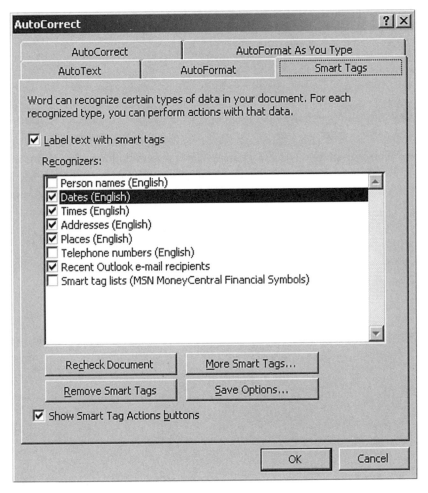

FIGURE 7.6 Smart Tags in Microsoft Office.

Smart Tags use syntax as a clue to interpret meaning. As we will describe in the next few paragraphs, this won't get you very far.

In each of these cases, if Microsoft Word (or Excel, etc.) detects you typing something like 12/21/01, it will assume that you have typed a date and tag it as such. Once tagged as a date, the application (Microsoft Office) assumes that it is a date and allows you to pop up a menu that would allow you to do something with the date. (In the case of date there are only two available options, but this is a programmable feature.)

The syntactic interpretation is easily fooled. Information concerning invoice terms structured as 2/10/30 (2% discount if paid in 10 days, balance due in 30 days) is interpreted as February 10, 1930. This style of punctuation is not used often, and the downside is minimal, but we need to be careful and not be lulled into believing that this is semantically verified information.

The rest of the tags are similar, are easy to parse, and charge little penalty for misinterpretation. Even at this level, though, there are a number of false positives (you typed in something other than a date that the application thought was a date) and false negatives (you typed in a date and the system did not recognize it). Here is a quick rundown on a few of the tags:

- **Person names**—This Smart Tag relies on capitalization and only finds full names. As a result, typing in only someone's first name or last name does not register. False positives are generated for company names that sound like personal names, and so on. Actions available include sending email, and adding to a contact list.

- **Dates**—As described earlier, any set of numbers with slashes is interpreted as a date. Jan 1 is a false negative, but Jan 1 2000 comes up right. There are also a few false positives on boundary cases (e.g., 2/30/2000). Alternate delimiters do not work (12.21.2000), but English style does (31/3/2001).

- **E-mail**—Anything that looks like an email address gets a hyperlink to send an email, but it is only a Smart Tag if you have corresponded via Outlook.

- **Stock tickers**—Curiously, the Smart Tag interpreter seems to know the difference between valid and nonvalid stock symbols. PPG (originally Pittsburgh Plate Glass) gets a Smart Tag, but PPD does not. There does not seem to be a syntactic clue in this case, which suggests that there is a database behind the scenes. However, there are many false negatives for the one-letter stocks (T for AT&T) and for lowercasing the names. The allowed options all send you to *www.msn.com*.

When Microsoft Office XP finds one of these tags in a document during typing, it puts an XML tag around it. This tagging is its connection to the right-click mouse behaviors.

I bring this up for a couple of reasons. The primary reason is that this is the starting point for some low-grade semantic interpretation of nonstructured documents. The Smart Tag interpreter is attempting to find a few semantic crumbs in documents that are otherwise opaque. Although this adds some information to a document, we need to be aware that very little semantic interpretation is going on.

Natural Language Processing

This brings us to natural language processing (NLP), which has been on computer science's Top Ten List of Holy Grails for more than 40 years. It is a difficult problem, but much progress has been made.

Scale Problems

One of the things that has dogged NLP since the beginning is the problem of scale. The problem is not amenable to demos, prototypes, or even incremental approaches (at least not yet). To get even the most rudimentary behavior out of a system it needs to have a vast amount of information organized in a way that will overcome the chaos that we deal with every day as we process natural language.

Common Sense

One of the less obvious problems has been how hard it is to represent "common sense." After making great strides with artificial intelligence (AI) in the 1970s and 1980s on "hard problems" such as specialist diagnostics and complex scheduling, we expected that some of the "easy" problems were just a "trickle down" away. As chess masters fell to the ever increasing power of computational intensity, wouldn't it be just a matter of time until a computer could engage in conversational English?

Doug Lenat rose to this challenge in the mid 1980s with a project that became known as Cyc (from encyclopedia).[31] The aim of Cyc was to organize a body of knowledge such that a program could reason with common sense comparable to that of a human. The Cyc knowledge base contains more

---

31. See *www.cyc.com/* for further information.

than 1 million concepts (assertions, facts, etc.), which gives an idea of the scale of the problem of achieving interpretation at the level of common sense.

Keywords

Keywords have been the brute force approach to mining information from natural language, but there is no semantic analysis occurring with keywords. Words are notoriously *polysemous*, which means that they are characterized by having more than one meaning. This plays havoc with keyword searches in general and natural language algorithms that are based on keywords, because there is no way to separate the references to the alternative meanings from the search.

Statistics

One of the promising areas over the last decade has been the use of statistical methods to attack machine interpretation of text. Various approaches (e.g., Bayesian statistics, Markovian analysis, and analysis of word distances and frequency) have helped greatly in reducing ambiguity in language interpretation by paring down the universe of possible meanings into a few that have been found in a reference set. Although this approach has made great strides, it seems to be limited because in the end there is no attempt to determine the semantics of the text.

Symbolic Logic

AI uses what is called *symbolic logic*. Symbolic logic is based on constructing databases of assertions, which have symbolically substitutable parameters, which are resolved at run time to make inferences. For example, we might say that any physical object x cannot be in the exact same location as another physical object y. We could say that my keyboard is a physical object. So is my computer mouse. Through symbolic logic, we could conclude that my keyboard and mouse cannot be in the exact same location.

Bottom Up

At the same time there has been a great deal of productive work from the bottom up, so to speak. Neural networks function on the principle of getting many small components to collectively work on a problem and generate solutions. However, there are problems with trying to direct this activity, and once directed it is not always apparent how the solution was achieved. Neural networks "grow" a solution of intermediate, interacting nodes that solve a particular problem, without necessarily giving any insight into the mechanisms used to solve the problem.

Agents

Some projects are based on the theories of Marvin Minsky and others, who hypothesize that complex intelligent behavior can be explained by the interaction of a limited number of not very complex "agents" if they are allowed to interact in a sufficiently rich fashion.

We have made considerable progress in each of the aforementioned areas. We have large-scale bodies of knowledge, terms, and concepts that are a necessary prerequisite. We have worked out many of the issues with statistical and bottom-up approaches to solving at least part of the problem, and we are beginning to see agent-based systems that are bringing all this together.

I believe we will soon create systems that can parse English (or any other human language) text and extract a semantically rich understanding of the meaning of the text digested. The understanding may or may not be expressed in a form we would recognize, but if the system can ask and respond to questions about the content of the text in a way that would convince an intelligent person that the system was intelligent (the Turing test), we can say that the system "understood" what it read (at least to some level).

Projects and Products that Embody Some Aspects of Interpretation

Several products are available that perform some aspect of the interpretation of unstructured data.

Verity,[32] Autonomy,[33] Inktomi,[34] and Inxight[35]

Verity, Autonomy, Inktomi, and Inxight each offer products that help with the categorization of unstructured data. Each uses a variety of techniques, especially statistical algorithms, to achieve an approximation of the meaning of the

---

32. See *www.verity.com/* for further information.

33. See *www.autonomy.com/* for further information.

34. See *www.inktomi.com/* for further information.

35. See *www.inxight.com/* for further information.

unstructured data in documents submitted to their servers. Each is also involved in document storage, publishing, and so on, but we are primarily concerned with the ability to infer knowledge from unstructured, uninterpreted data.

Applied Semantics[36]

A number of companies process documents and extract semantic information from them. One of them is Applied Semantics, whose Circa technology claims to be able to understand and categorize documents based on their content and a series of taxonomies. This is profoundly important. We should expect to see several derivatives of this emerging over the next few years. I expect that search engines based on semantic categorizations will displace keyword searches for most purposes. I also expect that mining a company's unstructured documents will create a treasure trove of useful structured information. Google has acquired this company.

Cyc

A project led by Doug Lenat, Cyc's ambitious goal is to create a common-sense AI rules base; that is, a rules engine and a set of rules that would allow a system to reason at a commonsense level.[37]

Commonsense reasoning allows us to take one set of discovered information ("John was reprimanded by his boss") and infer other information ("John has a job," "John may have transgressed some rules or performed at less than standard levels," etc.).

This is a powerful force in semantic interpretation, because often the literal information in a document, even if it is categorized into proper taxonomies, is not sufficient to reason about. Some of our most important information is extremely brief (e.g., emails) and involves a great deal of inferring based on prior knowledge or common sense to properly interpret.

After almost two decades of work, and with a knowledge base of more than a million concepts, Cyc is complete enough to be sold and used as the basis for other prototypes. Several large corporations have licensed the rule base for inclusion in products to make them more user friendly. There has also been some activity to make the rule base or some part of it available on a more open basis.

---

36. See *www.appliedsemantics.com/* for further information.

37. See *www.opencyc.org* for further information.

ThoughtTreasure[38]

ThoughtTreasure is an IBM research project led by Eric Mueller. It uses the agent-based approach described previously. The various agents run from parsers and lexical agents to analogy agents and planning agents. Although analogy agents may sound much more complex than lexical parsers, the insight is that once the other agents are in place the actual work an analogy agent has to do is minimal.

Summary

As we begin to interpret the unstructured documents in our companies and on the World Wide Web, we will blur the lines between unstructured and structured data, and between the documents and the database. Many products on the market and in development purport to help with this process, but there are no clear winners as of yet. What is clear is that this is a trend that will feed on itself, and our ability to structure our unstructured information will continuously improve.

As this happens, as query and search technology improves, and as we begin to standardize on a few ontologies, we will see a real breakthrough in the quality of meaningful information available to us.

Uninterpreted data isn't worth anything to businesses or individuals. The value of interpreted data varies greatly. In the next chapter we take up the issue of how business rules can aid in the process of interpreting and creating meaning from data.

---

38. See *www.signiform.com/tt/htm/tt.htm* for further information.

CHAPTER 8

Business Rules and Creating Meaning

Earlier, we examined how humans and software systems find unstructured information and interpret it. However, much more is going on semantically in business systems. Systems create new information and challenge that which is presented as new information. How it does this is the subject of this chapter. It is where semantics and business rules meet.

To clarify the distinction between a business rules–based system and a traditional system, we'll return to the factory analogy presented in Chapter 3. We then examine how the business rules approach builds on semantics to create vastly improved applications that are flexible. The chapter concludes with a discussion on the scope of applications and rules, and how that scope affects their building and deployment.

Note: The terminology in this chapter follows that established by the business rules community.[39] In some cases this terminology is slightly different from that used by the artificial intelligence (AI) community. Where I have found a difference, I've highlighted it to minimize confusion.

Business Systems as Semantic Factories

People process data, turn it into information, and take action (Figure 8.1). As we saw in Chapter 7, humans interpret stimuli. This chapter examines the process of determining what to do with this information. First, though, we turn our attention to the matter of partial delegation—specifically, delegating some of this processing to a software system.

---

39. See *www.businessrulesgroup.org* for further information.

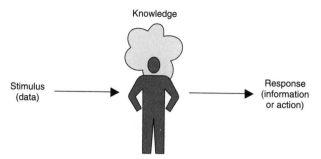

FIGURE 8.1 Human as information factory.

To delegate some of this "data processing" to a system, we have to build the system. Figure 8.2 is a schematic representation of this process, in which knowledge is transferred from one person to another, processed, and converted into a form that allows a machine to process it similarly. In this chapter, we look inside the box and see how this knowledge is represented, and just what that has to do with semantics. Chapter 9 takes up the issue of getting

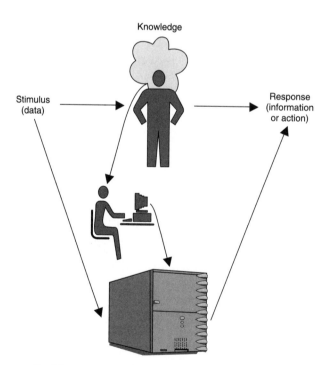

FIGURE 8.2 Partial automation of the information factory.

the information out of the heads of those who know and into a format that can be formalized, reasoned about, and implemented.

Traditional Business Software

Typically, what is "in the box" in a traditional business application is third-generation, procedural code. Still, as often as not, it is COBOL code, millions of lines of it.

These systems represent the "hard automation" approach to the information factory. We have all heard tales of how hard it is to make seemingly small changes to legacy systems. This is because these systems have developed the same characteristics as inflexible automation (recall from Chapter 3 the cost of change from rigid automation). However, in the case of application systems, the causes are mostly semantic in origin.

Before we dive into the business rules/flexible automation solution to these problems, let's spend a bit more time with the way things are now. We'll start with the question, "What is an application?"

What Is an Application, Really?

For 25 years I designed and built commercial and enterprise applications; in all that time, I never gave much thought to what an application was. We didn't have to. Applications were mostly bundles of functionality that vendors sold, such as "payroll," "human resources management," "shop floor control," or "enterprise resource planning." Some applications were leftover bits of functionality that didn't fit into any packaged application and therefore had to be built in-house. In most cases the boundary of what was in an application was what could be budgeted and managed. So "tool crib" might be an application, as well as "raw material stores" or "trip planning."

These boundaries are somewhat arbitrary, although guidelines and rules of thumb exist. Most applications are a coherent group of programs centered around some key entities and processes. Typically, applications that handle inventory transactions also have screens to update and report on inventory. However, these boundaries are becoming more and more arbitrary.

How Big Is an Application?

Applications have incredibly elusive boundaries. Once you've included some part of an application, it is easy to see that there are parts missing, but it is not so obvious on the front end what those missing parts are.

The smallest an application can be is large enough to perform a single type of interaction. For example, an application could capture time collection data. However, almost any application has a series of other interactions that are typically performed less often that would be greatly aided if they were also applications, and were integrated. So in the time collection example, the application is more useful if we have a structured way to create information about the person submitting the time report (i.e., employee record). That application, in turn, is augmented by information about the organization that employs the person (i.e., department record). In a similar fashion, the application needs information on the tasks or projects the person is working on.

Often the boundary of the application is extended to cover additional organization of the information. For example, a summary of time spent for the month, or time extended by billing rate, would each be additional information created by another application. (Whether it is part of "this" application, or part of some other, is an example of the arbitrariness of the boundaries.)

A second benefit to the partitioning of systems into applications is that each application has a manageable size and scope. This is discussed in more detail in Chapter 12.

The previous discussion merely restates what we currently think of as an application. If we look at applications through a semantic prism, we see that an application is a device for constructing more ordered information from less ordered information. To put it another way, it is a way to reduce information entropy. Let's explore this.

Noise

Applications exist in noisy environments. Not necessarily environments of high decibels, but environments where the orderliness of data is highly chaotic. The classic application is form-oriented software that is used by someone dealing with a customer.

Figure 8.3 shows what is still typically done in business systems. Either the randomness in the world is reduced to fields in a paper form, and then that paper form is entered and edited in a computer system, or (in the case of more modern systems) the "form-based entry" occurs directly in the system.

To appreciate how the application fosters the creation of orderly data, imagine what would happen in the absence of the application. A customer might walk in and start talking about what he wants, or some experience he has had. He might blather on for minutes on end. Have you taken an order?

FIGURE 8.3 Business applications are form-oriented data entry.

Have you checked on availability for the product or service? Have you even found out if you sell what the customer wants to buy? No, to all of the above.

With an application, the customer walks in (or phones) and says, "I'd like to buy something," or words to that effect. The salesperson takes out a form or starts an application, requesting the customer's name and account status; if the customer doesn't have an account, one is set up. The salesperson then asks about the product and quantity desired, and information is exchanged about the price. Ideally, the customer then commits to making the purchase.

The end result is a structured and simple set of information that represents the transaction. The key to the semanticness is the degree to which the application leads the user to create the most precise, accurate, and structured representation of what just happened or what is about to happen.

Other Types of Applications

Sometimes the noise that the application deals with is not from customers or users. An application that searches through vast tracks of data to find and extract information of interest (e.g., data mining, or trend analysis) is creating more ordered information from less ordered. But the direction is the same—using programming to create order, information, and meaning from chaos.

How Applications Create Meaning

Let's take a closer look at how applications create order out of chaos. Four major components are needed:

1. **Schema**—the structure of the end result

2. **Constraints**—rules about allowable information

3. **Production rules**—rules about generating information based on information supplied

4. **Query**—strategies for seeking out new information

Schema

The goal of the application is to create a structured and consistent set of data that is usable by downstream processes. The three most common forms of expressing structured and consistent data are the following:

- A database schema

- A transaction

- A message or document schema

What these have in common is a formal structure that has the potential to have semantic meaning. When we say "has the potential" we mean that the schema may mean something. The extent to which it is precise, consistent, and accurate is, in most applications, a judgment call. The degree to which another system could understand and rely on the semantics is unknown. However, the potential for semantic meaning is greater than if the data were in an unstructured format such as a word processing document.

A database schema might have a customer table, an order table, an order line table, and an inventory item table. The application takes the unstructured data from the environment and enables a user to put the "right" data in the "right" fields. The application contains some logic to move the data from the entered fields to the correct fields in the database, transaction, or message.

A transaction schema is a description of the layout of a transaction that can alter the data stored in the database. A transaction for an inventory adjustment might have the date when the adjustment was deemed to be necessary, the inventory identifier, the inventory location, the quantity by which to adjust the balance, the amount by which to adjust the value, and the reason for making the adjustment. Transaction schemas have been most formalized in business-to-business environments for electronic data interchange, as we discuss in Chapter 12, but are also highly formalized for internal transactions.

Message schemas, which we will take up in detail in Chapter 11, concern defining complex structures of documents or interapplication messages. The message or document schema is tagged in line with the instance data, which makes it verbose, but at the same time makes it easier to express more complex structures, and to express them in the presence of schema evolution.

Constraints

Another way that the application imposes order is through the expression of constraints. A simple constraint is a range check. For example, the number of wheels on a vehicle must be between 2 and 16, or the number of current spouses must be 1 or 0. Constraints are semantically interesting in two ways. First, their existence says that unless a new set of information passes the constraint tests, we'll disregard the information. "Unless you supply a fax number, I'm not going to accept your order." Occasionally this is exactly the intent of the requirements of the application. For example, we may not want to give someone a white paper until we have a valid email address. In this case, as we'll expand on later, the constraint ("must have a valid email address") is tied to an action ("send the white paper"). Most of the time, however, the constraint is there because it is far harder for downstream processes to deal with ambiguous or incomplete information. This may or may not be the actual intent of the requirements. Sometimes we would rather have some information, some indication that something happened, even if we don't have all the *i*'s dotted and *t*'s crossed.

The other aspect of constraints that is semantically interesting is how these constraints are expressed. Generally, they are described in the form of a rule. The rule is either about a single semantic property (e.g., "zipcode"), a predicate to express validity ("must be numeric"), or an action to take ("abort update transaction"). Constraints can involve multiple properties. A classic constraint is the "foreign key" constraint, which says that for a property of one entity to be valid, it must exist as a "primary" key on another entity. For example, the product number on a sales order must exist in the inventory table. Constraints can be complex and can be expressed at one of three times: before data entry (the constraint could make sure you get only valid choices), during data entry (interactive validation), or after data entry (when the transaction is being posted or even later).

Production Rules

Much of an application is really production rules. By production rules, I mean strategies for producing more data from existing data and an event. A simple production rule is "clone," and the simplest case would be to make a copy (e.g., making a copy of a document, or making a copy of a shape in a drawing package).

The most standard production rules in business systems are to create new records. However, the more interesting production rules are more elaborate than that. A class in an object-oriented language is a production rule. Sending the "new" message to a class causes it to execute code (the production rule) that instantiates (creates an instance of) an instance of the class to which the message was sent, and it often involves creating other associated classes.

More flexible production rules come from applications that allow users to build complex constellations of objects such that when the appropriate event is fired, they create a derived set of instances. For example, if we build a standard subproject in a project management system and then instantiate it, the production rules will create a new project.

Query

In most applications, aiding a user in finding information is an exercise in establishing which parameters are relevant, soliciting values for those parameters, and executing queries against predetermined tables in the database. Imagine what an application would be like if every time users needed information, they had to find it themselves. Queries ("select name from customer table where customerid = '12335'") are used throughout applications for validation and to get information to present to users.

Queries cover the following areas:

- **Scope**—Where should we look for our values? Historically this has been the database to which you are attached and a specific set of tables, but it could easily be broader or narrower.

- **Filtering**—Of the potential returned items, which do we exclude? In relational databases, the item in the "where" clause is excluded. Typically this is a set of predicates evaluated for each returned set.

- **Navigation**—In relational databases this is done with joins. More generally, what related data can you get to from the data you've initially selected? A rule-based approach specifies which rules govern the possible navigation and the chosen rules.

- **Projection**—Of the returned entities, which do we want to present? In relational databases, this is what is in the select class. It is a potentially interestingly structured return set.

Even Web-based searches, which seem to have no structure to them, are highly structured. The ability of Google or other search engines to find information rapidly based on keywords is made possible only through the use of various indexes and prefetched queries.

Interpretation versus Imposition of Meaning

Applications do one more thing in the realm of creating meaning: They impose themselves. The difference between interpretation and imposition is that interpretation is passive. It is something that we (or a system) does with data to try to find additional meaning in it.

As we can see in Figure 8.4, applications are not just passive processors of data. They participate, or, in other words, impose themselves on the world. That's the point. Sometimes this is direct, as with an application that opens a garage door or drops the cadmium rods in a reactor. More often it is indirect, but has just as much impact. The application says to move the raw

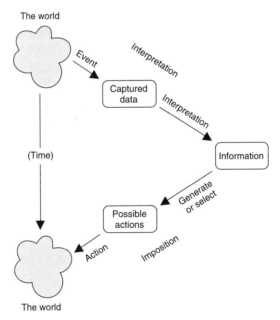

FIGURE 8.4 Applications affect the world.

material to production line 3, and sure enough the material moves. Or, as in a movie I recently saw,[40] one of the protagonists got into an argument with the other protagonist, which resulted in the second one breaking into the bank records of the first and causing him to be declared bankrupt. Despite his protests, the bank clerk wouldn't loan him any money, because "the computer says you're bankrupt."

However, applications, as we currently know them, run via "hard automation." Recall Chapter 2, in which we spoke of hard automation in the factory. Imagine a jib that drills holes in doors to accommodate hinges. Say you've been using the hinges in Figure 8.5 for years and you decide to automate the hole drilling. Someone builds a fantastic rig with gears and tracks and pulleys and the like, and sure enough, it drills the holes in the pattern you need, without human intervention.

Then you get a new supplier of hinges. These hinges look like the one shown in Figure 8.6. You have to bring the mechanic who built your first automation back to change the gears and tracks to drill for this new setup. You then have to test the new setup. And unless you completely duplicate everything, there is no going back, and no switching back and forth.

You may wish you had invested in flexible manufacturing, where you load a description of the hole pattern into the system and the system, without hardware change, switches to the new pattern and drills it.

Applications are more like the inflexible drill rig than something you would expect from a product called "software." I worked on a manufacturing resource planning project once where we had to change the field length of part number from 10 characters to 25 to accommodate the needs of the

FIGURE 8.5 Door hinge with screw holes.

---

40. *Changing Lanes,* Paramount Pictures, 2002.

FIGURE 8.6 New door hinge.

defense industry. You might think this would have been an afternoon's work, because it was an "easy" change that didn't touch the semantics or any of the logic, "just" the field length.

As only those of you who have had to work with the internal functions of large legacy systems can appreciate, this was a million-dollar change. Not only every screen and report had to be changed, but also every intermediate file and transaction. Most of the programs in this system of 10 million lines of COBOL code were affected. And of course what really wreaked havoc was the "Well since we're in here making these changes anyway . . ." kinds of additions that kept coming up.

We intuitively expect software to be "soft," that is, easily malleable and changed to fit our needs. However, the opposite is true. In the next section we review what causes software to be brittle and how business rules changes that.

How Business Rules Improve Systems Maintenance

In the previous section we described how application systems are constructed of rules about the domain. What we didn't discuss and will take up now is how those rules are implemented, and why that has such a profound impact on maintainability.

There are four main ways to construct an application:

- Procedural approach
- Declarative approach
- Model-based approach
- Rule-based approach

There are hybrids, and most systems have some combination, but fundamentally they represent four different ways to convert requirements to implementation.

Procedural Approach

This is application code as we are accustomed to it. The code in Figure 8.7 is called *procedural* because the computer carries out the procedure, pretty much as we have written it. Typically this is written in a third-generation language such as COBOL, C, or Java. The procedural code is expanded to its equivalent machine instructions and the program executes. You can predict what the computer will do in what sequence from the source code.

```
If purchaseOrder.amount > 10000
then call exceptionAuthorizationRoutine
Else call standardAuthorizationRoutine.
```

FIGURE 8.7 Procedural code.

Declarative Approach

A declarative language is one in which a developer describes what needs to be done but avoids many of the details about how it actually gets done at run time. Structured query language (SQL), the query language for relational databases, is probably the most common declarative language.

The SQL shown in Figure 8.8 will read the order table and the customer table and return the customer name and the order number for all orders over $100,000. Procedurally, how it does this is not known to the programmer. The SQL precompiler/optimizer will come up with an "execution plan" based on what it knows about the presence or absence of indexes, and the cardinality of the rows of the tables and histograms of the frequency of occurrence of values in each of the columns.

Procedurally, the optimizer may rely on the fact that only one customer has placed an order greater than $100,000 and read that record first, then join it to the customer table, and from there test the zip code. If that checks out, it then gets the customer name and order number and sends the output. However, it might just as well have tested the zip code first. You can see how

```
SELECT C.CustomerName, O.OrderNumber
FROM Customer AS C, Order AS O
WHERE C.CustID = O.CustID AND
      O.OrderAmount > 100000 AND
      C.Zipcode = 90520.
```

FIGURE 8.8 Declarative code.

one declarative statement could map to many different strategies for resolution as a procedural program, and therefore you cannot predict what code will be executed at run time.

Model-Based Approach

Model based approaches have become popular. Typically, instead of building a grammar for the language, the designer builds a model for the components of the request. Often the model is populated interactively or graphically (or both). A significant advantage of this approach is that the interactive build program can ensure that only valid models are built.

The graphic user interface tool kit is a form of model-based implementation (Figure 8.9). You pull "widgets" off a pallet and add them to your form. This is the visual representation. What you have really done is built a small model of a user interface and populated it with one object per widget, which has been parameterized with location, label, color, and binding information.

The model-based approaches typically have frameworks, or middleware, that execute the models; therefore you cannot easily predict which procedural code will execute, unless you have access to and understand the middleware.

Rule-Based Approach

Most of the rest of this chapter examines rule-based systems, specifically business rule systems. We'll discuss what types of rules there are and how they relate to semantics. First we need to distinguish them from procedural systems, which they resemble in some respects.

For example, we may have a "rule" that states that we would like to have all purchase orders over $100,000 approved by a vice president (Figure 8.10).

The rule in Figure 8.10 looks suspiciously like the procedural example from Figure 8.7. Therein lies the confusion. The "rule" is really a data structure that looks approximately like Figure 8.11. Sometimes it is referred to as

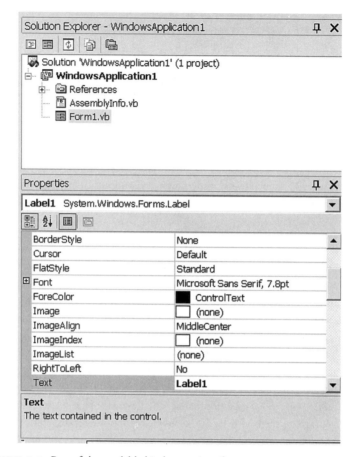

FIGURE 8.9 Part of the model behind a user interface.

having a head and a body, sometimes a predicate and an action (or a goal in goal-directed AI systems).

The significance of this difference may be more apparent in Figure 8.12, where we show the difference graphically. In the procedural approach, each new rule must be added somewhere in the structure, and where in the structure it is added is important. Each time we execute a predicate, the flow of control of the program moves us to a new point in the structure of the program. From this new point, a single rule can be evaluated, which moves the flow to a new point. This is true whether the code is a single large block of code, called subroutines, or objects. It doesn't matter. What does matter is

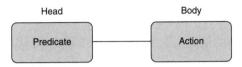

```
If purchaseOrder.amount > 100000
    then action: reviewByVicePresident
```

FIGURE 8.10 A sample rule.

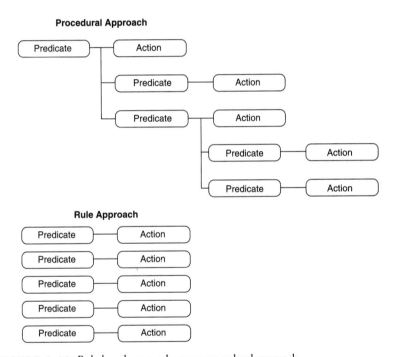

FIGURE 8.11 Rule as data structure.

FIGURE 8.12 Rule-based approach versus procedural approach.

that it takes a great deal of structural knowledge to know where to introduce a new rule.

In a rule system, we just throw the rules in a database, in any order, and a "rule engine" determines the sequence of rule execution dynamically. In a rule environment, figuring out which rule executes next is more indirect than in procedural code. In procedural code the next statement is the one that executes next. In a rule environment there is an algorithm that reads the rule base and finds rules whose preconditions have been satisfied. This set of rules is then queued up and each, in turn, is executed (or "fired").

Let's make this a bit more concrete. Say you have a program that sets the price for your products. The simplest version is shown in Figure 8.13; your price is just the list price for the item.

You then decide to offer your products at a 5% discount and your services at a 2% discount (Figure 8.14). All is well and good until you decide to offer your preferred customers a 10% across-the-board discount (off of the list price).

Now we have a problem. If we insert the new rule/statement ("If cust.type = "VIP" then price = listprice * .9") in the front of this block of code, the discount will be taken twice. If we insert it at the end, we might have overlooked some part of the algorithm in CheckProductAvailablity or ScheduleServiceTime that might have made use of the price. In this contrived example, we would probably put the test in twice and hope that we caught everything.

Multiply this a few thousand times and you begin to see why programs become so complex. For the sake of making a point, I'm going to leave out some of the complexity, such as how you determine when to fire a rule and how you determine which rules take precedence. The rule example looks more like Figure 8.15.

This isn't a rigorous example, because at this point I just want to convey the general idea, which has a profound impact on whether the automation of the business process is flexible or not.

```
Price = item.listprice
```

FIGURE 8.13 Simple price assignment, procedurally.

```
Price = item.listprice
If item.type = "product" then
     Price = price * .95
     CheckProductAvailability
ElseIf item.type = "service" then
     Price = price * .98
     ScheduleServiceTime
Endif
```

FIGURE 8.14 Slightly more complex procedural algorithm.

Predicate	Action
Item.type = product	Price = item.listprice * .95
Item.type = service	Price = item.listprice * .98
Customer.type = VIP	Price = item.listprice * .9
Item.type = product	checkItemAvailability
Item.type = service	scheduleServiceTime

FIGURE 8.15 Rules for the pricing algorithm.

To flesh this out, let's dive a bit deeper into the business rules approach, and then segue into the semantics of business rules.

Semantics and Business Rules

The Business Rules Group is a community of practice that has formed to promote and exchange best practices as they relate to applying rule-based architectures to business systems. The Business Rules Group defines *business rule* as follows:

Business rule   "A business rule is a statement that defines or constrains some aspect of the business. It is intended to assert business structure or to control or influence the behavior of the business."[41]

From a semantic perspective, we would say that a business rule is a declarative statement, made at the metadata level, that can be evaluated or asserted at the instance level. The reason for saying that it is at the metadata level is discussed later in this chapter, under "How Semantics and Business Rules Amplify Each Other."

It also generates new data. Sometimes this new data is trivial, as in a rule that validates an input field to determine its likely validity. This might be implemented by a rule that says that zip codes must be five digits long. Presented with a two-digit zip code, this rule would create a piece of data (an error number) that states, "Data supplied does not match our pattern and is likely not valid; please reenter."

However, many rules do much more complex evaluation and creation of data. The calculation of your net paycheck could be the product of a cascade of business rules.

---

41. From *www.businessrulesgroup.org.*

Two of the biggest advocates of the business rules approach are Ron Ross[42] and Barbara vonHalle.[43] In the following I will use their terminology and juxtapose it, where appropriate, with the equivalent terminology from the database domains and the AI domains.

Categorizing Business Rules

Business rules have been categorized several different ways. Generally, the first division is between those that primarily prevent things from occurring in some sets of circumstances and those that cause new actions to occur. The general terms *inhibitors* and *exciters* map to the different domains, as shown in Table 8.1.

For now let's consider only two types of rules: those that prevent or impede operations and those that enable, allow, or perform operations. Next we'll examine how rules are composed and organized. To do this, we need to take a semantic detour and ask, What do rules consist of?

Semantic Evolution of Business Rules

Rule-based systems have been evolving in their use of semantics. In the early days of AI, rules were expressed in terms of semantics that were made up at the instance level. Early AI systems said things such as "Daisy is a pet" and "Pets must be dogs, cats, or birds" and elsewhere might say "Veterinarians

TABLE 8.1 TERMS FOR RULE TYPES.

	Inhibitors	Exciters
Database	Constraints	Triggers
Business rules/Ron Ross	Verifiers	Evaluators
Business rules/Barbara Von Halle	Constraints	Enablers, computations and inferences
Artificial intelligence	Guards, truth maintenance Systems	Production rules
RuleML (XML)	Schema	Tranformers

---

42. Ronald G. Ross, *The Business Rule Book Classifying, Defining and Modeling Rules,* Houston: Business Rule Solutions, LCC, 1997.

43. Barbara Von Halle, *Business Rules Applied: Building Better Systems Using the Business Rule Approach,* New York: Wiley, 2002.

take care of domestic animals." But this doesn't resolve anything. Is a domestic animal a pet? Do we need to know if Daisy is a dog, a cat, or a bird? As rule bases grew, resolving these slight (and often not obvious) discrepancies became harder and harder.

Ontologies can help resolve these semantic ambiguities. However, it appears that starting with the semantics and the ontologies and then working toward the rules seems to be more productive than starting with the rules and trying to work out which ones apply to which circumstances.

To put it another way, the business rules movement tends to go through four stages, as shown in Figure 8.16. This seems to be a healthy progression: We start with the expression of the meaning and intent (rather than with the technology), and then gradually make it more and more formal. Michael Uschold describes a similar progression in the adoption of rule-based approaches in *Ontologies: Principles, Methods and Applications.*[44]

In the informal rule identification stage, organizations have heard of business rules and ask teams to "identify" the rules in their application. This typically takes the form of changing the design specification to have a separate section for the rules and then discussing these with users.

Formal rule definition is the stage where organizations begin to use the models, categorizations, and tools as described by Ross and Von Halle. This is the point at which the semantic model tends to enter the picture as a prerequisite, and the rules are expressed formally enough that designers can reason about them. Rules that are in conflict, or situations where there are gaps or ambiguity as to which rule to apply, can be discovered. This is also the stage where some organizations begin to use tools to extract the rules from their existing systems.

Code generation requires tools such as Aion[45] or Blaze[46] that can convert the formally expressed rules into code, which can be directly executed. Com-

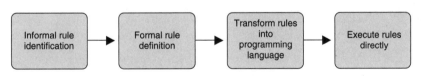

FIGURE 8.16 Evolution of rule usage.

44. See *http://citeseer.nj.nec/uschold96ontologie.html* for further information.

45. Aion is now part of Computer Associates; see *www3.ca.com/Solutions/Product.asp?ID=250* for further information.

46. See *http://www.blaze-advisor.net/blaze_rules_engine.htm* for further information.

puter aided software engineering (CASE) tools did some of this, but the rules were primarily at the presentation level rather than the business logic level. Scientio[47] has been working on a rules engine based on RuleML, an XML expression for rules.

In the final stage, executing rules directly, the rules are expressed as data and are changeable at run time. There are many compelling reasons to do this. A recent survey of large organizations found that 8% changed prices on a minute-by-minute basis. Organizations that do this have long ago shifted their pricing algorithms to be data driven, but they have typically done this in custom systems. There are many other areas where organizations would like to respond to change rapidly (and confidently). The main challenge is the infrastructure that must be built up around security (who can change the rules?) and predictability (what will be the impact of changing this rule?).

Terms and Facts Are the Semantic Basis for Business Rules

Business rule   "A business rule is one and only one of the following: term, fact, or rule."[48]

Business rule is defined as a term, a fact, or a rule. This appears to be recursive, but I believe the intent was for *business rules* to be an umbrella term and *rule* a specific subtype. Let's take a closer look at what terms, facts, and rules are, semantically.

Terms

A *term,* very loosely, is a vocabulary item. It is something that can be defined in a way that practitioners in a field of endeavor will agree on its meaning. As we will discuss in Chapter 9, techniques exist to create more precise and consistent sets of terms, but for now we can proceed with the idea that there is a set of terms on which the facts and rules will be based (or expressed in terms of).

Facts

Facts, in the business rule world, are expressions about two or more terms. As we will see in the Chapter 14, this maps nicely to an resource description framework (RDF) triple (term, fact, term). Figure 8.17 describes a "fact": A customer places an order.

---

47. See *www.scientio.com/* for further information.

48. Ron Ross, DAMA International Symposium, San Antonio, April 28–May 2, 2002.

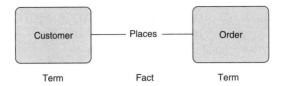

Term   Fact   Term

FIGURE 8.17 A declared fact.

This sounds good until you realize that we have no basis to know what "places" means. It is just a statement, with no clue about its meaning. This is a different definition of fact than that which is used in the AI community. In most AI-based methodologies, a fact is at an instance level and not at the schema level. Facts are generally "asserted." So at the instance level, we might assert a fact as in Figure 8.18.

FIGURE 8.18 An asserted fact.

Two things become apparent from this:

1. It is not obvious what "placed" means.
2. It is now obvious that without more information (e.g., what was the order for and who "placed" it), this statement doesn't mean much.

If we accept that the business rule type of fact is "prescriptive," in that it proclaims the type of facts that can be asserted, and the AI type of fact is "descriptive," in that it describes relations as they exist, we can make some headway.

Rules

Business rules, then, are expressed as terms or facts (or other rules). They either express conditions that must be held true ("A customer balance must not exceed $10,000") or they express rules to generate new information or actions ("The order total is the sum of all the order line amounts" or "Shipments will be held until customs releases them").

There are dozens of types of rules: rules for validation, rules for calculation, rules for typing and ordering, and rules for evaluating. I strongly suggest that anyone interested in how these approaches can improve the flexibility of their business systems should pursue the application of business rules.

Meanwhile, as this is a book on semantics, let's consider how rules and semantics work together.

How Semantics and Business Rules Amplify Each Other

There are two semantic ontologies to think about when dealing with business rules. The first is that business rules are built of instances from a business rule ontology (as shown in Figure 8.19). The second is that the terms in which the rules are expressed are taken from a semantic ontology from the domain that the rules concern. Figure 8.19 shows a small part of the rule ontology from the *Business Rule Book*,[49] in this case a few of the "verifiers." Each of the rule types is a proper subtype of its parent, and each has a prescribed behavior. As shown attached to the "unique" verifier, each has a set of templated properties that indicate how the verifier binds to the problem domain. Using a business rules system means committing to the verifiers' rule ontology.

The two boxes at the bottom of the figure represent two items taken from the domain being modeled. They must be in the ontology of the domain for the rule to have any effect.

The challenge to creating effective business rules is knowing how to deal with the potential complexity. A typical legacy system has tens of thousands or hundreds of thousands of business rules. If we re-create the rules at the same level of specification that we find in the source system, we will have even

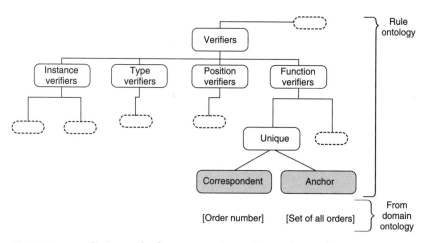

FIGURE 8.19 Business rules form a semantic ontology and use a domain ontology.

49. Ronald G. Ross, *The Business Rule Book Classifying, Defining and Modeling Rules*, Houston: Business Rule Solutions, 1997.

more. We can reduce the complexity somewhat by removing some of the order-specific rules and by getting all the rest of the code out of the way, but this won't reduce the complexity nearly as much as we would like. Having a rich ontology, and basing the rules on the most abstract aspect of that ontology, has the potential to reduce the size of the rule base considerably.

Say you have hundreds of rules about approving various kinds of expenses, commitments, purchase orders, and so on. Some of these rules concern orders at certain stages of commitment; others concern specific resources or specific funds. You may find great economy and ease of understanding when you express the rules at the highest level of each ontology. For example, you might say, "All commitment over $x must be approved before being released" or "All movement of hazardous materials must be accompanied by an MSDS label." Your ontology informs you as to what "commitment," "released," "hazardous materials," and "movement" mean, and if your applications share the same ontology, you have potentially saved yourself hundreds of special case rules.

Constraint Rules

Constraints are rules that prevent things from happening. The most common constraint is to prevent an update to the database. For example, a foreign key constraint will stop an update to a database if the foreign key is not resolved. (If there is a foreign key constraint that says all order line items must have an item number that matches a primary key in the inventory master table, any attempted updates to the order line table with missing or nonmatching item numbers will fail to update.)

In the relational database world these constraints are coded as declarative statements. In contrast, in business rules the constraints are subtyped into various types and then each one is instantiated with its appropriate parameters.

Each business rule practitioner and product vendor has its own taxonomy of rules. Some of the more common include the following:

- **Cardinality constraints,** also called instance verifiers, ensure that there are the proper number of related items or properties.
- **Type verifiers** ensure that related items conform to type.
- **Range and value constraints** ensure that a property is within a numeric range.
- **Logical connectors,** such as mutually exclusive or inclusive, restrict an item to be either one of a set of possible values or any number of a set of possible values.

Generative Rules

The way applications, and specifically flexible applications built from business rules, create meaning is not through their ability to constrain updates; this merely ensures that whatever is presented is consistent. The way applications create meaning is through the judicious use of *generative rules*. The act of "creating meaning" consists of soliciting new information from the environment (primarily users) or from inferences that allow the creation of additional information. For example, we may deduce a traveler's frequent flyer status from a set of data about his or her flight history.

Generative rules create new information when they execute. Many different varieties of generative rules exist, and they range from simple calculations to complex inferences. Each time they execute, something new is generated. All of these are done in some fashion in a traditional application, the difference being that in a traditional application they are not done flexibly.

Derived Information

Any new data that is created from old data is "derived." After some reflection, we realize that this is the case for most data. The main exceptions are measurements, where we record something from the real world, and assessments, where we discover something about the real world. Almost everything else is derived.

Calculated Data

The simplest derived information is calculated data. "Amount" is often the calculated product of price times quantity. It can be coded into the program where price and quantity are input, but there are reasons for making it a separately declared rule; for example, you can do the following:

- Express it in a way more likely to be understood by users and sponsors
- Change it more easily
- Reuse it more easily
- Defer executing it until you need it

Slightly more involved calculated data include those that deal with sets of data as opposed to discrete items. For example, we could declare an average over a set of values. We have to have a way of referring to that set. Other representative generative rule types include the following:

- Categorization rules, also referred to as projection controllers, establish that an item belongs to a particular category.

- Enablers set a behavior to be active for a given state.

- Copy, or clone, is a method to create new data.

For a thorough treatment of this subject, see *The Business Rules Book* (cited earlier in this chapter).

Generating User Interfaces from Rules

There are simple rules in almost any user interface (e.g., rules specifying the order of widgets on the screen). But user interface rules can go much further. The first set of rules would cover the minimum sizes of components based on device resolution and user visual acuity (basically a preference) and pointing resolution (the minimum button size on a kiosk is larger than that for a device with a mouse or stylus).

The content and ordering can also be expressed as rules. We tend not to think of these as rules because they are typically implemented as parameters on hard-coded interfaces. However, there are huge advantages to expressing them as rules, particularly when it comes to composing them.

Triggering the Execution of Rules

Virtually all of the database management systems have a triggering method that determines when a particular type of update (e.g., delete) is performed on a particular item (e.g., employee record bb104). The trigger tells us three things:

1. When to execute some set of business rules

2. Which business rules to execute

3. What context to use when evaluating the rules

One of the nice things about database-triggered rules is that you can be assured that they will fire regardless of what process (known or unknown) caused the update to occur. The downside is that the rules must be expressed in the language of the database triggers, which are typically proprietary extensions to SQL, packaged as stored procedures.

The context constraints are often convenience features (they restrict the scope of the context to the very items you wish to deal with). For example, a trigger that updates an accumulator for outstanding orders could be placed on the "order line amount" attribute. In practice you would have three triggers as follows:

1. Add/create trigger, which would add the order line amount to the accumulator

2. Delete trigger, which would decrement the accumulator by the old (predelete) value of the order line amount

3. Change/update trigger, which would add to the accumulator the (possibly negative) value of the difference between the order line amount and the old value of the order line amount

Sometimes you can't conveniently get to all the items you'd like to get to without making some unnatural additions to the database structure.

Alternatives to Database Triggers

Unfortunately, there aren't a lot of good alternatives to database triggering. The next most popular arrangement is to have the application call the rule engine when it needs to. This solves the performance and context problems at the expense of integrity.

I'm optimistic that as the message-oriented paradigm takes hold, there will be triggering mechanisms built to execute at the message level, which seems to be the right blend of granularity and guarantee.

Business Rules and Scope

When applications were stand-alone entities, scope was an issue only when building a new application. ("What is the scope of this new application?") Now, however, as we are contemplating separating our applications into finer-grained services, and at the same time opening up their access to a much wider variety of human and other systems, suddenly scope becomes crucial. The issue is magnified with the advent of rule-based systems because we have to be careful to indicate over what range of conditions the rule is valid.

Scope

One of the simplest, yet slipperiest, questions when getting started with an application is, "What is the scope of this application?" How we make this determination colors how we see rules in the building of the application.

The issue of scope arises because someone (usually either the sponsor or the builder of the system) wants to know how big the application is (how complex the application is, how long it will take to write and test, how long it will take to install and train people).

First, we have to separate those aspects that deal primarily with the implementation and not the application (although these are worth entertaining because they often raise application-building issues that we may not have thought about). These are some of the questions we typically hear first:

- What geographic areas are we implementing this in? This concerns areas that might imply foreign language for the application, as well as the documentation and training, but it also concerns travel, more sources of requirements, and so on.

- What organizational units does this cover? Is the application only for the use of the departmental finance group, or will it be used by all departments that originate financial transactions?

- What functions are we implementing? Does the application include order entry but not invoicing? This functional discussion always seems clear in a verbal statement but then often explodes in detail as the implementation proceeds.

- What other systems do we need to replace? Often a new system is meant to replace an existing one; however, the existing systems almost never have the same scope boundaries as the one you are introducing, which causes your scope to expand.

- What other systems do we need to interface with? As we will discuss later, these system are imposing semantics on ours, just as ours is imposing semantics on theirs.

- What data are we going to manage? First we need to determine this at the gross level (e.g., the application will manage data about employees, other than their payroll-related data). Then we get into more and more variations on these (e.g., hourly, salaried, or both? Temporary employees? Contract employees?).

Role of Schema in Defining Application Scope

In a traditional system the schema provides a convenient way to establish a boundary around the scope of an application. In a rule-based system we must use an ontology to serve this purpose.

Summary

The business rules movement is a significant step forward in building and maintaining business applications. Business rules and semantics go hand in hand. Business rules are much more powerful when they are built on a solid semantic foundation, and the business rules themselves form a semantic ontology of what it is possible to express in these nonprocedural forms.

This chapter has covered the following key issues:

- Applications built with current technology are expensive to build and maintain.

- Their complexity makes it difficult to change the system as the environment changes.

- Some of that complexity is in the rules that express the logic of the application, although they are buried in a great deal of code that procedurally determines when those rules can fire.

- The business rules approach is a major breakthrough in flexibility and expressiveness of application logic.

- Basing business rules on semantic-based ontologies, and concentrating on expressing rules at the highest level of those ontologies, will yield a great reduction in complexity of the rule base.

In summary, this approach will make it possible to change the nature of applications, making them more responsive to end users and analysts.

The next several chapters take the idea of semantic-based rules and examine the following questions:

- Since we application builders define the applications, how do we elicit or discover the semantics on which the rules will be implemented?

- Since everything beyond the most trivial application involves more than one person, how do we go about communicating a potentially complex semantic model to others?

CHAPTER 9

Semantic Elicitation: Uncovering Meaning

In the last section we saw that the application makes meaning. But how does the application designer determine what meaning to include in the application? Historically, application designers dealt with the data as presented and represented to them from users and existing systems, without giving a great deal of systematic thought as to what the data meant, whether this was the right data at the right level of abstraction, and whether these were the right procedures to deal with these issues.

This chapter is central in that up to this point we have been making a case for semantically based systems. We have been reframing common situations from a semantic standpoint. The chapters that follow explore what to do with this semantic information once you have it. This chapter deals with the central issue of finding the semantics in a particular domain.

This chapter deals with three keys aspects of the search:

- **Where**—Where are the productive areas to look for clues about the semantics of the problem domain you're addressing?

- **When**—When, relative to other system development tasks, should you be doing this search?

- **How**—How do you go about this process to maximize your likelihood of success?

Semantic Elicitation—Where to Look

Where do semantics come from? We've found the quest for meaning in business systems to be one part archaeology and two parts anthropology. In other words, we've found that some of the sources of semantics can be found in documentation and existing data, but a great deal of the meaning in systems comes from direct interaction with users and analysts. This chapter outlines practices and approaches that we have found useful from over a decade of structured observations.

Elicit   To bring or draw out (something latent); educe. To arrive at (a truth, for example) by logic.

The primary sources of clues as to the current and potential semantics of a given can be found in the following:

- Users
- Requirements documents
- Existing systems
- Existing electronic data
- Existing paper data
- Industry literature and trade associations
- Regulations

Users

Assuming there are users of a current system that is going to be replaced or upgraded, these users are good sources for information about the meaning of things in and related to the system. Within the community of users are often stakeholders and sponsors, and this process of elicitation also introduces them to the new system.

Humans are great at interpreting meaning. They can make distinctions interactively, and they can deal with the large parts of the system that are either not dealt with by the existing system or are dealt with in a nonsemantic way (e.g., in comment fields).

Requirements Documents

Most projects have requirements documents. There may still be one around from when the existing system was implemented. Generally, two or three are prepared for various approvals and false starts of the project. These documents are rich with semantics. Often they were written by the end users or their business analysts, and as such express their needs in their own language. Often they are imprecise, unrealistic, or not of much help to someone trying to design the system. You will probably be expected to summarize much of what you find into a requirements document, but that process is not part of the discovery process.

Existing Systems

The existing system is a validated expression of the semantics as currently understood, often called the "operational semantic" of the system. It isn't perfect, or there wouldn't be a project to replace it, but we have to keep in mind that the existing system can prove or disprove many assertions we might make about the semantics of the system. For example, we may wonder if a product can be in more than one category. Conduct an experiment using the current system. If it is not allowed, you may ask if this is a problem for users. If it is allowed, you might check to see if it is ever done.

Keep in mind that people have organized what they know about the domain of the business system structurally and terminologically from what they know of the current system.

Existing Electronic Data

The data in databases is a great clue to how people are really using the system. We will discuss data profiling, as a tool for finding meaning in existing databases, later in this chapter. For now, consider it a great source for clues about meaning.

Existing Paper Data

The "paperless office" is about as rare as the "paperless toilet." Despite, or perhaps because of, the great explosion of systems, we have more paper than ever. Two things are of interest to us:

- **What paper is retained**—The mere fact that people hang on to certain pieces of paper and throw away others is significant in itself. Check filing systems, as well as "piling" systems.

- **What annotations are made on the paper**—One of the main reasons people hang onto paper is because of the notes and marks they have made on it. Some of this is the data that is currently "outside" the system, and some of it places importance on the data that is in the system.

Industry Literature

Each company shares far more than they would like to admit with the characteristics of the industry they belong to. Any information you can glean from the industry trade association provides a good backdrop and potential challenge to the limited information from the company itself.

One source is literature on industry packages. The package developer has attempted to abstract as much of the differences between companies out of the package, while at the same time including as much industry-standard semantics (this is typically where software readers win points in the checklist-style evaluations). Other sources include white papers on issues in the industry or for the application area.

Perhaps the most fertile source is the ever-growing body of industry consortia standards for extensible markup language (XML). This effort involves numerous industry representatives coming together to agree on what terms mean precisely. Two good sources for XML standards are the Cover Pages[50] and O'Reilly's XML site.[51]

Regulations

Some systems more than others are driven by the need to comply with regulation (payroll and financial systems, material safety, workplace safety, etc.). Getting these regulations and extracting the semantics from them (a sometimes daunting but valuable exercise) can yield another great source of information.

The reason for doing this is due to the fact that features of a system often are justified based on some regulation. But on close study we find that the regulation prescribes a particular requirement, which has been historically implemented such that the regulation becomes synonymous with the requirement.

Semantic Elicitation and the Development Process—When to Analyze

We have some idea of where our sources are; let's now look briefly at project planning issues. The best way to think about this is relative to the development activities. Figure 9.1 shows key tasks in a traditional waterfall-style application development project. I will describe where semantic elicitation fits in each of the major stages.

---

50. See *www.oasis-open.org/cover/sgml-xml.html* for further information.

51. See *www.xml.com/* for further information.

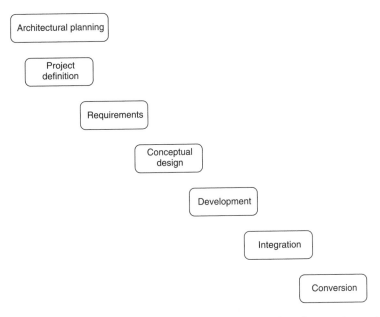

FIGURE 9.1 Typical tasks in an application development and implementation project (waterfall method).

Architectural Planning

The most powerful time to elicit semantic information is when you are doing your architectural planning, in particular the application architecture. Information uncovered at this stage has a profound impact on decisions regarding the size and boundaries of applications. As we will discuss in Chapter 13, it will have a major impact on the types of reusable services you implement later on.

It is typical for semantic analysis done at the time of architectural planning to uncover shareable services and major areas of overlap between existing systems. These opportunities can lead to consolidation of applications and reuse of services, both of which save considerable development and maintenance effort.

Project Definition and Scope

Another good time for semantic discovery is in the project definition and scope phase. This occurs when the projects are being approved, and there is considerable involvement with users and analysts.

Requirements

Another excellent time to elicit semantic meaning is during the requirements gathering phase. This is because the requirements will be expressed in terms of semantics and because of the leverage at this point in the project. At the requirements phase, you are still refining the scope of the system and are still determining what is important and what is going to be done.

Semantics help the requirements process considerably. Figure 9.2 is an excerpt from a requirements document for a psychiatric hospital system. The paragraph shown in Figure 9.2, which is just one of hundreds, is rife with semantics. Some of the semantic entities are straightforward, such as physician, county, and admission, but some are not. For example, unless you had considerable background in the health insurance industry, it would take some interrogation before you would realize that a "utilization review" is a form of authorization. Semantic analysis is consistent with and will clarify other requirements gathering approaches such as functional decomposition, use case design, scenario-based design, and quality function deployment.

Conceptual Design

Most projects have a phase where they do most of the packaging of logic into buildable modules and do the logical design of the databases. This is another productive time to introduce semantics into the project. In some ways the best time is when some work has been done on the conceptual design, but

```
The proposed system must capture and store the clinical data included on
the hospital's Admission Notification form (Exhibit I). The required
data includes, but is not limited to the following:
  Date and time of admission
  Admitting diagnosis
  Type of admission (eg civil, involuntary, voluntary)
  Court commitment (eg 72 hour)
  Identification that patient is in seclusion or under restraint
  Admitting county and Certified Mental Health Professional
  Admitting Physician/ institution
  Identification that patients rights have been read
  Utilization review requirements, including authorized days and
    authorization number
  Indication that the liability notice, release and
  Assignment form has been signed.
```

FIGURE 9.2 Excerpt from a requirements document.

not so much as to create a commitment to the design. Once people start defining and designing screens and reports, they often are reluctant to entertain changes, even if they are constructive (see sidebar).

The Report/Check Tracking System

We worked on a system for a federal agency. A General Accounting Office (GAO) report had revealed that the agency was conservatively losing $1 million per day in lost interest and lost receipts of money due. We had worked on a similar state system and were called in to assist with the design of a new system to address the problems. After a bit of looking around we discovered that one of the problems the agency had focused on was how to avoid a situation they had had historically: large (multimillion-dollar) checks getting lost while they were being processed. (There was a complex process to reconcile these checks and make sure they were for the right amount.) We suggested that they photocopy the check, put it in the bank, and do the reconciliation to the copy.

Unfortunately, this had not occurred to any agency personnel earlier, and they were deeply into the conceptual design of what they called the "report check tracking system." This was a system that was intended to keep track of the movement of a check from desk to desk as it was being processed, such that it wouldn't get lost. We might have been able to dissuade them from this, except that for the 2 years they had been working on this problem, this was the only area where they had made any real progress (the substantive problems, as you might imagine, were elsewhere).

At conceptual design time, designers will often have designed a great deal of variety into their models. For example, a recent design we worked with had entities and tables for licenses, permits, and apprenticeships. As we semantically modeled these we found that they were far more alike than different, and therefore we created an abstract entity (called *permission*) that subsumed the three. Although there were still some views for setting up the differences between these entities and tables, most of the other processes that dealt with them were reduced in number and complexity by two thirds.

This hints at how great the payoff can be from semantic modeling. Even greater payoffs were hinted at in the chapter on metadata. In most cases we've found that semantic investigation has led to the discovery of areas to which we could apply metadata design. In one case, a client had built 24 fairly similar "modules" each for a disease-specific health care outcome. This approach, besides requiring new development every time they wanted to introduce a new disease protocol, prevented any combined reporting, any comorbid analysis, or any modification to the modules. After some analysis it became apparent that a single, more generalized "instrument" could be designed in which the protocol and the inclusion of questions to the instruments were metadata.

Development

For reasons discussed earlier, once past conceptual design, few projects will entertain fundamental changes to the design, even if the changes are beneficial. However, occasionally a project will find that its assumptions have been violated midway through development, and semantic analysis can be applied to find out how to correct the problem.

Systems Integration

There is great opportunity to apply semantic analysis to the task of systems integration. The main reason this is true is that pretty much everyone expects interfaces, or other integration points, to be harder to build than expected and to require a great deal of rework in test, conversion, and even postproduction support. Developers are ready to hear the argument that the source of the difficulty is semantics—specifically, that the semantics of the system they are interfacing with are not what they are purported to be. Further, they know that their problems are not syntactical, mechanical, or technical, because they typically work through these problems early on.

Semantic modeling of a target system will proceed differently than for new development. Specifically, the investigation of an existing system will rely far more on data profiling of the existing data than it will from interviewing users. However, the result is generally the same.

You should also take this opportunity to model the aspects of the new system (if there is one) to make sure the semantics on the other side of the interface are what they are purported to be. In this case, you will not have data from its use to rely on and will have to work primarily from specs and code.

Variations for Package Implementation

Packages these days are incredibly configurable. SAP, the most popular enterprise application package, has more than 10,000 configuration options in its setup tables. The net result of this (besides running up the billing rate of people who know what these settings mean) is that you impose meaning on the application by setting these parameters. Figure 9.3 shows the major tasks in an application package implementation. Most of them are similar to the custom development described earlier.

There is no substitute for experience in these cases, but what we'd advise anyone to do would be to build a semantic model of the system as you intend to implement it with the package. The elicitation process for this model will be similar to the process you would go through for a custom system. The model will help with scoping the implementation. (Sometimes its not obvious which of the many modules in a package you want to implement; for example, do you want to implement the vendor's pricing algorithm, which is based on a complex set of tables, or is the algorithm you have hard coded into your legacy system more appropriate?) It will help with the inevitable data conversion and systems integration, and it will help rationalize your conversation with the experts you have assisting with the implementation because you won't remember what values you authorized for the 10,000 variables and certainly won't be able to predict their interactions.

With the growing popularity of XML, it is likely that most vendors will publish at least an XML version of the public semantic model interface of

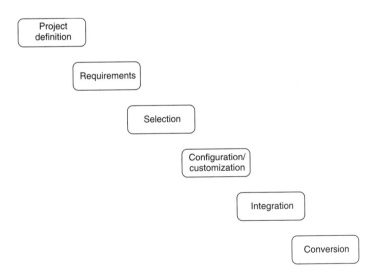

FIGURE 9.3 Typical tasks in a common off-the-shelf (COTS) package implementation.

their packages. SAP (the largest of the enterprise package software vendors) began supporting XML with its 4.6c version.[52]

Variations for Iterative Development

Various iterative development methodologies are currently being practiced, with Extreme Programming (the original XP[53]), Agile Methods,[54] and the Rational Unified Process (RUP[55]) being the most popular. How does semantic analysis fit in with iterative development?

Figure 9.4 characterizes the iterative methods: Development is done through a series of iterations, each one resulting in a functional system, which is tested and evaluated to determine what changes should be made in the next release. One of the basic tenets of iterative development is that getting the design right up front is expensive and unlikely to be successful. It is cheaper to build a working system and use that to determine the real requirements. This requires that the system be easy to refactor and change with each iteration.

This approach works very well for many projects, especially smaller projects with highly skilled developers. Given that semantic elicitation adds little overhead to this or any other kind of development project, we would recommend it for all iterative development projects.

Because of the nature of these projects, it doesn't make as much difference when you do the semantic elicitation. Doing it before the project starts

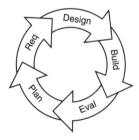

FIGURE 9.4 Typical tasks in an iterative development methodology.

52. See *www.sap.com/solutions/r3* for further information.

53. See *www.xprogramming.com/* for further information.

54. See *www.martinfowler.com/articles/newMethodology.html* for further information.

55. See *www.rational.com/products/rup/index.jsp* for further information.

may help with the scoping and initial iteration plan. Doing it after an iteration or two ensures that the users and developers are well versed in their domain.

Semantic Elicitation Techniques—How to Uncover the Meaning

We believe that experienced users hold a great deal of the semantic intent of a system in their heads, but of course it has not been organized in any usable manner. To ask a user "What are the semantics of your system?" would be even less productive than to ask the user to design it.

We have conducted more than 100 semantic modeling elicitation sessions with users and analysts in dozens of industries. We can generalize several things from this experience and suggest several techniques for making it more productive. I have summarized the recipe behind the primary approach as being three parts anthropology (talking to the natives) and two parts archaeology (digging through the ruins).

Anthropology—Part 1: Organizing Semantic Modeling Meetings

To date we have used only face-to-face meetings. Teleconferenced meetings or collaborative, asynchronous approaches may be fruitful, but we have found the face-to-face setting so powerful that we have not experimented with the less interpersonal approaches.

Defining the Sessions

A semantic modeling session should be between 2 and 3 hours long. Few groups can stay on task at the level of involvement needed longer than that. A single moderator should not plan more than one session in a day; we have done as many as four in a day, and they are not nearly as productive (it requires a certain energy to conduct these well, and it requires time between sessions to digest and document what you've learned).

You will need a scribe who is also a semantic modeler. The action will be moving fast and furious, and an untrained scribe will not be taking down the appropriate information.

To keep the sessions to the 2- to 3-hour limit, as well as to figure out who should be invited, you will want to divide your scope into a set of "topics."

You needn't worry too much about the size of the topic; the discussion will expand or contract as it needs to. Topics for a health care system might include "diagnosis and disease," "patient scheduling," "physician scheduling," "coding a visit for financial remuneration" "patient insurance."

Who Should Be Invited?

Once you have the topics you must determine who should be invited. You want at least 5 people (in addition to the moderator and scribe). You do not want more than 12. You want as many valid and varying viewpoints as you can get on a given topic. For example, on "patient scheduling" you might invite two physicians, preferably with differing opinions about how patients should be scheduled. You will want an administrator who is involved with routine patient scheduling, as well as someone who deals with emergencies and exceptions. You will want people affected by scheduling, such as office managers and nurses. Ideally, you would like a patient or two. You will want someone who deals with insurance (you'd be surprised at the insurance issues that come up with scheduling). You should include one or two people familiar with the current systems; you want to avoid having them dominate the conversation, but at the same time there will be many misperceptions about how the current system works that they will be able to clear up.

Setting

It's best to have everyone around a conference table, but auditorium seating can work. You'll need a lot of white board space. In the absence of white board, or as an adjunct to white board if you only have one board, you can paper the walls with flip charts.

Facilitator's Preparation

You will want to do some background reading before you go in, especially if you are not familiar with the vocabulary and concepts, but avoid trying to design the model on your own. If you do, you won't be listening to the dialog.

You will want to have some provocative questions ready in case things slow down, especially in the early part of the dialog. When we did "diagnosis and disease," the facilitator for that session opened with the question, "So what is the difference between diagnosis and disease?" The answers started as glib definition, but after returning to this question several times, a rich vein of meaning was opened.

Finally, you will want to cultivate what the Zen masters call "beginner's mind," meaning you want to set aside what you know long enough to hear what is being said, as if you were hearing it for the first time. (If you are asking leading questions and feel like saying "That's not the answer I was looking for," you're not in beginner's mind.) I have been involved with project management for years, and was certified as a Project Management Professional (PMP) from the Project Management Institute (PMI). I once started a session with architects, engineers, and project managers by asking the question, "So what is a project anyway?" Apparently I was sincere enough that I got a blank stare that seemed to say, "Who is this guy who purports to be a project management expert and doesn't know what a project is?" After the awkward silence, we had a great conversation.

Anthropology—Part 2: Conducting the Meeting

So you've decided what sessions to have, who to invite, and what to cover in each session. Now comes the actual conducting of these sessions.

Socratic Method

The best technique I've found is continual use of leading, open-ended questions. Unlike the typical Socratic dialog, which is meant to bring the questioner to a particular point, these questions should not presuppose the answers. You are there to find out.

Opening with a very general question about the topic will usually elicit one of two responses: either a glib definition or unbelieving silence. You could also open with a naïve question (even if you know better); for example, "So there really isn't much to this loan approval process, is there? You just look up the credit rating and make the determination." This will invariably result in the participants helping you understand that "it really isn't quite that simple."

Once the ice is broken, and you get them to talk, you'll want to start writing on the board, to create a public short-term memory. Don't try to draw the semantic models (see Chapter 10) during the meeting; I have found that to be distracting to the business at hand, which is mostly brainstorming.

Enumerating Types

Once you've identified a "type" of thing that seems to be somewhat central to the topic, such as "loans" from the mortgage example, it often helps to ask,

"What types of 'loans' are there?" People seem to be much more inclined to contribute when they are enumerating variations on the type theme.

Splitters and Lumpers   In taxonomy, as in life generally, there have always been "splitters" and "lumpers". The splitters are most impressed by the differences between entities, and they therefore advocate small taxonomic entities and tend to make more species, more and narrower genera, etc. The lumpers are more impressed by similarities than by differences, and they will always prefer larger species and fewer, broader genera.[56]

This process will turn over a lot of stones, very rapidly. At some point you want to shift to one of the following techniques to elaborate further.

Definitions

You will want to periodically ask for definitions of the terms being brought forward. You will find that most definitions are trite and aren't much use semantically, but they are good jumping off points for further clarifications. In particular, you will want to challenge why something isn't more like something else; you might say, for example, "So, 'explanation of benefits' is really just a set of error messages to explain why certain procedures were outside the scope of the particular medical plan." (This led to a lengthy conversation because most people in health care are convinced that explanation of benefits is something important and specific because they deal with it on an almost daily basis.)

Making Distinctions

As people list variations on some basic type, periodically you will want to interject with some distinctions. This is far easier than it sounds, and it generates a lot of new data that the participants often hadn't thought of themselves.

We were discussing receivables (monies owed to us) in the context of workers' compensation systems. One of the main sources of receivables in this domain is inadvertent overpayment of claims. One of the questions posed was, "What is the difference between a receivable on a claim overpayment and a pension overpayment?" This led to a series of comments that unearthed the fact that in some cases the pension overpayment concerned someone who

---

56. Wim Vader, "Splitters and Lumpers," personal communication via email, May 6, 1998.

is no longer living. This creates a very different scenario than the typical claims overpayment, where it is very likely that the payer has a continuing payment obligation against which the debt can be netted.

Using Semantic Primitives

We are building a set of semantic primitives based loosely on the work of Charles Peirce[57] and Anna Wierzbicka.[58] Peirce had a system of dividing everything in the world into a categorization involving 12 orthogonal axes of categorization. Wierzbicka's study of language has led her to believe that there are a small number of semantic primitives that are so fundamental that all people know them; they cannot be fully defined but are experienced as a by-product of being human, and all other concepts are built on them.

When the conversation slows, we ask people to attempt to categorize anything they've discussed into one of the following:

- Person
- Identifiable biologic entity (pet, tree, etc.)
- Organization
- Building
- Discrete made object (equipment, parts, etc.)
- Homogeneous made object (chemicals, etc.)
- Historical event
- Measurement
- Planned activity
- Intellectual property
- Document
- Agreement
- Relationship
- Transaction
- Category
- Generative rule
- Constraint

---

57. C. S. Peirce, *On A New List of Categories.* Proceedings of the American Academy of Arts and Sciences, 1868. *http://www.peirce.org/writings/p32.html*

58. Anna Wierzbicka, *Semantic Primes and Universals.* Oxford: Oxford University Press, 1996.

Most items are one of these or a composite of them. In almost all cases, the act of attempting to assign a proposed "type" of entity to a semantic primitive results in greater understanding of what is being said. It is important to make some of these distinctions semantically as the concepts are uncovered, otherwise the participants are going to be unsure of what is being discussed.

For example, in a discussion of work flow tasks, you need to ask whether the participants are discussing a task that has occurred (recording what really happened as opposed to what was supposed to happen), a task scheduled or assigned, or merely the category of a task (editing, for example, as opposed to editing a specific document, which could be a scheduled task). This may sound obvious, but this is exactly where most systems get confused.

Going to Extremes

It is also useful to test the boundaries. In a discussion about the definition of *patient,* you might ask, "When a patient dies, is he or she no longer a patient? When did they cease to be a patient?" "When a woman gives birth in the hospital, are there two patients or one?" "Does the patient have to be a human? A living thing?" "Is a tissue sample a patient? If not, what is it?"

Completeness/Wholeness

Somewhere around an hour and a half into this, you will want to begin checking for coverage and completeness. Given what you know about the topic, are there areas that haven't been discussed yet? You might want to write these on the board and include them in the conversation later.

Archaeology—Part 1: Data Mining

Talking to people shouldn't be your only means of accessing semantic information. The existing systems often contain a wealth of data that the users are not aware of or forget to bring up.

The real trick with data (and system) exploration is knowing how much to do before interviews, how much concurrently, and how much later (as well as how much to do at all).

Data Mining and Profiling

Two sources of data are of interest here:

- **Official data**—Official data is the data that is in the database. It has passed all the official validation and editing and represents the book of record as far as the company is concerned about what happened.

- **Unofficial data**—Unofficial data is all the data that didn't make it into the system, or is in unstructured formats such as memos. A great source of this information is notes annotated on the margin in forms or on reports. This is one of the reasons that systems designers like to work with forms that have been used. You will often need to interview the user to find out what the annotations mean.

For the official data, data profiling and data mining software exist, and if you have the luxury, it is handy for finding data anomalies and patterns. Some of the major vendors offering data profiling software are Evoke,[59] Ascential,[60] and Avellino.[61]

If you don't have data mining or data profiling, you can still do a lot on an ad hoc basis. Here are some strategies:

- Review existing reports, especially if you can find any that are exhaustive. The closer you can get to a file dump the better. You are looking for the anomalies, which are often excluded from some of the more widely distributed reports.

- Use the client's report writer. Many systems will have a report writer, which you can use to extract this data. One of the advantages is that while it often takes a lot of effort to get a nice-looking report from a report writer, it is usually simple to get tabular output.

- Use the client's query system. You may need to rely on their query system, which might include a structured query language (SQL) input if you're lucky, and may have you reviewing pages of data on a screen. Still, you'd be amazed at the patterns you will see just from paging through almost at random.

- See if they have an ODBC attachment (ODBC is a widely used abstraction popularized by Microsoft that allows many general purpose tools access to a wide variety of relational data bases). Many systems now allow ODBC access to their databases. (From a security and integrity standpoint it is not a good idea to have this sort of "back door" on your system, but if the capability exists you might as well use it.)

What you do is scan for certain cases. If you have managed to download data into Excel or Access you can sort each column, which will make searching for the interesting cases much easier. You are looking for the following:

---

59. See *www.evokesoftware.com/* for further information.

60. See *www.ascentialsoftware.com/* for further information.

61. See *www.avellino.com/* for further information.

- **Values that might indicate subtypes**—If you scan through a file that has an order-type code field, you might see an "N" in the column followed by a "W." In most cases these indicators will not be self-explanatory, although you may be able to determine the meaning from the context. In this case the "W" meant it was a warranty order (the rest being "normal"). Often blank will be normal.

- **Values that indicate temporal status**—This requires the same sort of review, although you'd be looking for values that typically change over the life of the order. You might want to list these next to some key dates, such as order close date, to see if the status correlates with the order close date. Once you find a correlation, you immediately want to look for examples that violate the correlation, which you will want to quiz people on. "I noticed that order 1234 has a closed date of 12/31/2001, and yet the status was 'P' (pending)." This will most often bring up some unusual special case.

- **Unusual numeric values**—For any measurement or dollar value, look for negative numbers or extremely large numbers ("high values" aren't used much anymore, but you may want to check just in case). Often the presence of negative numbers where you wouldn't expect them to be represents some other special case. Also look for 0 or very small values. (For example, $0.01 shows up with surprising frequency; often there are systems that will not allow $0 transactions, yet users want to enter some sort of memo transaction, and they are willing to have the cash total be off by small amounts in order to accomplish what they are trying to do.)

- **Dates**—There are all sorts of odd conventions around dates. You may find many transactions on an obvious border date (e.g., 12/31/2001 or 1/1/2002). The number of them relative to 12/30 or 1/2 should tip you off that they aren't really what they appear to be. Also look for dates out of range, such as dates that should be historical but are in the future. You should look for invalid dates, not so much to bust the validation routine, which obviously isn't working, but to start a question about what this means or how the output copes with it. You also want to compare some dates; for example, it is often a good idea to compare the posted-on date/time with the effective or occurred-on date/time. If they are always the same you either have a system that is completely contemporaneous (highly unlikely) or one that isn't making this distinction. More interesting are the cases where the posted-on date is before the occurred-on date.

- **Unusual text values**—You'll want to sort most text values and also search for special characters. You'll get all sorts of weird stuff here; look for patterns. We've had several clients put "*** do not use" as the address line for a vendor that they wanted to take off their approved vendor list, because integrity constraints in the system prevented them from simply deleting vendors with whom they had ever done business.

- **Referential integrity (not!)**—Explore fields that should be foreign keys, but aren't always. If you have some ability to execute SQL against the database, or a copy of it, try doing the opposite of a join: Look for tables that don't join (i.e., tables that either have a blank foreign key or one that does not match). We have found cases where there appeared to be referential integrity, but there were fields that didn't match. Sometimes this was because the master file was changed and the integrity was not checked in that direction; in other cases there never was an integrity check, but the users had been mostly very good at keeping them in synch.

Each anomaly is either a bit of semantic information about how the existing system has been used or at least a conversation starter for the user groups.

Archaeology—Part 2: Metadata and Legacy Understanding

The existing data is the "horse's mouth" in terms of how the system has been used up to this point. It highlights what people have been doing in fields that have little semantic validation. It doesn't shed any light on what they might have done, or what the system allows them to do. To obtain this information, we look at the systems that are enforcing the current semantics: the metadata and the existing applications.

Metadata Review

Somewhere, there is data about the data model. Maybe it's in a repository, or maybe it's in comments in the data definition level (DDL). Maybe it's in copybooks for the code. Maybe there is some separate documentation. Regardless of where you find it, you will want to review it from two standpoints:

- Does it indicate any understanding you haven't come across already?

- Does it agree with the data? If not, consider the metadata to be the intention. You may wonder why the intention is not currently executing, but that's all you can know at this point.

Legacy Understanding

Finally, much of the semantic validation is done in the existing application code. There are three main ways to gain understanding of this:

- Interview the maintainers of the existing system (this is perhaps the most efficient).
- Read the code (this doesn't scale very well).
- Employ legacy understanding software.

Legacy understanding code reads the source code to the application systems and "slices and dices" it into data that can be interrogated. Legacy understanding software can cross-reference where certain fields are being accessed, and it can also help you find all the hidden types we discussed earlier. This sofware can uncover every place there is an "if" statement and report on what it appears to be distinguishing. Some of the key vendors of legacy understanding software are Relativity, Merant, and SEEC.

Anthropology—Part 3: Uncovering the Semantics in Work Flow

Business process, or work flow, is another rich vein for semantic investigation. Initially it is useful for discovering semantics that may not have come up in the more data-oriented review described previously. As the project progresses, we can use semantics to better understand what options are available and how routing should progress at each stage along the way.

Classic work flow starts by interviewing a large number of people to document the current flow of information. In any large company, this rapidly becomes extremely complex. This is because users, and often the people interviewing them, are more comfortable with specifics and not abstractions. They are likely to remember, discuss, and go on at great length about each minor variation or exception in the process. This is their job, and they typically have many years of experience working through special cases.

Unfortunately, this isn't very helpful. Work flow proponents believe that by documenting the "as is," you can cross out a lot of the boxes, achieve a more streamlined flow, and save the company lots of money. The reality is that the level of detail obscures rather than reveals what is essential.

You may be tempted to integrate the process I'm about to describe with the semantic modeling sessions described previously; many of the same participants will be there and many of the same topics will come up. We have found, though, that having a separate meeting is more productive. People come with an expectation of talking about process, and they will be armed with forms, examples, and exceptions.

The biggest trick is to avoid descending into the detail of the "as is," while still capturing the richness of the current problem (and the economics, because many projects are still justified by savings defined and denominated by work flow simplification).

Essential Long Duration Business Transactions

A long duration business transaction (LDBT) is an interchange between an organization and another party (usually, but not always, external) that takes a long time (hours, days, months, or in some cases years) to complete. A traditional short duration business transaction, such as a retail sale, is processed in its entirety. The transaction is posted to the database and it is complete.

With an LDBT you enter into a relationship, centered around a transaction, and over the life of the transaction much information is added and changed. The transaction goes through many states. It occasionally branches into multiple transactions.

A canonical example is a purchase order. It may start as a request for a quote, become converted to a purchase order, and involves the shipment of goods, acceptance, and invoicing. When all the goods have been received and paid for, we declare the LDBT "complete."

Many LDBTs have longer lives than the organization that deals with them, and in those cases we have found it useful to examine the entire life cycle of the LDBT and then note where, currently, the organization that is dealing with it picks it up and drops it. Mortgages, for example, start with a home owner desiring a loan, and run until the loan is completely paid off. It is rare that the company that originates the loan is the same one that services it, and nowadays this is not the organization that owns the underlying contract.

The Essential LDBTs

Most organizations have a few essential LDBTs. One of the first places to check is the taxonomy of business processes we introduced in Chapter 2, and determine which of these generic processes are conducted by the enterprise:

- Extraction (mining, agriculture, forestry, oil, and gas)
- Conversion (manufacturing, generation)
- Transportation (planes, boats, trains, conveyors, pipelines)

- Facility service (janitorial, construction, maintenance)
- Personal service (health care, haircutting, entertainment)
- Business process (legal, accounting, information service)

Each will have a few LDBTs that define what business the organization is in. "Sales" may be an LDBT, or it may be the front end for a longer-term LDBT of delivering a product or service. In any event it may imply and be nested within another, longer-term LDBT, "customer acquisition and maintenance." If you are in a business where you do not deal with the same customers repeatedly, you may have customer setup as part of the sales process. But most businesses expect to have repeat business and therefore have a customer relationship management process that lasts much longer than any sales transactions.

So you define a few essential LDBTs and schedule your work flow meetings around them.

The Predominant Flow

There is some default or most frequently occurring process flow. You need to start with this. You will need to annotate this with transaction volumes and financial value to the enterprise. Say the LDBT is loan origination through to resale to the servicing organization. You will document how often this is currently occurring, how much it costs, and what it is worth to the organization. Study all the semantic entities that are related to it, in the most common or default case. There will be some things that are essential even at the default level. In the loan example, there will have to be some process to value the pledged property, some process to establish the creditworthiness of the borrower, some process to ensure that the borrower has title to the property, and some process to select and configure the particular loan instrument (term, rate, points, etc.).

Variations

Each variation is based on some subcategory of one of the semantic types in the primary flow that at some time was deemed worth handling differently. This is the time to investigate whether these variations are still worth treating differently. With the loan, one of the first variations is "new purchaser" versus "refinance." On the first category you may find differences between "new home" and "existing home." You have a series of categories based on credit ratings. At each point you want to document what is different, why the difference is worth treating differently, and what the work flow "rules" are related to the difference.

This process will smoke out most of the work flow variations. It will sort between those worth distinguishing and those not worth distinguishing. It will also keep you out of the detail of the existing work flow.

Semantic Scope

Once we begin finding the semantics of a system, we need to consider and organize these semantics according to their "scope."

"Universal Truths"

Is the semantic term or statement "universally true?" Few things are universally true. Those that are, we are trying to work into our semantic primitives. For example, we could say that an object that recorded an event that has already occurred should have an occurred-on date, and that date should be in the past. It should have an occurred-at place, but that place may be fairly imprecise (Illinois) or extremely precise (latitude 41.872833, longitude −087.62441; street address: 720 S. Michigan Avenue, Chicago, IL).

We might uncover a subtype of historical event that is not a physical, real-world event, such as a Web search or a chat session, and only be able to say that it occurred at a place but not know where that place was.

Geographic Scope

Some assertions are true in some places and not in others. In Singapore, vehicle tax (which is some 250% of the value of a new vehicle) can be drastically reduced by retiring another, older car from the island population.

In many western states, property owners are obligated to build fences to keep animals (primarily cattle) out of their property; in most eastern states the obligation is on the animal owner to keep them in.

In the United States, a sport utility vehicle (SUV) is considered to be a small truck and therefore is exempt from certain mileage and safety requirements.

Industry Standards

There is a much larger set of facts, terms, axioms, and so on that are true for an entire industry. If nothing else, the semantics of most of the vocabulary will belong to the industry.

For example, in the mining industry a *claim* is the deed to mineral rights on a given unit of land, whereas in the health care industry a *claim* is a bill for services. A mineral claim must have a precisely defined geographic boundary, and to be enforceable (a subtype or status of claim) it must be registered with the county or counties within which the claim is located.

Corporate Conventions

Although it may seem that many items are company specific, on closer examination, we see that few of them are. Most items reflect policy, "the way we do things here," identification of products, channels, subclassing relationships with customers and vendors, and so on.

Rules relative to categorizing a customer as a "cash only" customer or a carrier as a "preferred carrier," or definitions of what constitutes a "full load," are examples of items that have a company-wide scope.

Personal Interpretations

There is a branch of philosophy that holds that each person lives in his or her own world, created by his or her perceptions and categorizations. This seems to be an extreme view, and if true it invalidates most of this book, to say nothing of 2000 years of science and philosophy.

However, there are things that are true only for an individual or a small group. To make this manageable it needs to be an extension of what is true for everyone. Preferences fall into this category, especially preferences for user interface display. However, many items that have worked their way into a company-wide categorization actually belong in only a few individual's semantics. For example, rules about categorizing tasks for the purpose of reestimating or calculating reserves can be restricted to a small number of people.

Summary

Semantic information is hidden in plain sight. Almost everything we would want to know about the semantics of a company's business systems is easily obtainable, yet it takes a rigorous process to uncover and refine the essential information.

We call this process *elicitation* because that term evokes the sense that what we are looking for has to be drawn out of the participants and their systems. What we are looking for cannot be found in the form in which we need it, nor can it be manufactured through any existing mechanical process. It must be interactively created.

This creative process is an intellectual exercise in that it requires the participants to inquire deeply into how they categorize and deal with the world. It requires starting with a blank slate and putting on it only that which is necessary.

This sounds difficult, but at the same time easy. It sounds difficult because it requires a passion to continue to probe for meaning when it may seem like the meaning is obvious. It sounds easy because you may think you already do this. At some level you do.

The challenge is to blend the difficult and easy aspects of this process. Use the familiar structure as a scaffold, and pursue the meaning as deeply as you can. Whether you get to the deepest, most elegant representation of the meaning (and whether there even is a deepest and most elegant representation of the meaning) matters far less than that you uncovered meaning and structure that you can profitably use as you build your systems.

It is one thing to uncover some profound insight into the meaning of your systems, but to ensure that it does not get lost we need ways to store, organize, and communicate what we have found. This is the subject of Chapter 10.

Understanding and Communicating Meaning

To be useful, the semantic information you've collected, whether it is from interviews or from existing data or data definitions, must be organized and presented. A fully expressed semantic model of anything at an enterprise level is quite complex. This chapter deals with issues in recording, organizing, and rendering a complex semantic model in a way that is understandable by humans and deployable in systems.

In Chapter 9 we showed where semantics lurk and some structured ways of uncovering them. We'll start this chapter with some techniques for capturing and cataloging the semantics. After that we'll deal with organizing and presenting the semantics.

In practice, the elicitation and representation of semantics greatly overlap. I have separated them into different chapters to focus on each.

Capturing the Semantics

Capturing the semantics is primarily a matter of expressing the terms, facts, and relationships in a standard syntax. To make this more tangible, we'll use a single concrete example throughout the rest of this chapter.

Bill Swets is something of an institution in the Fort Collins area. His business is real, but I have made up these systems, because he has what may be the most semantically straightforward business imaginable. Bill has been welding sculptures from surplus car and tractor parts for more than 20 years (Figure 10.1). He occasionally sells one of his creations, and he has set up a park where families can enjoy the sculptures and have a picnic. The "zoo," as he calls it, is supported by anonymous cash donations.

For the purpose of our narrative, let us assume that the zoo donations cover the cost of the welding supplies and that all the parts are donated scrap.

Let's say that Bill decides he needs a system. We'll use his requirements for the examples we develop in this chapter.

Capturing Concepts

The main thing is to capture and organize the concepts of a domain. To refer to concept we use labels that we call *terms*. Take terms to be the same as entities, or vocabulary entries.

For each term, we should have a *distinctionary* entry for it. This will include the following:

- **Term**—A word or set of words that describes the concept in business terms.

- **Synonyms**—Other phrases or keywords that are either used interchangeably with this term or would be used by someone looking for this term.

- **Scope**—Most terms are not "universals." That is, most of the terms you will uncover will be specific to a line of business, an industry, or a department. Capturing this is essential, because it avoids confusion of false synonyms.

- **Primitives**—Record the primitive of which this term is composed.

- **Definition**—A concise definition that users would agree to.

FIGURE 10.1 Sculpture from Swetsville Zoo. (Photograph by Marek Uliasz.)

- **Specialization/generalization**—If it is a subtype of another type, specify what type that is and how it is distinct from other subtypes of the same parent.

These can be difficult to construct. A good example of high-level business concepts expressed similar to this can be found in "The Enterprise Ontology."[62]

Distinctionary   A type of glossary. It is different from other glossaries in that it assigns each item to a broader category and then sets up the characteristics that distinguish it from its peers.

Figure 10.2 shows a few of the key cataloged items from the Swetsville Zoo. Some of the terms aren't defined here (such as Physical Persistent Object and Made Item) because the task of defining them back to their ontologic roots is beyond the scope of this chapter. You can assume that their meaning is close to what you might expect from the name. Note that "isa" is the traditional specialization/generalization relationship.

Capturing Facts and Relationships

Facts, in the business rules jargon, are assertions about possible relationships between terms.

For example, we can say "Customer places order." This is the same as declaring a relationship in a semantic model or an entity model. We need to record slightly different information for relationships than for terms:

- What type of relationship is it?
- Part/whole (meronomy)
- Type of relationship (hyponymy)
- Reference (the relationship is a one-way pointer to some reference material or standard)
- Member/collection
- Subarea/superarea
- Composition/assembly
- Dependency

---

62. Mike Uschold, "The Enterprise Ontology." Available at *http://citeseer.nj.nec.com/uschold95enterprise.htm.*

```
Sculpture
Synonyms:  creature.
Scope:  Swetsville, the term sculpture elsewhere typically
means something that was carved from a large homogenous
mass.
Primitives: Discrete Made Object
Definition: a figure made from welded together surplus
parts.
Specialization/Generalization:

Location
Scope:  Swetsville,
Primitives: Geospatial (a place on the earth)
Definition: The sculptures are relatively large, and most
are bolted in place.  For most of them, their location is
given by a numbered position on the path that winds through
the Swetsville zoo.  The entrance to the zoo itself is
represented by latitude and longitude positioning.
Spec/Gen: isa Place

Price
Scope: Swetsville
Primitives: Currency, Offer
Definition: The amount each sculpture is offered up for
sale.  Price is at Swetsville zoo, there are no delivery
arrangements.
Spec/Gen: isa Amount

CommittmentDate
Synonyms: SoldOnDate
Scope: Swetsville
Primitives: Historical Event
Definition: The date on which the transfer was committed to
Specialization/Generalization: isa Date

PlannedTransferDate
Synonyms: ShipDate
Scope: Swetsville
```

FIGURE 10.2 Term repository.

- Agent/result
- Valence (number of end points to the relationship and how they inter-relate)
- What are the cardinality constraints? For each end of each relationship, we need to know whether it is
- Mandatory (i.e., there must be at least one)

- Multiple (i.e., there can be more than one of the items at the end of the relationship)
- A plain English description of the relationship
- Attributes that might be associated with this fact (date, effectivity, etc.)
- Any other constraints on the fact or relationship (a person cannot be one's own parent, grandparent, etc.)

Figure 10.3 shows some example relationships (or facts in business rule jargon). As you do this analysis you may be unsure whether something is a term or a relationship. For example, is an "order" a term or a relationship? We have been discussing "order" as if it were an object. We have "reified"

```
OfferForSale
Valance:2
Referents (Domain/Range):Offeror; MadeItem;
Cardinality: offeror (1); madeItem (0+)
Attributes: price, effectiveFromDate, effectiveToDate.
Description: indicates an offer to sell a particular product or group of
like products at a given price.  Offer is potentially date limited
Scope: Swetsville
Basic RelationshipType:
Constraints: Offeror must have ownership rights in madeItem, price must
be > 0

Sale
Valance:3
Referents (Domain/Range):Owner; MadeItem; Customer
Cardinality: owner (1); madeItem (0+); customer (1)
Attributes: price, committedDate, plannedTransferDate
Description:  This is the recording of a sale (not a special price
offering)
Scope: Retail, physicalgoods
Basic RelationshipType:
Constraints: prior to sale, owner must have ownership rights in
madeItem, after sale customer must have ownership rights

MadeFrom
Valance:2
Referents (Domain/Range): MadeItem; Material
Cardinality: MadeItem(1); Material(0+)
Attributes: quantity
Description: billOfMaterial relationship at the as built level
Scope: Swetsville
Basic RelationshipType:
Constraints: Must be acyclic
```

FIGURE 10.3 Fact repository.

what was a relationship. This is normal. For years we have reified relationships in database design, because there is no good way to deal with high valence relationships or attributes on relationships. Until we have systems that can directly implement a semantic model, we will be confined to treating relationships as entities, so that any misclassifications in this area won't be too serious.

Reify To regard or treat an abstraction as if it had concrete or material existence. Note that we do this at many different levels. We treat corporations as if they were people for legal reasons. We treat agreements as if they were things, and we treat relationships as if they were things.

Capturing Rules

At this point we are not attempting to build fully expressed rule-based systems from our semantic discovery, but if you studied the business rule methodologies you could see how they would lead to the ability to fill them in here. However, we should capture what we have found; not to do so would be wasting valuable discovery.

Figure 10.4 shows some examples of the information you might capture on rules for storage in your repository. Rules that will come up that can be dealt with at this time include the following:

- **Validation**—In the discussion, validation issues will come up regarding terms.

- **Temporal status**—There will be rules that describe how an item moves through various defined states (pending, open, in process, complete, closed out, etc.).

- **Calculations**—People will volunteer scoring systems. For example, you may know the entities that make up an algorithm, but not the algorithm itself. This is OK; at this point knowing what goes into it is most important.

- **Description**—An English-language description of the rule so that it can be verified by the user.

```
CommitmentDate Must Precede PlannedTransferDate
Terms: CommittmentDate; PlannedTransferDate
Rule: CommitmentDate must be <= PlannedTransferDate
Rule: CommitementDate must be <= timeNow
```

FIGURE 10.4 Rule example.

Tools and Approaches for Cataloging the Semantics

The preceding gives an idea of the detail and structure of the semantics to be captured. It should be apparent that even in the simplest business the volume of semantic information being gathered will quickly overwhelm any effort to keep track of it in a simple textual format. The sheer volume makes communicating the semantics difficult. This section discusses strategies and categories of products for storing and organizing this information, reviews products and approaches for communicating it graphically to others, and discusses formal methods for expressing the semantics.

These are the major tool-based strategies for dealing with this complexity:

- Dictionaries
- Database do-it-yourself options
- Document management systems
- Content management systems
- Knowledge management systems
- Metadata repositories
- Ontology editors

Dictionaries

Typically, when people begin gathering information about terms and relationships, the first reaction is to want to put them in a dictionary. The first problem that comes up with dictionaries is the synonym and homonym problem: The dictionary works best if there is one and only one word for each concept. If these problems aren't solved, you will get multiple definitions of the same word or multiple meanings commingled.

The homonym problem is not that serious, because we aren't trying to interpret natural language. The synonym problem, however, is more subtle. We have no problem with exact synonyms, and this is how we would do foreign language versions of our dictionary and, by extension, our semantic model. However, as pointed out by John Saeed, there are few true synonyms.[63] Most things that we refer to as synonyms contain slight variations in meaning

---

63. John I. Saeed, *Semantics.* Oxford: Blackwell Publishers, 1997, p 65.

and are not in fact synonyms. A rule of thumb is to ask yourself whether it is likely that we would write code (or make the distinction in a model) that would cause us to treat the near synonyms differently. In the Swetsville example, if there were a real distinction between a statue and a statuette (say, statuettes are small enough to be shipped by parcel post), you should set it up as a different term; otherwise, just note it as a synonym (Figure 10.5).

We need to avoid the urge to catalog every word we can think of related to the application; only those that will cause the system to do something behaviorally different are worth capturing.

```
If (item = statuette ) then routine1
Elseif (item = statue) then routine2
```

FIGURE 10.5 Behavioral difference indicating different type.

How System Lexical Scope Affects Complexity

I believe the *lexical scope* (the number of distinctions an application makes) is the real reason that the same system implemented for a large company is more complex and costly to write than if it were implemented for a small company. As we discussed in Chapter 2, a small company will not make a capital investment in creating a procedure for a variation that for them will occur very infrequently.

What is needed is a way to track the lexical scope of each distinction made, and ultimately whether the distinction is ever referred to; if it is not, it could be eliminated. The tricky thing is that there may be distinctions that humans will use in making decisions that will not be used by the system, and it will therefore be difficult to find which ones are really being used.

The next step up from a simple dictionary is some form of storage that can capture some of the richer aspects of the metadata and its interrelationships.

Database Do-It-Yourself Options

It would be handy to store this information in a database, which would allow sorting and searching by various attributes. In most cases this will mean building your own system. This section is an outline of some of the considerations if you decide to go this route. Note that the database schema should be arrived at through the same reasoning process as that which is used for the schema of any other application created this way.

If you decide you're going to "roll your own," there are four basic patterns you might structure your metadata around. Figure 10.6 is the simplest starting point for a metadata repository: Everything is a node that might be related to another node. This is the structure of document object model (DOM[64]), which is one of many ways to process an extensible markup language (XML) document. It has the advantage of simplicity, but requires that any inference you make about the structure be in the code that accesses it.

Figure 10.7 is a highly simplified version of the repository for a relational model. Each entity can have many attributes and has many relationships, each of which is binary (attached to two entities). In practice you would embellish this with domains, constraints, and so on, but this is the basic structure. To build a database from this, entities become tables, attributes become columns, and the relationships must be implemented as foreign key and primary key pairs.

Figure 10.8 shows a repository model for an associative model of data.[65] The associative model promotes the association ("relationship" in entity relationship terminology or "fact" in rule-based terminology) to a first class object. I haven't actually built any repositories or systems off this model, but it is very much in line with the semantic modeling approaches.

Figure 10.9 shows a repository oriented more toward the rule-based approach. You would expand the rule hierarchy, because each rule type has its own attributes to store, but this is the essential structure.

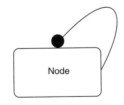

FIGURE 10.6 Generic repository model.

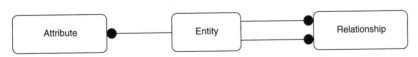

FIGURE 10.7 Repository model for ER model.

---

64. See *www.w3.org/DOM/* for further information.

65. Simon Williams, *The Associative Model of Data*. Great Britain: Lazy Software Ltd., 2000, p 215.

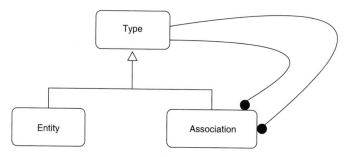

FIGURE 10.8 Repository model for associative model.

Any of these approaches will work. As you can see, the essential structures are simple and should not deter you if you do not have other tools at hand. By storing the metadata in a database, we have a reasonable way to cross-reference synonyms, and we can find out which terms are being used by which relationships or rules.

This is the route you might take if you needed to design your own system. Purchased metadata repositories have a similar schema.

Document Management Systems

Document management systems began life as a place to store and retrieve "documents." This initially meant images of documents that were scanned in and documents that were internally generated, in their native word processor formats. The main features of the system were to add indexing and work flow on top of the documents, which was useful for traditional "paper-centric" work flow procedures.

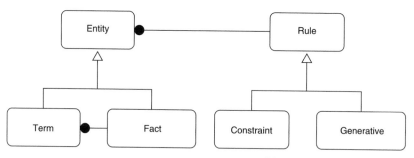

(Many more rule subtypes possible)

FIGURE 10.9 Repository model for rule metadata.

More recently, document management has been extended to include markup, which begins to put it in the realm of something that could be used to keep track of the semantic information gathered. From the document management systems I've reviewed, this would not make a particularly good repository, but if it were the tool at hand you could do something with it.

Content Management Systems

Content management became popular with the advent of the corporate web and the need to manage far more content than was easily tractable just by storing HTML pages in the file system. Content management systems have gone a bit further than document management systems in terms of structuring content and supporting more complex linkages between documents and fragments of documents. This is the type of solution that you would not buy for this purpose, but you might use it if you had it in house and were familiar with it.

Content management systems tend to focus on four areas:

- **Authoring**—helping with the process of building content
- **Work flow**—routing content around for approval and editing
- **Repository**—organizing, cross-referencing, and storing the content
- **Publishing**—reformatting and repurposing content to different viewing devices

We are primarily interested in the repository functions. Don't buy this just for a semantic repository, but if you have one and have completed the learning curve you should be able to put it to good use.

Knowledge Management Systems

Knowledge management has become an umbrella concept covering many different technologies. Most practitioners agree that the implementation is far more important than the tools. The knowledge management vendors make various distinctions between explicit knowledge (that which can be expressed as storable information, such as a recipe) and tacit knowledge (the often unexpressed skills or abilities we possess). Knowledge management systems typically focus on these areas:

- **Synthesis**—tools to help create knowledge or information from existing data
- **Communication**—tools that help with sharing and collaborating

- **Storage**—storing, indexing, and searching the knowledge base
- **Gathering**—tools to acquire data, including data mining and optical character recognition for getting data from scanned documents
- **Publishing**—technology for disseminating the information

Again we're most interested in the storage features, for use as a repository.

Ontology Editors

Several products are available that make it easy to construct and maintain your evolving ontology. One of the more popular is Protégé, which is available free as a download. Figure 10.10 is the main window for Protégé and shows the buildup of an ontology.

Protégé is freely available from Stanford.[66] It is representative of a large family of ontology editors that includes Ontolingua,[67] Ontosaurus,[68] and

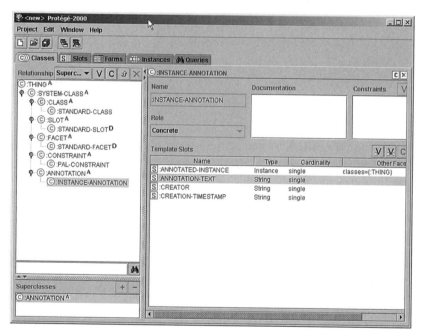

FIGURE 10.10 Protégé, an ontology editor.

66. See *http://protege.stanford.edu* for further information.

67. See *www.ksl.stanford.edu/software/ontolingua/* for further information.

68. See *http://sevak.isi.edu:8900/ploom/shuttle.html* for further information.

OilEd.[69] Their main strengths are that they are applications specifically built for the purpose of building and reviewing complex ontologies, and as such have many of the features that would be needed. Most of them export the ontologies in standard formats such as rescource description framework (RDF) glossary (see Chapter 14) or the knowledge interface format used in many artificial intelligence tools.

The primary weakness is that ontology editors are not primarily graphic. Although they can export data that might be graphed, the primary input and display are not graphic (other than an outline view), which is a disadvantage for nondedicated modelers. In the next section we discuss graphically oriented approaches to semantic modeling and look at what is needed to communicate the vast amount of knowledge that will have been accumulated through this process, and how some of the current approaches stack up.

The main point with any of these repositories is to gather as much of the semantic information as you can and capture it in an electronic format that can be indexed and searched. Anything you do to increase the likelihood of reusing this information will be useful; the tool itself is secondary. In the next section we take up the issue of building and reviewing semantic models graphically, which may be done based on extracts from these repositories, or these tools may be used instead of the repository.

Graphically Oriented Approaches

With graphics the first question is, "Do we adopt something someone else has built, or start from scratch?" The argument in favor of using an existing graphic depiction is that people will be familiar with it. The argument against is that although they are familiar, we are allowing them to confuse the semantic with the nonsemantic. Graphic notations by their nature emphasize some aspect of a problem and deemphasize others. For example, as we will see, the unified modeling language (UML) graphics would emphasize the class structure if we were preparing to implement an object-oriented system. Entity relationship models emphasize the persistent stored data and help shepherd it through the normalization process.

Requirements of a Semantic Graphic Model

Many graphic tools and modeling approaches are currently available. We discuss each of the major ones in this chapter. However, none of them is really

---

69. See *http://oiled.man.ac.uk/* for further information.

adequate for the problem. This section outlines the requirements of a notation approach and tool, as a point of reference for the following tool evaluation.

Many of the notations currently available either don't scale to industrial-sized problems or don't have features that make using the models easy. This section outlines requirements of a graphic semantic model editor:

- **Classes and instances**—One of the most difficult requirements is the need to represent what is traditionally "instance level" data (specific instantiated objects), as well as class or schema level data. The reason we need one tool and graphic representation to represent both is that increasingly we will find that a model will mix and match both levels. Classes or templates at one level will be instances at another. Any approach that doesn't allow for this will require us to shift models and representations at points where we don't want to.

- **Semantic primitives and static types**—We need to have some way to indicate which semantic primitive type that each instance, class, or type belongs to. We posit that there are fewer than 100, and more than 20, semantic primitives, and every other instance or class "is" one of them. Further, they are primitive enough that there is no temptation to include the capability for an instance to change its type over its life-time. To put it another way, there are a limited number of fundamentally semantically different base classes. There will probably be too many of them to distinguish them by color or shape, so we will probably have to rely on some sort of labeling.

- **Dynamic types or classes**—There are far, far more dynamic classes. These include state, status, and temporal change or behavior. For example, a request for materials may become a requisition, may later (dynamically) become an open order, and may eventually become a closed order. Its properties change as it morphs through these transitions. We need to be able to indicate at an instance level which dynamic types an object is. It is not as important that we be able to trace from the type to the instances. Note that an instance can be many dynamic types at once, and it might have been any particular type in its lifetime (we might want to show this). A typical application will have hundreds of dynamic types, and some will have thousands. Each one will correspond to a "type" in business rules.

- **Properties**—For any instance (or class, dynamic type, or template) we need to be able to indicate what properties it can take on, and potentially what its current properties are. Each property needs to have its name, value, and type. Most instances will have few properties and many (3 to 12) relationships (which are a special form of property).

- **Relationships**—We need to show what relationships are allowed (at the template level), including cardinality, and in some cases we may need to show what relationships are instantiated. We also need to indicate what "kind" of relationship it is (containment, assessment, reference, etc.) and indicate whether versioning or effectivity is in effect.

- **Templates**—A template is a semantic primitive. It is a special kind of generative rule. It creates new instances or constellations of instances. It can be created by other templates. We need to be able to indicate what static type of instances this template creates, as well as what dynamic types this can or does give them. We will have hundreds of templates. Many won't need to be shown in a diagram because they won't be interestingly different from their peers.

- **Generating properties on templates**—A generating property on a template is one that executes to create new data for the instance that the template is creating. We have to be able to distinguish between the properties of the template and those that it engenders in its offspring (analogous to class variable and instance variable in object-oriented systems). We need to be able to show the concept of default, and whether it is a lazy default or an ambitious one. (This has bearing if we later disconnect the item from the dynamic type.)

- **Rules**—We need a way to indicate rules, as well as which instances or types they govern. (Note that in most cases it has to be at a higher level of abstraction than instance.) A typical system will have thousands of rules, so we need ways to show and hide them, and perhaps have ways to show just one type of rule at a time, or centered on one object.

- **Behavior**—We need a way to indicate what an instance or type can "do." This is analogous to methods in object-oriented systems, but they are dynamic and can be changed at the instance level. Behavior will be reified and represented as data in the model.

- **Volumes, subsetting, and navigation**—The most important issue is that most models will consist of tens of thousands of things and relationships that need to be represented. There is nothing currently available that will deal well with that level of complexity on a single diagram.

To build these new modeling tools and approaches, we will need to borrow from other disciplines. Cartography deals with a great deal of complexity by rendering special-purpose views. Cartographers have the advantage of one fixed view (the physical land structure) against which many other values can be juxtaposed. Tim Bray (one of the codevelopers of XML) has started a company, called Antarctica,[70] to build content maps that are analogous to geographic maps.

We may need to borrow from the biosciences, which have done incredible work in the area of visualizing complex protein structures as a way to understand and predict biologic behavior. Most of our systems will not be as complex as organic molecules, but the biosciences do have the advantage of modeling a physical system that they can test things against. Our system models are not models of physical structures.

We may need to adopt some techniques such as hyperbolic trees to help us with information density. More broadly, to show complex temporal relationships, we will be greatly aided by animation and three-dimensional visualization. One of the advantages of three-dimensional representation is that it allows one more way to hold things in proximity, which is one of the things we want to do when we model. But no matter what we do, we are going to have to find ways for defining and using relevant subsets of the model.

Using Entity Relationship Modeling to Model Semantics

In entity relationship (ER) modeling, we would define the key entities in the problem domain. Figure 10.11, a simplified ER model of the Swetsville sales

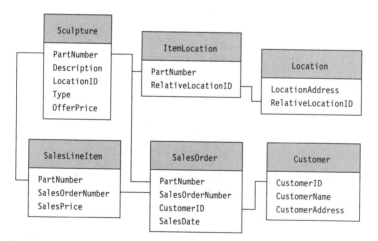

FIGURE 10.11 Relational version of sales order.

---

70. See *http://antarctica.net/* for further information.

system, shows Sculpture, Location, and Customer and the relationships that would join them: ItemLocation, SalesOrder, and SalesLineItem. Each of the entities would have attributes as shown.

Each of the boxes would eventually become a table. The terms in the gray areas are the entity names. The rest are the attributes of each entity, which will become columns in the tables. Lines represent where foreign keys will establish relationships. In other words, the way we know that an order is going to a particular customer is by "joining" the SalesOrder table to the Customer table via the Customer/CustomerID relation. If things go well, for any given order there will be exactly one matching customer, and therefore one delivery address.

Note that most of the design choices here are completely arbitrary. There is a body of knowledge, and a lot of patterns of better designs, but nothing really in the methodology to guide toward better or worse designs.

Also, to be fair, the more advanced practitioners of ER and especially Extended or Enhanced Entity Relationship (EER) produce designs that look very much like object-oriented designs, but they eventually have to reduce them to tables and rows. Most relational modelers that I have come in contact with in industry go straight to a relational design, pretty much as close as possible to the target table design.

Unified Modeling Language

The UML has become the most popular way to draw object-oriented designs. You identify the key "classes" (entities) in the problem domain, and their key attributes.

However, UML breaks with ER modeling in three key areas:

- Behavior, showing methods on the diagram
- Inheritance, in particular of behavior
- Relationship type and cardinality, with emphasis on the difference between aggregation and association semantics

With inheritance we would search our already available class library and see if there were classes similar enough to the ones we were designing that we could "subclass" and inherit a lot of their attributes and behavior. In object-oriented systems, we delegate some of the key behavior in the system to the objects themselves. So rather than have a program that calculates the order total or updates the average on-hand cost, there will be "methods," small units of callable code, that behave as if they are directly attached to the objects (instances, or analogously "rows").

In UML designs, we distinguish between relations where one entity effectively "owns" the other, which is called an "aggregate" relationship, and those where there is only a reference to the other entity, which is called an "association." Relationships also have cardinality information, indicating how many of the target objects there can be for each of the source objects.

The methods are shown below the line with () after them, to indicate that they are going to be implemented as method calls, with arguments and return values (Figure 10.12). One of the first changes is that some of the attributes in the first design have become methods.

Object Role Modeling

Object role modeling (ORM) is a method developed in Australia in the 1980s, originally called Nijssen's information analysis method (NIAM). It has recently been adopted and popularized by Microsoft. Figure 10.13 shows a part of the model in ORM. The focus is on the relationships, which are shown as double and triple boxes. The notation is verbose, but it is powerful. The emphasis on the relationships, especially the high valence relationships, is very

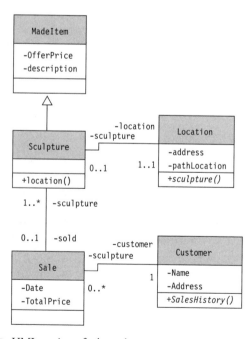

FIGURE 10.12 UML version of sales order.

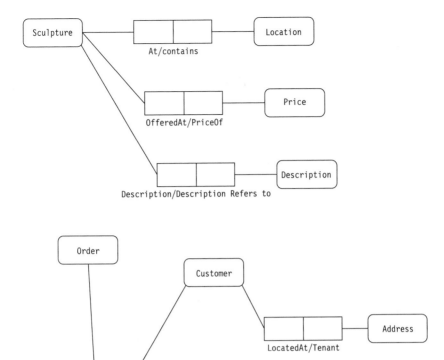

FIGURE 10.13 ORM version of sales order.

useful semantically. The model can also be translated into sentences, which may make reviewing them with users easier. Notice how the sale was modeled as a ternary relationship.

Formal Methods and Semantics

There is one other way to represent semantics, called "formal methods." Formal methods have two primary advantages:

- They can be reasoned about with mathematical precision. Truth can be deduced and proven, based on a set of assertions and rules of logic.

- They can be more easily, reliably, and predictably translated to machine-executable instructions. This means that if you can express your semantics completely in formal terms, translating them to executable systems is usually straightforward.

Formal methods have two downsides:

- Few people are comfortable reading or writing formal descriptions. They glaze over when they even look at them.

- They don't scale very well. They rely on human retention of a large number of semantics expressed in Greek symbols, and after a few dozen assertions many people cannot assimilate any more.

Some tools, such as OilEd,[71] allow the construction of an ontology graphically and then convert it to formal notation.

We'll discuss formal semantics briefly. I have not done any work with them, but found in the research for this book that many good sources of semantic insight use these notations extensively. I've assembled a brief "decoder ring" (Figure 10.14) that you can use if you find yourself faced with a semantics book with many non-English characters in it.

If you find yourself getting more involved with this you may want to consider John Sowa's *Knowledge Representation: Logical, Philosophical and Computational Foundations*[72] or Richard Epstein's *The Semantic Foundations of Logic*.[73]

This allows us to make assertions about the problem domain such as the one shown in Figure 10.15. The graphical description is equivalent to the formal notation underneath (this example uses the notation as per John Sowa's *Knowledge Representation*[74]). Read Figure 10.15 as "for every sculpture (x) there exists a location (y) such that (x) is 'at' (y)" or "every sculpture has a location."

Obviously, this is a simple example. However, these systems can become extremely complex, and the challenge is in reasoning about these complex structures.

Conclusion

The semantics of a typical business application are complex and voluminous. We can't escape that. There is a certain amount of essential semantic

71. See *http://oiled.man.ac.uk/* for further information.

72. John F. Sowa, *Knowledge Representation: Logical, Philosophical, and Computational Foundations.* Pacific Grove: Brooks/Cole, 2000.

73. Richard L. Epstein, *The Semantic Foundations of Logic: Predicate Logic.* Oxford: Oxford University Press, 1994.

74. See Sowa, p. 477, for a similar example.

Symbol	Read as	Official Name	Means
∃	There exists ...	Existential Quantifier	There is at least one ...
∃!	There is exactly one ...	Exactly One Quantifier	There is one and only one ...
∃!!	There is one unique	Unique Existential Quantifier	There is a one to one relationship between the two things noted
∀	For every ...	Universal Quantifier	This is what is true for all things of this type
⊃	If ... then ...	Material Implication	if x is true then y must be true, but no implication if x is not true
∧	And	Conjunction	And
∨	Or	Disjunction	Or
⊻	Either	Exclusive Or	XOR
≡	If and only if	Equivalence	Two expressions represent the same thing
∈	Is a member of	Set	Is in the set
@	Count	Count	Count
~	Not	Negotiation	Not
⊨	... implies ...	Semantic Entailment	the second statement is inferable from the first within a particular context
⊢	... is provable from	Provability	second statement can be proven from the first without contextual information
∩	... intersect ...	Intersection	everything that is part of a and b
∪	... union ...	union	everything that is part of a and b

FIGURE 10.14 The formal semantics "decoder ring."

complexity in the systems we build. That is the bad news. The good news is that the essential semantic complexity is nowhere near as complex as what we have been doing to date, which is to work around the semantic complexity. The complete semantic description of a typical business application consists of thousands, and in some cases tens of thousands, of semantic expressions. This is a lot to comprehend, as well as to maintain and configure as things

$(\forall \text{ x:Sculpture }) (\exists \text{ y:Location }) \text{ At } (x,y)$

FIGURE 10.15 Each sculpture is in a location.

change. But it is two to three orders of magnitude less complex than the current implementation of the same system, which will typically run to millions of lines of code.

In this chapter we've described the type of information that needs to be captured to translate the semantics you've uncovered into semantics that can be converted into a system. We've described major types of tools for cataloging the semantics that you've captured, as well as the major modeling approaches currently in vogue. Although each of these can be used for expressing and communicating semantics, and you will probably use the tool or approach that you are familiar with or have already purchased, none of them is ideal. I've laid out the requirements as best I know at this point, and I hope that some enterprising software developers will come forward and build something into this outline that will make semantics far easier to express and convey.

Finally, we dealt with the issues of expressing semantics formally and the role this will play in converting our semantic models into systems that actually do something.

The remainder of this book picks this thread up and explains the key role of semantics in some key technology initiatives as we enter the twenty-first century, specifically XML, enterprise application integration, Web Services, and the Semantic Web.

CHAPTER 11

Extensible Markup Language (XML)

The common myth is that Extensible markup language (XML) exploded onto the scene in the late 1990s as a semantic alternative to hypertext markup language (HTML).[75] In this chapter we'll dismantle that myth and reconstruct an even more interesting reality.

The reality is that economic and technical forces have aligned for XML to be the common denominator of all our semantic initiatives, for at least the next decade, including most content management, application integration, service invocation, knowledge management, and rule expression. However, as we will discuss in this chapter, XML is not a semantic language; it provides a place to store semantics.

I'll describe in this chapter how this has come to be and how we can be so certain about the role of XML. I'm also going to delve into some aspects of XML and its many derivatives that will aid the transition to semantically based systems. We'll examine the essential nature of XML, as well as the many technologies that have evolved within the XML ecology.

What Is XML?

XML is short for extensible markup language:

- **Extensible**—That is, we are not stuck with a predefined set of tags or identifiers

---

75. There wasn't anything in the language of the original proposal (see *www.w3.org/TR/PR-xml-971208*) that indicated an intent for XML to be a semantic alternative to HTML, but the press soon caught on to the idea.

- **Markup**—A way to add information about structure or content from within a document or transaction
- **Language**—A standard syntax and grammar for the markup

To put it another way, XML is a tagged markup language that allows anyone to define their own tags. On the surface that sounds like a prescription for anarchy, and there is some of that, but as we'll discuss in this chapter, it is this flexibility that lends itself to semantic expression.

Figure 11.1 is a tiny snippet of HTML. It is a tagged markup language. The <h1> and matching </h1> are "tags" around the name "John Smith." But in the case of HTML, all we know about John Smith is that it is a heading.

```
<h1> John Smith </h1>
```

FIGURE 11.1 HTML snippet.

The XML fragment in Figure 11.2 is also tagged, but in this case we have some clue as to what or who "John Smith" is. "Author" is something other than a formatting hint, but at this level we can't tell any more about it. The difference is between format tags and content tags. But before we get into the difference let's take a look at the motivation behind the creation of XML.

```
<Author> John Smith </Author>
```

FIGURE 11.2 XML snippet.

Where XML Came From

Document markup languages have been around for decades. In 1973 IBM developed the generalized markup language (GML). This was a markup language that was inserted into documents, primarily for formatting. However, it was a proprietary markup language.

Eight years of development, with input from hundreds of people in the document management community, led to the standard generalized markup language (SGML) in 1985. SGML was a comprehensive and widely adopted way to annotate documents with structure.

However, SGML was complex. It was complex to learn, and writing parsers and interpreters was also complex. In 1991 Tim Berners-Lee developed HTML as an application of SGML, tailored specifically for displaying text and graphics and supporting interdocument links. Due at least in part to its great simplicity, HTML and the World Wide Web took off.

HTML is a tagged markup language, but there is a fixed set of tags. The tags don't represent semantic concepts; the tags are layout and presentation clues. The tags that indicate "bold face" or "table" do not determine what the bold-faced item is, nor whether the items in the rows of the table have any relationship to the column headings.

By 1996 several people had come to the conclusion that the World Wide Web would eventually outgrow HTML. The Web needed the expressiveness of SGML without its complexity, and XML was created out of that vision. The team that authored the XML specification did so with the goal to get 80% of the expressiveness out of 20% of the grammar. The result is that XML is a derivative and a subset of SGML.

What we have in XML is a simpler and more consistent language, with a high degree of extensibility. XML is stricter than HTML about grammatical elements such as tag matching. The original spec was 28 pages long, and even after years of debate and revision it is only 38 pages long.

XML's Popularity

XML has gone from relative obscurity to virtual ubiquity in just a few years. By 2002 it was rare to hear of a software product, an industry consortium, or a large-scale integration effort that wasn't based on XML. Let's take a look at some of the features that have led to such rapid adoption, and set the stage for semantic markup.

Rendition Preserves Composition

The success of the relational model popularized the idea that data, in their native state, are tables. In all but the simplest cases, however, the data are likely to be complex graphs. A graph in this context is not line art or graphics, but refers to a relationship in which the data items refer to each other through a network of interrelationships. The graph in Figure 11.3 is meant to represent part of the composition of the metal sculpture from the Swetsville Zoo shown in Figure 10.1. The sculpture has a location, an offer price, a body, and a head. The head in turn has several parts, including two eyes, each of which is a "gear."

In the relational model, the graph is still there, but it is implemented as tables and foreign keys (Figure 11.4). To build the sculpture out of the

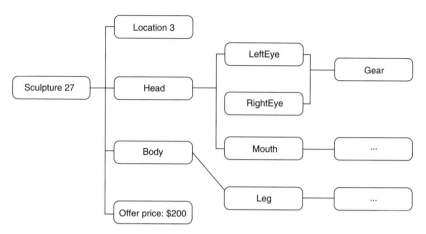

FIGURE 11.3 Sculpture as a graph.

components, as they reside in the tables, you have to "join" the appropriate rows in the tables, until you have a structure that resembles the graph or tree shown in Figure 11.3. Reducing a complex structure to its primary tables before storing it in the database has been likened to dismantling your car into its elemental pieces every time you drive it into your garage. This mismatch between how data is typically stored in a relational database and how it is typically used in a program is the primary source of contention between object-oriented programmers and database administrators.

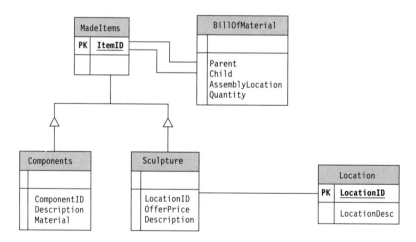

FIGURE 11.4 Sculpture as tables.

The data in the tables is shown in Figure 11.5, and a query to put the tree back together again is shown in Figure 11.6.

When a user wants to access a subset of data from the graph, he or she typically describes a tree of data that is arrived at from some starting point. On the left side of Figure 11.5 we have the graph of the sculpture as it normally exists. This would be the object-oriented instance representation. However, XML is primarily hierarchic (i.e., each node can have only a single parent), so it can't represent the graph easily or directly. Instead, in most usages the graph is converted to a tree, as shown in the right side of Figure 11.7. The only difference is that the "gear" is repeated in the two places it is referred to. (Note: You do not have to repeat the data every time it is needed; you can use XML's ID/IDREF features to refer to a subtree stored elsewhere.)

XML preserves the tree structure. The structure is captured in an XML document as shown in Figure 11.8.

Components			
ItemID	Component ID	Material	Description
G1	Part	Gear	Differential Gear
H1	Assembly	Metal	Insect Head
B1	Assembly	Metal	Insect Body
M1	Asembly	Metal	Insect Mouth
L1	Part	Exhaust	Exhaust Pip

BillOfMaterial			
ParentID	ChildID	Location	Quantity
27	H1		1
H1	G1	LeftEye	1
H1	G1	RightEye	1
27	B1	Posterior	1
B1	L1	RightFront	1
H1	M1	Mandible	1

Sculpture			
ItemID	LocationID	OfferPrice	Description
27	3	200.00	Six Legged Insect
28	4	600.00	Diplodocus

Location	
LocationID	Description
3	MainPath Station 3

FIGURE 11.5 Data in the sculpture tables.

```
SELECT LPAD (" ", 2*LEVEL) U.ItemID, U.Description
FROM U,
CONNECTBY PRIOR B.parentID = U.itemID
START WITH U.itemID = "27"
 (UNION SELECT ItemID, Description
    FROM Sculpture, Component
    ORDERBY ItemID, Description) AS U
```

FIGURE 11.6 A query to get the "tree" from the tables.

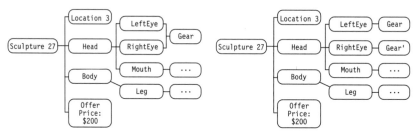

FIGURE 11.7 A tree from a graph.

```
<sculpture>
<location> </location>
<head>
   <lefteye>
      <MadeItem> Gear </MadeItem>
   </lefteye>
   <righteye>
      <MadeItem> Gear </MadeItem>
   </righteye>
</head>
<body>
   <leg> L1 </leg>
</body>
<offerPrice> 200 </offerPrice>
</sculpture>
```

FIGURE 11.8 XML version of sculpture.

Readable by Humans and Systems

One of the advantages of the XML syntax is that it is readable by humans, as well as systems, although it's not optimal for either. Further, what the human and the machine understand is not the same. As we discussed in Chapter 5, a completely unstructured document (e.g., a memo) is understandable only by humans, and a compiled program is understandable only by systems. Having one grammar that goes both ways is more powerful than it first sounds. It means you can build an Application Program Interface (API) that is meant for use by another program, and with very little adjustment allow a human to use it. This greatly rationalizes a system and ensures that the inputs from people and other systems are being subjected to the same edits.

Document/Transaction Duality

Light exhibits *wave/particle duality*, which means that sometimes it behaves like a wave and sometimes it behaves like a particle. XML has what I call "document/message duality," meaning that sometimes it behaves like a document and sometimes it behaves like a message or transaction.

Really it doesn't have any behavior at all, but sometimes we treat it one way or the other. What is interesting about this is that SGML and many other document markup languages were treated exclusively as documents, and the world of messages was pretty much in the domain of Electronic Data Interchange (EDI) and other non–self-describing approaches.

What is refreshing about XML is that it has this dual nature, which causes us to think a bit longer about the question, "What is the difference between a document and a message?" Indeed, we find that there really isn't any difference. Documents can be messages. Messages can be documents. Having one representation allows us to reuse interfaces, treat messages as documents, and treat documents as messages, as it is convenient.

Data Describes Itself

There was a pattern in the object-oriented pattern community called "data describes itself," which advised that a system was likely to be easier to maintain if the data and the definition of the data (at least some part of the schema) traveled together.

This is an interesting insight. The state of the art at the time for inter-application data communication was EDI, which relied on the sender and receiver "knowing" the precise layouts and sequences of all the record types in the communication. (Chapter 12 goes into this in more detail, as well as strategies for using XML and semantics in situations that were previously in the domain of EDI.)

With XML the structure and the labels (tags) for the values are transmitted with the data, in every invocation. This is inefficient, but the incremental cost of doubling or even tripling the size of each message packet is becoming a smaller and smaller penalty to bear.

"Standard Gauge"

Perhaps the most important thing about XML is that, like another great standard, it has become almost universally adopted (Figure 11.9). The standard gauge for railroads in the United States is 4 feet 8.5 inches (the Stephenson gauge). It is not superior in any significant way to any of the more than 120

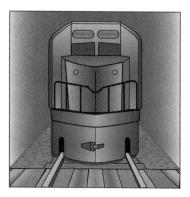

FIGURE 11.9 Standard gauge.

gauges that have been developed and used commercially, or the 60 or so that are still in use in some applications or in some areas.

However, virtually all passenger and freight in North America is carried on rails that are 4 feet 8.5 inches wide, because once a majority of the railroads conformed there was a great benefit to all of them conforming. Before the Civil War about half of all railroads used the Stephenson gauge. After the war a consortium (the Master Car Builders Association) committed to this standardization, and it became nearly universal.

The point is that even if XML were not vastly technically superior, it has been adopted enthusiastically by virtually every software manufacturer, and its use as a lingua franca is pretty well guaranteed.

The Stability of XML

Many people are concerned about the variety and stability of XML. The currently approved standard is XML 1.0 (second edition).[76] Unfortunately, the practices of the software community over the last two decades have conditioned users to avoid 1.0 releases of anything. "Wait until they iron out the bugs," "Don't be a guinea pig," and "Wait for the 3.0 release" are common rules of thumb.

But XML really is different. There is a huge amount of history behind it. The originally proposed specification from 1996 is scarcely different at a level that most people would recognize from the current spec. There is a 1.1

---

76. See *www.w3.org/TR/REC-xml* for the W3C XML 1.0 spec.

spec, and although there are differences that would be important to parsers and tool writers, the average user will not recognize some of the suggested improvements (e.g., changes to the "new line" conventions).

To the best of my knowledge there is no 2.0 spec in the works, and anyone who waits for the 3.0 release is going to be waiting a long, long time.

Some of the perception of the unstableness of XML is really meant for the many derivatives that have been built on top of XML. We will deal with them later in this chapter in the section on XML derivatives. Before we get to that, though, we need to clear up something we've left unsaid—namely, that nothing we have said yet sheds any light on XML as a semantic tag language.

Syntax and Semantics

As mentioned earlier, XML was heralded as a semantic alternative to HTML. Let's take a closer look at this claim. Before we do, we need to say a few words about "parsers" and "well formedness."

Parsers

For software to make use of an XML document or message, first it must parse it, or separate it into its tokens. Many parsers are available, and many products now contain them. This process of taking an XML document and separating it into its component pieces is also called "shredding," especially if the intent is to store the pieces atomically in a relational database.

A parser looks for the matching tags and turns everything it finds in between into a token (which may or may not be further subdivided if it has matching tags within it).

Well Formedness

The parser can evaluate whether the XML message (or document) is "well formed." Basically, *well formed* means that the tags match up and there are no characters out of place. Well formedness says nothing about what the data means or whether it agrees with its schema, or even if there is a schema. We'll discuss XML schemas later in this chapter, but at this point we should note that XML does not require schemas. An XML document can be well formed whether it has a schema or not.

Semantics in the Tags?

We have yet to ask the question, "What do the tags mean?" In other words, where do the semantics come from? Looking back to Figure 11.2, there is nothing inherent in the tag or anything else that creates meaning for the tag "author," other than the fact that many of us humans recognize it and think we know what it means. As far as an XML parser is concerned, it could just as well have been as shown in Figure 11.10.

```
<xyz>  John Smith </xyz>
```

FIGURE 11.10 A tagged value.

The XML web is still really a syntactic web.[77] We have agreed on the syntax, the matching of the tags, and so on, but little else. Even where we have schema, which we do most of the time, the systems are not aware of the semantics; only the humans who agreed on the schema are aware of the semantics.

Let's address this now by looking at schemas and namespaces.

Schemas and Namespaces

XML has two concepts that help bridge the gap between syntax and semantics: schemas and namespaces. A *schema* is a document that describes the tags used in the XML document. Schemas have two main functions: descriptive and prescriptive. If we have an XML document and would like to get some more clues as to what the tags mean, we use a schema for its descriptive value. If we are building a new XML document and need to know which tags can validly follow which other tags at any point in the document, we use a schema for its prescriptive value.

Many Standards for Schemas

The first standard for XML schema was document-type definition (DTD), which was borrowed pretty much intact from SGML. Subsequent to that, dozens of schema standards were proposed. Some of the more notable include the following:

---

77. Jonathan Robies, "The Syntactic Web." Available at
www.idealliance.org/papers/xml2001/papers/pdf/03-01-04.pdf.

- **XDR**—XML data and XML data reduced were originated by Microsoft.

- **SOX**—Schema for object oriented XML was promoted by CommerceOne, primarily to aid with its business-to-business (B2B) initiatives.

- **DCD**—Document content description was an XDR/resource description framework (RDF) hybrid.

- **DDML**—Document definition markup language focused on the logical structure as distinct from the physical structure.

- **RELAX and RELAX NG**—Regular language description for XML was promoted by Murata Makoto and James Clark through Oasis. RELAX uses patterns to define things such as cardinality constraints in the schema.

Although these and many other efforts essentially created prototypes, the two enduring schemas are DTD and XSD:

- **DTD**—This is still widespread, but it is essentially a legacy standard. There are still many tools that support only DTD, and there are many DTD-defined documents out there, but most new work has moved on to XSD.

- **XSD**—XML schema definition language was heavily promoted by a consortium of vendors (including Microsoft, IBM, Sun, and Oracle) and is the current standard for XML schemas.

We'll discuss the differences between DTD and XSD for the remainder of this section in the context of description and prescription.

DTD

XML stores its structure and validation rules in its schema. Originally the schema was stored in a data-type definition file in the same manner as SGML. DTD is a different format than XML (it is not a tagged language), so a DTD schema might look like Figure 11.11.

XSD

XSD has made three major breaks from DTD:

```
<!DOCTYPE sculpture
<!ELEMENT sculpture (location, head, body, offerprice)>
<! - the location is the relative location on path -->
<!ELEMENT location (#PCDATA)>
<! - all sculptures must have right& left eyes and mouth -- >
<!ELEMENT head (lefteye, righteye, mouth)>
<! - sculptures can have any number of legs including zero (like the
  snake)>
<!ELEMENT body (leg*)>
<!ELEMENT offerprice (#PCDATA)>
>
```

FIGURE 11.11 DTD schema. PCDATA is not "politically correct data," it is "parsed character data." In other words, data in this position is expected to be ASCII or Unicode data that the parser will interpret. CDATA is character data that the parser is not meant to interpret (e.g., an image).

- *The schema is now expressed in XML.* As can be seen in the portion of an XSD schema shown in Figure 11.12, the schema is now expressed in XML itself, and not in a special language. The first benefit this brings is ease of working with the schema, because you use the same tools that you use to work with an XML document. More interestingly, schema can now refer to other schema.

- *XSD has much stronger data typing.* Many more data types are available and can be used in the XML document creation process, such as the decimal type shown as the next to the last line in Figure 11.12.

- *XSD supports namespaces.* As we'll discuss in more detail in the next section, the use of namespaces in XSD allows us to overcome a number of potential ambiguities.

Semantic Scope and Namespace

Chapter 2 examined how words become overloaded when they are used in many different contexts. Imagine the problem we'd have with XML schema if we had to use a new word every time we had a "name clash" (i.e., we used a word for a different meaning than someone else did). This approach would not get us far.

Namespaces are a way to scope the tags. For example, the tag "sculpture" would be in the "Swetsville" namespace, and we wouldn't have to worry that our trading partners have used the tag "sculpture" in some more traditional

```
<?xml version="1.0" encoding="UTF-8"?>
<xs:schema xmlns:xs="http://www.w3.org/2001/XMLSchema"
elementFormDefault="qualified" attributeFormDefault="unqualified">
<xs:element name="sculpture">
  <xs:annotation>
     <xs:documentation> </xs:documentation>
  </xs:annotation>
</xs:element>
<xs:element name="Location"/>
<xs:group name="Head">
  <xs:sequence>
     <xs:element name="LeftEye"/>
     <xs:element name="RightEye"/>
     <xs:element name="Mouth"/>
  </xs:sequence>
</xs:group>
<xs:group name="Body">
  <xs:sequence>
     <xs:element name="Leg"/>
  </xs:sequence>
</xs:group>
<xs:element name="OfferPrice" type="xs:decimal"/>
</xs:schema>
```

FIGURE 11.12 XSD schema.

sense. This prevents the problem of having to achieve universal agreement on all the terms we use. We only need to agree on the terms we share.

XML's Many Dependents

XML's great strength, its extensibility, has led to the creation of approximately 500 XML-based languages, standards, tools, and so on. The rapid and decentralized opportunity presented by XML has ignited a stampede of opportunistic groups (trade groups, academic groups, government regulators, and software vendors) to stake a claim in the eMarket. This ferment is a major reason that "outside" people tend to become confused and tend to believe that XML is unstable.

The 500 dialects can be grouped in three main categories:

- Tool vocabularies
- Industry-specific vocabularies
- Generic vocabularies

Tool Vocabularies

Most of the XML specifications that are not industry specific, one way or another, are ways of describing a tool or capability. The use of the tool is described in a specific XML dialect. For example, the extensible stylesheets language (XSL) tool is a way of describing how one XML document can be transformed into another XML document, into an HTML document, or into any other type of document (this is handy for displaying XML).

I call this a tool vocabulary, because somewhere behind the syntax of XSL is a tool that reads the XSL tags and does something to the XML. In that sense it is a tool. There are many tools, largely because each tool does few things. This leads to a modular style of assembly.

Some of the other tools of most interest include the following:

- **XPath**—XPath is a language for addressing part of an XML document. This seemingly simple ability is amazingly useful. By describing, in the form of a pattern, what tags you are interested in, and contextually where you are interested in them, you are able to withstand many changes to the XML document without requiring any changes to your interface.

- **XQuery**—There are many query languages built for making interrogation of XML documents or XML databases. This is just one of them.

- **SVG**—Scalable vector graphics is an XML representation of vectorized drawings, which allows them to be rendered or interrogated.

There are many more, and more are being invented all the time, but these are some of the more important ones. They are representative of the breadth and depth of support that is available to operate on XML documents, which in turn can be expressed in XML.

Industry-Specific Vocabularies

Virtually every industry has built a schema on which to base its future inter-operation or internal systems. As we discussed in Chapter 2, each industry has a long history of having invented its own terms. These initiatives represent an attempt to codify and normalize them. To the extent that they are comprehensive and accepted, they will provide a great deal of value to the industry participants. To get broad agreement within an industry, most industries have formed *consortia,* or committees of sponsors who represent the interests of the industry in general.

In many industries these consortia are led by vertically oriented software companies. A vertical software company is one that specializes in a particular industry. In many ways these vertical software companies are the natural choice for this assignment. They make a living going from company to company within the industry. They have had to capture the semantics of the industry in the schemas of their databases. They have had to resolve some of the semantic mismatches in intercompany integration (the topic of Chapter 12).

However, there is a downside to allowing the software vendors to drive this process: It is in their conscious and unconscious best interest to define the industry vocabulary such that it closely resembles their current (legacy) database schemas. Most of these schemas are based on very old models. The schemas of most of the leading vendors in most verticals were defined 10 to 20 years ago.

Representative consortia-led XML dialects include the following:

- Health language 7 (HL7) is an XML version of an EDI standard that is at least 10 years old, and likely much older. It has been heavily represented by the software vendors.

- ACCORD is the consortia-led XML dialect for the insurance industry, primarily property and casualty.

- ChemXL is primarily a markup language to allow for B2B purchasing of chemicals.

- NewsML is a markup language to manage news throughout its life cycle, including production, interchange, and consumer use.

This list just scratches the surface. It seems that every time we turn around there is a new announcement. I'm waiting for the rebuilt carburetor markup language to know that it has finally reached saturation.

One final problem with this proliferation is that it is perpetuating the tower of babble. Each industry is potentially getting further entrenched in its own vocabulary to the detriment of communicating with other industries. As we mentioned in Chapter 2, no industry is an island; all industries have to communicate with others for their basic needs, and many have most of their customers in industries other than their own. To address this, we'll introduce generic vocabularies. Chapters 12 through 15 will then take up three different aspects of this problem.

Generic Vocabularies

Some initiatives cut across all industries. The most important include the following:

- **Web Services**—We won't go into this here because Chapter 13 is devoted to this new, XML-based way for programs to interact.

- **The Semantic Web**—Chapter 14 examines this initiative, which adds a layer of shared and discoverable meaning to the data stored on the Web. The Semantic Web includes RDF and the ontology Web language (OWL).

- **BPEL4S**—This is the latest of many standards to support work flow, both within an organization and across organizations.

- **xCBL, cXML, and RozettaNet**—These are XML dialects intended to support generic cross-company and cross-industry B2B eCommerce. We will discuss these in Chapter 12 in the context of systems integration.

These initiatives offer the most hope for total interconnection and scale. Each is aimed not at a specific industry and not to support a particular tool function, but is aimed at supporting broad-based interconnection.

Adding Behavior to XML

A seemingly inevitable extension to XML has been a move to include behavior, or programming logic, to the Web. XML is widely regarded as "data" and therefore passive. However, the tool usages described previously showed how XML could be used to parameterize the use of a tool. RuleML is a markup language for rules that can be used to implement a wide range of behaviors.

Summary

XML is well on its way to becoming ubiquitous. XML is highly likely to become more common, more important, and more stable than HTML, and it will rival ASCII as a foundational technology.

XML's strengths lie in its stability (few changes are even contemplated at this point, and no one has the leverage to make proprietary extensions to it); its flexibility (it handles documents, transactions, and behavior); its self-disclosing structure (it either describes or points one to a description of the meaning of its tags); its expressiveness (it maintains complex structures such as bills of materials in their native format); and its neutrality (it has allegiance to no particular company).

XML's only real downsides are verbosity and roundtrip throughput. An XML transaction may be three to five times the size of a traditional transaction. The fact that this message not only has to be transported over the network, but also must be parsed and marshaled at each end, leads to a total end-to-end performance penalty of almost tenfold. However, just as the performance penalty of relational databases was overcome in the 1980s, the performance penalty of XML will be overcome—partly through technology and partly as companies come to accept the penalty because the flexibility is worth so much more than raw performance.

The rest of this book concerns important semantic initiatives that are partially or completely dependent on XML: enterprise application integration, Web Services, and the Semantic Web.

CHAPTER 12

Semantic-Based Enterprise Application Integration and Systems Integration

Systems integration (SI), or enterprise application integration (EAI), consumes the lion's share of SI maintenance and development budgets. It is estimated that between 20% and 67% of the annual SI budget is devoted to building and maintaining integration, with the consensus seeming to be in the 30% to 40% range.[78-80] This is value-added work in only the most limited sense of the term. It is worth doing, and it provides some value; otherwise people wouldn't do it. However, the amount of effort it consumes is far out of proportion to what it could and should cost.

More important for the topic at hand, it has been estimated that 95% of this cost is attributable to semantics.[81] That number seems a bit high, even to a semantic fanatic like myself, but my experience would suggest that at least half the cost of integrating systems comes down to resolving semantic issues. In this chapter we cover the mechanics of systems integration; we will look at integration within your enterprise and integration with your trading partners. Then we'll look at two approaches that help with the semantic issues in integration: enterprise message modeling and semantic brokers.

---

78. Mario Apicella, "Making Application Ends Meet," *Infoworld,* Feb 22, 2002.

79. Dr. Wolfgang Martin, "The Second Wave," Meta Group. Available at *www.ids-scheer.com/sixcms/detail.php/15360?_country=3582.*

80. See *www.csc.com/solutions/enterpriseapplicationintegration/offerings/717.shtml* for further information.

81. Jim O'Leary, "Tying it Together," Feb 9, 2000. Available at *www.omg.org/news/meetings/workshops/presentations/eai_presentations2/Tying%20it%20Together.pdf.*

What Is Integration?

Before we examine how integration works, or how it should work, I'll spend a brief moment on the industry and the acronyms, so that the remainder will make more sense. The exact size and shape of the "systems integration" market is hard to pin down, but by almost any source it is a multi–hundred-billion-dollar industry.[82–85] The "industry" consists chiefly of the following:

- Professional services firms (Accenture, EDS, CSC, BearingPoint, etc.) who integrate existing and new software systems on a consulting basis

- Software firms (Web Methods, Tibco, BEA, IBM, etc.) who sell software that makes it easier to integrate existing systems

- The share of internal Information Systems (IS) staff devoted to building and maintaining interfaces between existing and new systems

This "industry" was originally called SI, but more recently it has specialized into EAI for internal integration and business-to-business (B2B) and supply chain management (SCM) for interorganizational integration. A study of 400 enterprises by PwC and the Meta Groups found that the average organization had 68 application systems.[86] We have encountered firms that have thousands. There is a great deal of redundant information in those systems, as well as events recognized in one system that must be reflected in another. A study of 600 enterprises by the Hurwitz Group found that only 10% of the enterprises had fully integrated their most mission-critical processes.[87]

On top of this vast and underpenetrated need, the industry has added another dimension. The hot topic in the industry currently is the "need for speed." This shows up in a number of acronyms, including zero-latency enterprise (ZLE), straight-through processing (STP), and real-time enterprise (RTE). Each of these is based on the theme that it is not enough to integrate your systems; they must be integrated in a way that removes time delay.

---

82. Gartner Group IT Service Market Statistics, Oct 31, 2000.

83. Kim Girard, "Middle Management Enterprise Integration Software's New Home on the Net," *Business 2.0*, June 13, 2000, pp 92–93.

84. "The $700 Billion Help Desk," *Industry Standard,* July 30, 2001, p 27.

85. "This Decade's Trends," *Application Development Trends,* May 1, 2001, p 64.

86. Reported in *VAR Business,* Nov 11, 2002, p 102.

87. See *www.massecomm.org/news/news.asp?NiID=231* for further information.

So hundreds of billions of dollars are being spent annually on a need that seems to be insatiable, and the majority of it seems to be related to semantics. Let's take a closer look.

Where the Need for Integration Comes From

To understand this better, we need to delve into the nature and mechanics of the dark art of systems integration. To put this in context, let's imagine that Bill from the Swetsville Zoo did what so many businesses do: He bought an application software package to handle his inventory. Let's call this the *inventory management system.*

Traffic picks up at the zoo. Bill opens a gift shop and decides he needs a *point-of-sale system* (a cash register with a computer appendage). He does a detailed requirements project and a software selection project and buys a state-of-the-art point-of-sale system. There's only one problem: It is not integrated with his inventory management system. What does this mean?

Integration

Here's a good operational definition of integration for business systems:

Integration Two systems are integrated if an event in one system (system A) that might potentially affect decisions being made in another system (system B) is always reflected in system B in "business real time."

Whether or not you fill in the question mark in Figure 12.1, and how much you are willing to spend to do so, depends almost entirely on the value of the decisions to be made or the efficiency in automating the action to be taken. How rapidly and reliably it needs to occur depends on what "real time" is for these functions.

"Real time" is relative for all business functions. For stock trades it may be milliseconds, whereas settlement is still measured in days. For many business functions it is measured in seconds or minutes. Industries that rely on

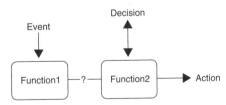

FIGURE 12.1 Where application integration fits in.

physical movement, such as trash collection, can measure time in days and still be in "real time." The issue is whether your system's end-to-end latency matches up with your business requirements.

At the Swetsville Zoo, Bill will only notice this when he adds a new sculpture to the zoo and someone wants to buy it, or when someone buys one and it must be marked as sold. This example is intentionally simple, but many businesses waste millions of dollars from information leakage of this type.

The other issue that rapidly comes up is the number of applications, and therefore the number of interconnections, that must be supported. The number of possible interfaces goes up geometrically as the number of applications increases. Systems integrators are fond of pointing out that the number of possible interconnections between n systems is $[n(n - 1)]/2$. Whereas there are only 3 possible interconnections between 3 systems, there are 45 possible interconnections between 10 systems and 2278 possible interconnections between the 68 systems that the "average" company has. These are only the theoretically possible number of interconnections. Nobody comes anywhere close to that. First, just because there is a theoretically possible connection between two systems doesn't mean they have any data in common. Second, it is usually not economical to build all of the possible interfaces.

Integration Is Harder than It Looks

Integration is hard for two reasons: technical and semantic. By technical I mean the issues involved with the implementation technologies, especially binding to languages and communication protocols.

Technical Issues with Integration

The nonsemantic issues with integration can pose some difficulty, but they have a tendency to be about as complex as they look. Typical nonsemantic issues include the following:

- **Language mismatch**—Often the first issue that comes up is incompatible languages. Are we interfacing a system written in COBOL with one written in FORTRAN or Java? The language issue sometimes restricts the design options.

- **Platform boundaries**—Are the two systems to be integrated on different platforms? A different platform might be a different database. It might also be a different computer. The issue is more acute if it is a different type of computer. Are we interfacing an AS/400 with a DEC

VAX? The platform boundary eliminates some of the options, and it requires extra effort to overcome the rest.

- **Character sets and byte order**—Some interfaces have to deal with EBCDIC (mainframe character sets) to ASCII (minis and PCs). Different computers represent numbers in a different byte order, and some domain names have their order reversed. These are issues that must be dealt with somewhere in the interface.

- **Binding issues**—Some sets of components or applications have constraints on how they bind to other systems. For example, most integration with Microsoft technology must bind to some variety of component object model (COM) object.

- **Temporal issues**—Many integration projects operate on the assumption that the second system will be available and have adequate response time when we need information. But this is not always the case, and sometimes we don't find this out until long after the integration has been implemented.

These are the straightforward issues; most integrators spot them immediately and plan accordingly. The level of surprise is rarely great with these issues.

Semantic Issues with Integration

The root cause of the semantic issues with integration seems to be human gullibility. There is a tendency to believe that information is more reliable than it actually is, and we have to learn to be skeptical and question our information sources. It's hard to be cynical enough to be good at this.

Let's go over the sources of information and why they aren't reliable:

- **Metadata**—Most of the time, systems integration starts with metadata, some sort of description of the data in the systems to be integrated. The metadata might be as simple as the table and column layouts of the database from which data will be retrieved. The integrator will form opinions about what the data fields are going to be, how valid they will be, and so on, based primarily on what can be deduced from the names of the fields. As we know, names can be deceiving.

- **User interviews**—Often the integration process is driven from discussions with the users. The users have been doing an interface manually for some time and they would now like it automated. They describe a process, and maybe they tell you what the source data is like. Only they don't see all the source data and when you run the interface, spurious results appear. Or there are many subtle differences in the data that they have been finessing and had forgotten about.

- **Program specs or program code**—Occasionally integrators will resort to reviewing code, but this is tedious work, and it isn't done all that often. The downside, if there is one, is that sometimes the programs you review are not the only ones that create data or events that you need to know about. Also, as we discussed in Chapter 3, the less semantic rigor there is in a given application, the more it is subject to procedures and training, and more variability can show up that will not be detected in a code review.

- **Review the existing data**—In many ways this is the most reliable method. It has two possible drawbacks: The sample size may be too small (if the review is manual) or something may change in the future so that the system is not used in the same way that it was before, creating a different profile of data in the future from what was observed in the past.

So why is it said that these types of issues are semantic issues? And what can be done to address them? They are called semantic issues for two reasons. One is that they are not technical issues; typically the integrators have resolved the binding, language, and platform issues, and the interfaces still aren't working. The other, a bit more subtle, is that each of these approaches to attempt to integrate the two systems is built on an impoverished semantic model.

We know the model is impoverished after it fails. We run the interface, and somebody notices that some of the sales orders didn't come across. On further investigation we notice that some of the sales orders have duplicate numbers and the posting program rejected them. Or some of them had negative numbers for the amount and therefore were rejected or treated as credits. Three things are going on here:

- The two systems had different implementation models. That is, they describe and implement the same part of the business in different ways. If they had identical implementation models (including the enforced definition of the terms), there wouldn't have been a problem. But that isn't the case.

- The integrators created—usually in their heads, occasionally explicitly in a spec—their own version of a model that would bridge the two discrepant models, and they also had mental models of the semantics of each of the systems and a model of how they would resolve to the

intermediate model. (Analysts don't often articulate this; they more often think in terms of "mapping" from source to destination, but if probed there is generally an abstract notion that they are going through. For a trivial example, if they have Julian dates [dddyyy] in one system and American Gregorian dates [mm/dd/yyyy] in another, in the back of their minds they know they are translating one of them into an abstract representation of time, and then reexpressing it in the other format.)

- Evidence shows up, in a delayed fashion, that indicates that something is wrong with the model. Changes are made, the system is retested, and they proceed until they get to the next violation of the model.

This process is harder than it looks, and it doesn't always go as planned, but it is worth an incredible amount. Hundreds of billions of dollars have been invested on integration, most of it cost justified by return-on-investment analyses. This suggests that even poorly done integration is better than no integration at all. Let's take a look at how companies actually attack this problem.

Strategies for Coping with Integration

There are five major strategies for achieving integration. We'll touch on each briefly and then cover the semantic implications that each brings to the party. The following list is five patterns we have seen toward approaching integration projects. They are not mutually exclusive in that many projects use some elements from each, but each requires a predominant mindset that determines much of the direction and economics of the project. The five most common approaches to systems integration are as follows:

- Manual
- Big database
- Direct connect
- Point to point
- Message based

Manual

Most integration is still manual. In many cases people don't even know they are doing integration; they are just taking a report from one system and keying it into another. This has the disadvantage of being operationally expensive,

and it doesn't scale well. It is semantically imprecise (remember Chapter 3?), but these disadvantages have a counterbalance: The semantic mismatches that grow up between systems can be finessed by the human that is doing the integrating.

Big Database

An approach to integration that has a lot of intellectual appeal is the big database approach. This approach is based on the premise that if we can just get the two functions to run off the same database, they will be as integrated as possible. If they share a customer table and one of them updates it, it is immediately available to all the other functions.

The semantic problems with this approach are that the different applications may still treat the data semantically slightly differently. This cost shows up in the "systems" or "integration" test, which is typically the last and most expensive phase of a development project. The system is exercised with every combination of transactions from the various applications that might affect the system, in the most varied sequences, and the semantic discrepancies show up.

The more important argument against the big database approach is that it doesn't scale well. The scale problems come in two varieties. The first is that the database schema is essentially the same as "global data" was to early programming. In the early days of programming, programmers used to define all the variables they might access in one area ("global storage"), which was available to any subroutine to access. As programs became more complicated, people discovered that the variety of subroutines that might access the global data (and therefore create the potential side effect of changing something) became unwieldy. The database schema is essentially the same, and as applications scale up, the side effects become more complex.

The other issue is that as applications become larger (and that's really what we're talking about when we put multiple applications on the same database; they essentially become one larger application), they become less and less productive to build and maintain, and the chances of a successful project drop precipitously. The Standish Group has done a comprehensive study on more than 23,000 software projects.[88] To summarize the findings: Projects that cost less than $750,000 had a 55% chance of successful completion. Each doubling of the project cost cut the chance of success roughly in half, until

---

88. Jim Johnson, "Turning Chaos into Success," *SoftwareMag.com*, Dec 1999. Available at *www.softwaremag.com/archive/1999dec/Success.html*.

at $10 million there were statistically no successful projects (presumably less than 100 for the sample size).

Direct Connect

By direct connect we are referring to techniques that allow one application to directly access the programs of another application. The technique could be a remote procedure call mechanism or it could be through the sharing of components, such as COM or DCOM. In either case the applications soon become highly interconnected and complex.

There are semantic problems with this approach. The calling program has to accept the semantics of the called routines whether they are made explicit or not. The main reason this approach runs out of steam, though, is not semantic. In this case it is that there is no decoupling mechanism, and a set of highly interconnected systems will be brittle and hard to adapt. By directly connecting applications we turn several small applications into one large one, with all the attendant antiscale issues.

Point to Point/Store and Foreword

Perhaps the most popular and viable strategy of integration currently is what we call "point to point/store and forward." The term *point to point* refers to the fact that one system is sending data to another. There is one sender and one receiver. The term *store and forward* refers to the fact that the sender need not be directly connected to the receiver. The most common form of this uses the file system, in which one system writes transactions to a file, which is picked up later by the receiving system. This strategy includes most forms of electronic data interchange (EDI).

The semantic shortcoming of this approach is that the sender and receiver must agree on the semantics of the record formats ahead of time. Because the semantics are not fully expressed in the structures that define these transactions, this agreement often gets worked out in a trial-and-error process. This is generally done though some sort of specification (either an independent standards body, in the case of most EDI, or an internally written specification). The other problem with this is the point-to-point topology, which limits reuse and makes applications dependent on one another.

Message Based

This category includes most of the modern EAI approaches, including the use of integration brokers, message-oriented middleware (MOM), message buses, and self-describing messages (i.e., XML).

Message Broker, Integration Broker, Message-Oriented Middleware

These technologies address the topology of application integration by placing a software component (the broker) as a hub that all the applications talk to, instead of talking directly to each other. This topology can greatly reduce the number of interconnections that must be made.

The message-based approaches have the potential to overcome the semantic issues by expressing the messages in a format that could potentially be evaluated by a system for semantic consistency. They address the point-to-point issues by "anonymizing" the sender and receiver (each knows about the bus, but not each other) and by encouraging multicast of messages through publish and subscribe mechanisms (one application can publish a change message, which may be subscribed to by many receiving applications).

The message-based approaches have the potential to provide a semantically rich interface while leaving the sending and receiving systems loosely coupled, but this is only potential. The rest of this chapter discusses issues that must be resolved before that potential can become a reality.

Issues with Internal Integration

We haven't yet made a distinction between integrating applications within your enterprise and integrating your applications with other enterprises. The five strategies we described work in both scenarios; however, the emphasis is different. Between enterprises, most of the interfaces are manual. In most cases, the producers of the information don't know there is an interface; they publish information (on paper or a Web site) and someone keys it into a spreadsheet or database. The big database and direct connect strategies are not used much between companies, but point to point in the form of EDI is used extensively. Finally, the message-oriented approach is about to gain currency between firms in the form of Web Services, as we'll discuss in Chapter 13. Although the mechanisms are similar, the semantic challenge is quite different.

Within an enterprise the primary semantic integration challenge is to avoid implementing a large number of point-to-point interfaces. With new technology coming on line it is easier to write individual interfaces, but we must discipline ourselves against doing more of the same damage that we have done in the past, only faster and cheaper. As the old adage advises, "When you find yourself in a hole, stop digging."

Once we have built interfaces to a particular system, it becomes harder and harder to change the system, because more things (the interface and the downstream systems that are connected to the interface) will break. In most organizations we've examined, the problem is worse than this: The organization may not know all the processes that depend on a particular system, database, or interface, because those processes or systems may not be under the control of the people who manage the application. Some of the key activities to be performed include the following:

- Create an intermediate representation of all interfaces such that each system need only know about the intermediary, and not about the other systems. This reduces the geometric explosion of interfaces, but it requires some semantic analysis.

- Dictate to the applications what their interfaces will be and what the semantic contract for them will be. The reason for doing this is that the default behavior of application developers is to allow applications to define their public interface, or worse, expose their data model, which opens up many more points of access. This will typically be poorly defined and not designed to interoperate with the rest of the systems.

- Redefine the number and borders of the existing applications. Even if we don't change them immediately, we will want to define the interfaces as if the new systems were in a more rational configuration. If we don't do this now, we'll be stuck with the configuration of applications we have at this point.

- Maximize the flexibility, resiliency, and stability of the intermediate model, so that changes to one application are buffered through the intermediary and cause little or no change to other systems.

The Semantics of Integration between Enterprises

Integrating outside the boundaries of your enterprise is completely different. This is the world of B2B and SCM. You do not have the luxury of defining the most elegant model and integrating to that. You have a host of different consortia and standards to deal with, as well as specific point-to-point interfaces.

A few prominent standards cross many industries and should be the first consideration for these efforts:

- **ebXML**[89]—sponsored by the United Nations Centre for Trade Facilitation and Electronic Business (UN/CEFACT) and the Organization for

---

89. See *www.ebxml.org/* for further information.

the Advancement of Structured Information Standards (OASIS); has developed open standards for intercompany commerce

- **xCBL**[90]—originally developed and sponsored by CommerceOne, now an open standard for promoting eMarketplaces

- **cXML14**[91]—originally developed and sponsored by Ariba, now an open standard primarily focused on eProcurement

These are some of the key standards for B2B across all industries. However, you may find that you need to deal with vertical industry particulars. You may want to use your industry's consortia-led XML standard and start building onto it, but you may not be doing most of your external transactions within your own industry. Say you build injection-molded plastic parts, and your biggest customers are automotive manufacturers. You have a lot of transactions with people in the automotive supply chain. You also have transactions with customers in other vertical chains, perhaps consumer electronics and office furniture. You make purchases from the chemical industry, and may deal with a human resources XML consortium for recruiting. Assuming you can sort through these and determine which are more important and less important, you next have a topology issue to resolve.

The principle topology questions are as follows:

- Do I want to integrate directly with some of my key partners?

- Is there a "market maker" who fulfills the role of an intermediary for an industry?

- Do I want to allow many partners to integrate to me?

These are strategic questions with semantic overtones. Strategically, and historically, if you were a significant trading partner with another company, you would want to invest in some sort of point-to-point interface with that company. The interface represents a capital investment in your relationship and helps raise a barrier to potential competitors. You might prefer to leave the semantics of the interface ambiguous and change it over time, which again keeps out competitors.

If a particular partner or class of partners does not represent a large part of your business, you may want to participate with a market maker. A market maker fulfills a role in a market where there are many buyers and many sellers, and it would be cost prohibitive for each of them to find and negotiate with

---

90. See *www.xcbl.org/* for further information.

91. See *www.cxml.org/* for further information.

each other (it's the combinatorial explosion problem again); instead, each deals with the market maker. For example, eScout has created a marketplace for procurement, primarily of "indirect" items, and Neoforma and GHX have created marketplaces for health care supplies.

If you have a product or service that you believe many other partners (or consumers) would want to integrate to, you may want to invest in making this as easy as possible. In the past this meant allowing email or bulletin boards of files, but now it means an easy-to-use Web site (business to consumer) or a Web Services interface to your applications. We'll discuss the Web Services angle more in Chapter 13. It should be noted that many firms have built an on-line presence only to realize that their on-line presence wasn't integrated with their delivery systems, turning the external integration problem into an internal integration problem.

If you find yourself in the first scenario (integrating with key partners), the semantics of the defined interfaces will be of great interest, and your primary approach will be as described in Chapter 9.

In any of the scenarios, an important issue to address is how to reduce the number of internal applications that are dealing with outsiders. If you deal with 50 key partners, three marketplaces, and thousands of on-line customers, your systems development effort will gridlock if you allow all of your 68 applications to access any or all of these outsiders. To manage the complexity, run your internal systems through their semantic intermediary and then to the outside world through a common gateway.

Why the Implementation Level Makes Things So Much Harder

Occasionally applications are built from a sound semantic or conceptual model of the domain. Usually before the implementation project is completed, and certainly before the application is retired, the conceptual model gets shelved. The implementation is there, and all bugs must be fixed in the implementation. The implementation has its own data structure (often because of real or suspected performance problems) and its own naming conventions. The conceptual model is no longer relevant to the maintenance programmers, because the implementation model is more germane to their task.

What happens is that the conceptual model gets violated at every turn. If it is possible to overload some field that isn't being used all the time, with a value that essentially subtypes the object, that is what will be done. For example, an analyst might note that no one is using the "inventory source" field and might decide to put substitute part numbers there. If another field needs to be tacked on somewhere it will, and generally at the most concrete level possible. If someone requests a "price per ounce" field, that is what will get added, and there will be little or no consideration to whether there is a need for price per unit; it will be price per ounce. A few maintenance programmers would actually go through the analysis, but most wouldn't (largely because it wasn't requested, isn't appreciated, and is outside their sphere of training). Often the original models and analysis can't be found or are out of date. However, I don't mean to single out maintenance programmers; the issue is the general state of applications systems as we typically encounter them after years of in-the-field adaptation.

Why You Probably Don't Have the Right Applications Anyway

One other aspect of the implemented systems is even more profound for the business of integrating efficiently: The applications themselves have arbitrary boundaries. Typically what is in one application is a product of what was needed at the time to fill some other gap, or it reflects the scope that was offered by an application software vendor. Based on our observations, it is highly likely that some applications share too much data, and they should be combined instead of integrated; many nearly duplicated systems should be rationalized; and a few applications are too big to be economically maintained and should be partitioned.

If you accept these boundaries, you will build an integration infrastructure that will ensure that these boundaries stay in place. In effect, you will have calcified the existing configuration at a time when you need to be moving toward more flexibility. An approach that enables the repartitioning of application boundaries and redefinition of application interfaces, if needed, is the enterprise message model.

Enterprise Message Model

The solution is not to start with the existing Application Programming Interfaces (APIs) or data model, which is the path of least resistance. The solution is to begin at the center with a model of the shared interaction, independent of the current implementation. The techniques to do this mostly follow from the elicitation techniques described in Chapter 9, with a few variations. Figure 12.2 shows an outline of an approach to this task. Space doesn't permit an

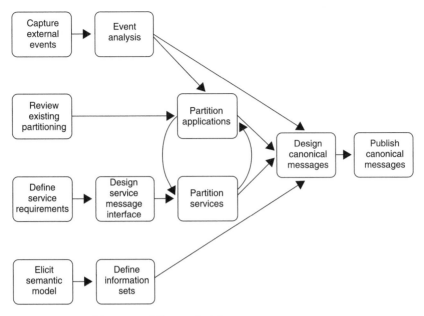

FIGURE 12.2 Message modeling methodology.

exhaustive treatment of all the steps, but they should be self-evident. The approach shares with the more general semantic modeling approach the idea of building a semantic model of the concepts to be addressed. Where it differs is in the emphasis on business events, as these will generally translate into messages that will track between the systems, and in the recognition that some of the messages are there to accommodate the fact that the business has been split into application areas, which generate some of the need for messages.

Part of this analysis, again in the area of event analysis, is to look at the potential traffic from partner companies (B2B opportunities and existing relationships). To be consistent, these will need to be translated into messages and fed through this approach. The "canonical message" in Figure 12.2 refers to the creation of an authoritative version of a particular message, rather than letting each application project and each system integration project define its own.

Semantic Brokers

One more development adds nicely to the concept of an enterprise message model: the concept of a semantic broker. Most integration brokers provide message routing and message mapping, but no further semantic translation. A semantic broker is similar in concept to a message broker in that it is an intermediary between application systems, but it goes considerably further than a message broker.

The semantic broker is a product that greatly aids the process of building and maintaining an enterprise message model, and especially the process of adapting each of the application systems to the model. A semantic broker contains a semantic model that is a core representation of the shared concepts in the enterprise. With the aid of tools provided by the semantic broker vendor, the integrator defines a mapping from the application to the semantic model. Each of the products differs somewhat in what is done next. I'll describe how several representative products work to help with the semantic broker concept.

Contivo

Contivo[92] is a design-time semantic broker. Its tool set allows the integrator to build a map from the source system to a semantic model. The tool then translates the map into a run-time component based on the middleware and architecture in place. One of the strong points of this approach is that it does not tie the enterprise to a proprietary run-time product. Another feature of the tool suite is "transitive association," meaning that once a map has been created from one application to the semantic core, all other interfaces that use the shared concepts are ready to go. This dramatically reduces integrator workload.

Unicorn

Unicorn[93] is a semantic broker that has many of the same features as Contivo, such as supporting a single central representation to which each of the applications is mapped. Unicorn has its own run-time engine, which enables it to support EAI and "extract transport and load" (a technique for loading data warehouses) without the need for additional middleware. Unicorn is able to import existing models captured in entity relationship diagrams (e.g., ErWin) or UML-based tools, such as Rational.

---

92. See *www.contivo.com/* for further information.

93. See *www.unicorn.com/* for further information.

Ontoprise

Ontoprise[94] is a German company that also provides a semantic broker capability. Ontoprise's primary tools are ontology editors. Its primary market is in the B2B marketplaces, where resolving the discrepancies between product vendors' catalogs is a huge semantic problem.

Summary

Two systems developed and evolved independently will share some superficial semantics. Perhaps they will both be concerned with sales orders. They may have been built on different technologies or purchased from different application software vendors. This situation leads many to believe that the technical barriers may be difficult to overcome, but once done, the resolution of the data will be easy. The truth is almost always the opposite: There are technical difficulties, and sometimes they are tricky, but they rarely create major overruns in integration projects. The semantic issues, which are routinely discounted, assert themselves late in the project or even in the post-conversion phase, where they are very expensive to deal with.

Hundreds of billions of dollars are at stake in doing this well, to say nothing of getting companies in a position where they can respond and adapt more easily. This chapter examined this issue in detail, and outlined two strategies for mitigating this problem with the enterprise: the development of an enterprise message model as a reference point for flexible and economic integration, and the use of a semantic broker so that each application would not have to understand the semantics of every other application. For external integration (B2B), we outlined the key role of cross-industry consortia and industry-specific consortia and outlined strategies for dealing with each. In Chapter 13 we examine another technology that is growing in popularity and that is often used in connection with enterprise integration: Web Services.

---

94. See *www.ontoprise.com/* for further information.

Web Services

Web Services are the hottest thing going these days; you've probably heard the hype. One of the problems with new technologies is that definitions tend to become overloaded with vendors' and the media's claims about the value and benefit of the new technology, with the result that it is often difficult to determine just what the technology is or does.

In this chapter we start by grounding ourselves in a succinct definition of Web Services and cover the mechanics of Web Services in just enough detail to allow readers to follow the rest of the chapter. There are many excellent books on the subject and many more coming out every month for those who want to pursue the mechanics in more detail.

Because this is a book on semantics, we will spend most of the chapter discussing the implications of this style of architecture and the semantic tools and methods that will be needed to help it achieve its potential.

Web Services: Definition and Implications

For something as simple as Web Services, there seems to be a lot of confusion even at the definition level. Here are some representative definitions:

- David Rosam: "Web Services are reusable software components based on XML and related protocols that enable near zero-cost interaction throughout the business ecosystem. They can be used internally for fast and low-cost application integration, or made available to customers, suppliers or partners over the Internet."[95]

---

95. From *www.dangerous-thinking.com/stories/2002/02/16/webServicesDefined.html.*

- Hailey Lynee McKeefry, ZDNet: "Web services are self-contained, self-describing, modular applications that can be published, located, and invoked across the Web. They perform functions that range from simple requests to complicated business processes."[96]

- The Stencil Group: "Loosely coupled, reusable software components that semantically encapsulate discrete functionality and are distributed and programmatically accessible over standard Internet protocols."[97]

- W3C Glossary: "A Web service is a software system identified by a URI [RFC 2396], whose public interfaces and bindings are defined and described using XML. Its definition can be discovered by other software systems. These systems may then interact with the Web service in a manner prescribed by its definition, using XML based messages conveyed by Internet protocols."[98]

Web Services Defined

Here is a simpler and more operational definition:

Web Service   A Web Service is a remote invocation method. It is different from other remote invocation approaches in that it uses XML for its binding, and it can support both asynchronous and synchronous interaction.

A typical example is a Web Service that returns a stock quote. The calling program formats an extensible markup language (XML) request containing the symbol for the stock, and the Web Service returns an XML message with the current price per share.

There are several implications to this simple definition:

- **Platform independence**—The caller and receiver need not share a technology base, as long as each is able to send and receive an XML message over a network.

- **Internet scope**—These calls can be made across the Internet, including to computers that are behind firewalls, which is difficult for other approaches.

- **Loose coupling**—Using XML has a double benefit: Because it is "just" text, there aren't any binary compatibility issues to deal with, and XML

---

96. From *http://techupdate.zdnet.com/techupdate/stories/main/0,14179,2803166,00.html.*

97. From *www.stencilgroup.com/ideas_scope_200106wsdefined.html.*

98. From *www.w3.org/TR/ws-gloss/.*

has features that allow both participants to pick the parameters they are interested in out of a potentially larger and changing message.

- **Promotion, or at least possibility, of asynchronous interaction**—For most other distributed architectures, it involves considerable extra effort to get the interaction to be asynchronous. As we'll discuss, this is much easier with Web Services.

Before Web Services, if you wanted to invoke some functionality on another computer, you had to have a mechanism to bind to that other functionality. These mechanisms, such as CORBA or DCOM, were closed (i.e., a CORBA object called another CORBA object) and did not operate well over the Internet, especially in the presence of firewalls.

People avoid seeing the simple definition because there is so much marketing hoopla around Web Services that they have a tough time believing that that is all there is to it. Simple as it is, though, there are many implications to it, and much more technology is being built up around it to make it work reliably. These things are in the Web Services ecology, but they aren't Web Services. To understand how to plan your semantic-based Web Services strategies requires mapping the current ecology's likely evolution. This evolution will include both technical and organizational changes.

End of the Platform Wars

Before the advent of Web Services we were in the midst of the "platform wars." Vendors of computer hardware, operating systems, middleware, and database management systems all believed that the only logical outcome of the trend for distributed processing would be a "winner take all" scenario, where one platform would dominate. Because it was far easier to intercommunicate between homogeneous platforms, they believed that one would prevail.

Web Services potentially renders this moot, because there will be competition at the add-on or tool level by vendors who will try to make their tools the easiest on-ramp for Web Services. However, Web Services are built on open standards and any platform can invoke Web Services from any other platform.

Distinction from Component Architectures

People sometimes liken Web Services to component-based architectures. A component-based architecture is focused on building and using "reusable" chunks of program logic to construct a solution. At some level that is what Web Services do. The difference is that in a component-based architecture the components are brought to the problem. The components become part of the product that delivers the solution. In the Web Services world, the service stays where it is and delivers the information or side effect requested.

Web Services and Firewalls

One of the great strengths of Web Services is their ability operate over the Internet, including their ability to tunnel through firewalls. Many consider this also to be one of the great weaknesses of Web Services. This technical capability enables wide-scale deployment, attracting many people to the idea. However, in the short term there are many impediments to actually using Web Services over the public Internet, because of the lack of the contracting infrastructure. This in turn restricts the options for producers of services. As a result, most of the early work with Web Services is at the intranet level.

Consumers and Producers

One way to think about Web Services is to distinguish "producers" and "consumers" of the service. The consumer is the process that invokes the service and gets the result. The producer is the owner of the service that handles the request. The advantages for consumers are obvious—they receive some value-added service without having to build or support the system that delivers it.

However, the business model that ignited the World Wide Web—advertising—is available only to a very limited degree in the Web Services model. Web Services are designed for application-to-application (A2A) communication, rather than the application-to-human (A2H) model of the Web. As a result there is no one to read the advertisements. (The consuming application will consume the stock quote, put it in a spreadsheet or graph, and ignore any ads, if there were any, that accompanied it.)

In the absence of the advertising model, three other models may entice producers to play:

- The producer and consumer are owned by the same entity. (This is the intranet scenario, in which a company may shift processing from one system to a service where it can be shared and reap the benefit purely from the sharing). This is where the early adopters are putting their efforts now, but this model will not scale out to the broader Internet.

- The producer is paid to deliver the service. This is where Web Services ultimately must go. As we'll discuss in the section on contracts, a great deal of infrastructure must be built to make this work. In the short term, people will try to work out the financial arrangements separately from the service invocation. This is similar to the application service provider (ASP) arrangements that were much promoted but little used over the last 5 years.

- The service directly contributes to the producer's mission. For example, Amazon.com has a Web Service interface that allows people to access books, prices, reviews, and so on. The Web Service also allows users to put books in their Amazon shopping carts and can execute a purchase. Amazon doesn't need to get paid for delivering the service, as long as it contributes to selling more books. Another example would be companies that use the service to increase their own internal efficiency; for example, the U.S. Post Office could supply a Web Service to normalize addresses and supply nine-digit zip codes, knowing that every time it gets used their ability to deliver mail more efficiently would increase.

Enterprise Application Integration

Given the prerequisites for producers on the public Internet, we expect that most of the activity in the short term will be on intranets. In particular, people will be looking to solve their enterprise application integration (EAI) problems (see Chapter 12).

Web Services is a two-edged sword for EAI. On the plus side, the platform neutrality is a great feature. All that's needed to be a producer is to set up an XML adaptor for some piece of functionality on a legacy system.

The main negatives (all of which can be overcome) are as follows:

- **Performance**—As we'll discuss in the section on service-oriented architecture, there can be a steep penalty for using Web Services, especially for high-volume transactions. Many companies may not want to incur this penalty.

- **Polymorphism**—The ability to get a varied response, depending on the specific nature of the item interrogated, is generally considered to be a big plus. For example, if a stock ticker encounters a stock symbol for an American Depository Receipt (ADR; these are shares of foreign companies traded in U.S. dollars on U.S. exchanges) in addition to the current price on the U.S. stock market, it might return the foreign stock symbol, market, and current price in the foreign currency. This might be useful on a modern system, but it confuses most legacy systems that expect a fixed-format response. If we had set up our application to display the results generically, based on the XML it receives, it would be able to handle this gracefully.

- **Point to point**—The default topology for Web Services is *point to point:* A single consumer calls a single identified producer. The rest of this chapter examines how to overcome this, but we need to start by realizing that "out of the box" default behavior for Web Services is point to point. Point to point refers to the caller knowing the presence and identity of the receiving program, there being only one receiving program, and the caller blocking and waiting for a response. (Blocking and waiting means cutting in half program execution and waiting for the responses before proceeding.)

All of these issues can be resolved with a combination of tools and standards already available, as well as a more rigorous application of the semantics of the service to be delivered. Let's start with some of the mechanics.

Web Services Mechanics

There are several more difference between Web Services and other remote methods.

Vendor-Neutral Application Program Interface Exposed as Extensible Markup Language

To reiterate, the essential part of Web Services is creating an interface that can be bound with XML. Some Web Services are XML interfaces on legacy systems, and some are new programs built specifically with an XML interface. Using XML as the binding mechanism decouples the consumer and producer. The primary decoupling is at the binding level; the two systems no longer need to use the same binding scheme, and indeed need to know very little about each other.

Document-Style Application Program Interface

In a traditional remote procedure call, the called routines must agree on number and order of parameters being passed back and forth. By default, Web Services calls are set up exactly the same. (Default refers to the use of tools that promote the use of Web Services, such as Microsoft's Visual Studio Programming environment; the behavior that results when you set up the Web Service using Wizards; or the behavior that results when you don't override the default behavior). If you define a service with three parameters, you will get the stub of a calling program with the same three parameters.

However, this behavior can be overridden.[99] By putting the interface in "document mode" (kind of an odd way to describe it), you essentially allow the producer the option of "finding" the parameters in the incoming XML document. Clearly there are limits to what you can find, but if the information is in the document, tagged as agreed on, and in an equivalent structure, you can extract the parameters. This can drastically reduce the impact of a change to a message, and it allows the same producer to handle multiple different requests.

Asynchronous Processing

Another level of decoupling possible with Web Services, but not the default, is support for asynchronous processing. A *synchronous process* is one where the initiator of a request waits for the response before doing anything else. An *asynchronous process* doesn't wait. For humans, a phone call is synchronous; voice mail is asynchronous.

People become confused on this concept with computer architectures when they start talking about many "layers" simultaneously. Generally, asynchronous processes need queues to buffer up requests in case the respondent is busy servicing another call. The confusion comes when people see a queue, and assume the process is asynchronous. Some part of the process probably is asynchronous, but the end-to-end process may not be. A Web site may have a queue and may process requests asynchronously, but if the end user (or requesting process) is waiting on the response, the end-to-end process is synchronous. Note that this makes the definition of *synchronous* somewhat subjective (it depends on which process you're reviewing).

Programmers and programming environments by default promote synchronous processing. However, synchronous processing is extremely inefficient. Synchronous processing environments must be set up and tuned to average (or really two standard deviations around average) response time. Imagine you have a compute-intensive service that requires 1 second of server time for each request. If the requests come in asynchronously—that is, you don't care about the response time—you could handle 60 requests a minute and wouldn't care if they were bursty (came in bursts) or leveled. If it is

99. See *www-106.ibm.com/developerworks/webservices/library/ws-docstyle.html?dwzone=webservices* for a description of how to set the parameters to override this default behavior.

set up for synchronous processing, the configuration is greatly dependent on the response time requirement and how bursty the arrival rate is. So if your requirement is to supply 2-second response time, and the arrival rate averages 60 per minute, but could be as high as 10 per second, you would need five servers to handle the load (each on average used only 20% of the time).

Most developers immediately respond with, "But our system has to be synchronous." Processes do work better synchronously, but all processes could be done asynchronously, and many at very little penalty other than some additional design time. Many interesting hybrids of interfaces can be partially synchronous, or synchronous for default case and asynchronous for other cases.

It is beyond the scope of this book to go into how to do this, but in the context of the semantics of Web Services, the important point is that the Web Service interface can be set up to handle messages asynchronously, which is exactly what you will want to do in many cases.

Getting around the Internet in a SOAP Envelope

SOAP originally stood for standard object access protocol, although there is some movement toward a rename to service-oriented architecture protocol, to take advantage of where this parade is headed, or just dropping the expansion altogether.[100–102]

Regardless of the terminology, SOAP is just an envelope (Figure 13.1), a container in which to ship an XML payload. The SOAP envelope was designed to allow for easy routing around the Internet, including through firewalls (over port 80, the port that Internet Web servers us to service http: requests). The SOAP envelope transports its payload to the destination, where it is released in the form of an XML message that can invoke a Web Service.

Describing the Interface with Web Services Description Language

Web Services description language (WSDL) is an XML language used to describe the interface to a Web Service. It is possible to use Web Services

---

100. See *http://archive.devx.com/javaSR/articles/smith1/smith1–1.asp* for further information.

101. See *www-106.ibm.com/developerworks/webservices/library/ws-mvc/?dwzone=webservices* for further information.

102. See *www.vbxml.com/soap/articles/tk2/* for further information.

FIGURE 13.1 SOAP is an "envelope" for transmitting an XML message.

without WSDL. If you already know the interface to a Web Service, you can just access it. But WSDL was invented for those cases where you don't already know the interface to the Web Service.

Figure 13.2 shows the basic sequence of activity. The requestor gets the WSDL file, which describes the location of the service and the messages that can be called on it. The requestor then calls the service.

This would be a good time to pause and note that the time between message 2 and message 3 in Figure 13.2 might be short or long. By "long time," I mean human time. The current state of the practice is that a human finds the WSDL files and then configures the request, by hand, to make the Web Service call. We call this *design time*. It is usually hours to days. We'll discuss later what needs to be in place to convert this to a run-time activity.

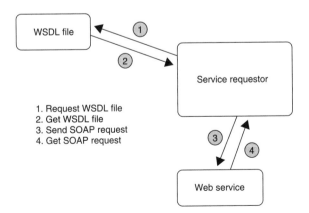

FIGURE 13.2 Using WSDL.

Finding a Service with Universal Description, Discovery, and Integration

Universal description, discovery, and integration (UDDI) is a registry for Web Services. It serves the same function as the Yellow Pages, in that it lets you find out about services that you may not have been aware of (provided the service has registered with the registry). Figure 13.3 shows the sequence of steps and technologies used to invoke a previously unknown service. First the provider of the service registers the service with a UDDI service registry (step 1 in the diagram). Later, potential consumers of the project look for and eventually find a service that will do what they want. Their search was a UDDI search; what they received was a WSDL description of the messages they would use to invoke the service. As in the WSDL-only example, there is a step, which is currently manual (step 4), where the consumers take the WSDL and incorporate it into their system. At the time of use, they construct an XML message with their request, stuff it in a SOAP envelope (step 5), and send it to the destination they learned about from the registry.

The service provider accepts and processes the message, composes a reply (also an XML message), and sends it back in a SOAP envelope (steps 6, 7, and 8). Finally the consumer consumes the message.

Service-Oriented Architectures

A Web Service is an integration technology. To achieve the potential benefits, companies will need to create a service-oriented architecture.

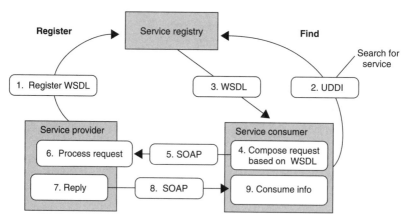

FIGURE 13.3 A UDDI-based registry of Web Services.

Putting a Web Service Interface on an Application Doesn't Reap the Benefits

It's been called many things, including service-oriented architecture (SOA), service-oriented development architecture (SODA), and service-oriented integration (SOI); however, at the heart of all three is the realization that the benefits of Web Services are not going to come accidentally.

A service-oriented architecture is a company's explicit blueprint for how it is going to implement Web Services within the enterprise. It covers a lot of the ground we discussed in Chapter 12. When companies begin experimenting with Web Services, there will be a tendency to use them as direct replacements for remote procedure calls. This will merely replace one form of spaghetti integration with another (admittedly, one for which it is easier to develop applications).

The SOA needs to define what the applications are going to be in the future, especially where any major functionality can be pulled out of applications and reused. The SOA needs to encourage publish and subscribe–style interaction, asynchronous communication, and composite applications, because these define where the real benefits will be realized.

The benefits of using Web Services are not going to come automatically, merely from adopting the technology, just as switching from C to C++ did not deliver on the benefits of object-oriented technology until people learned how to design and program in a different way.

Performance Penalties

There is a significant performance penalty in using Web Services. It consists of several bits of overhead added on top of each other, including the following: converting binary representation to Unicode, tagging each value, including more data than is generally needed for each message, encrypting, and parsing and marshalling at each end. As Dan Davis and Manish Parashar of Rutgers point out in an unpublished manuscript, the latency involved when using SOAP over http can be as much as 10 to 100 times as great as using CORBA or RMI.[103]

I'm a complete believer that the performance hit will turn out to be worth it for the flexibility, and that people will engineer in ways to speed this up or

---

103. Dan Davis and Manish Parashar, "Latency Performance of SOAP Implementations," unpublished manuscript. Available at *www.cse.ogi.edu/~wuchang/cse581_winter2002/papers/p2p-p2pws02-soap.pdf.*

make it less of an issue. This is exactly what happened with relational databases in the 1980s: They had a huge performance shortfall compared with hierarchic or Codasyl databases, yet now no one is implementing any new systems based on hierarchic or Codasyl models. (Codasyl was a prerelational database standard that had much better performance characteristics than relational databases.)

However, while we are waiting for these performance problems to be sorted out, we would do well to adjust the way we intend to use Web Services. As mentioned earlier, everything that can be done asynchronously should be. Another area to investigate is whether the services being implemented are large enough make the performance penalty workable.

Fine-Grain and Coarse-Grain Services

Grain refers to the size of a service. A fine-grain service might be one that adds two numbers together. A coarse-grain service might prepare your corporate tax return.

At this stage in the market adoption, most of the services publicly available are fairly fine grained: currency conversion, unit-of-measure conversion, and even simple calculator functions. I believe that for the next several years, coarse-grain services will be the most economical to implement. Not only is performance overhead an issue, but the management tools aren't in place and the registry services are not yet mature. This means that there is a management overhead, and managing a few hundred medium- to coarse-grain services is going to be far easier than managing thousands or tens of thousands of fine- to medium-grain services.

Composite Applications

The widespread presence of Web Services will enable and encourage a new style of user-oriented application: the composite application.

Navigation Giving Way to Composition

Traditional applications have evolved to become what is sometimes called "navigationally oriented" systems. The basic user interface is to go from screen to screen filling in whatever data is requested of you. Although this is true by necessity in mainframe systems with limited screen real estate and no possibility of local processing, it has become the paradigm of choice for most transactionally oriented Web sites. Often many of the screens will be in different systems. The user may have to set up the customer in one system, take an order in another, check inventory availability in yet another, and arrange the freight in yet a fourth. Figure 13.4 shows a small part of this schematically. Each interaction may have four or five screens. Many of the transitions are directed by the system, but the user has some choices along the way. The net result has been a lot of interest in procedures, training, and work flow. For example, a standard scenario might involve the user going to seven different screens in three different applications to complete one unit of work.

Each of those screens represents either available information, or a transaction that can be processed. Preferably the information behind each function should be abstracted out as we discussed in Chapter 12, but even if all you do is extract the screen information into an XML representation you are ahead of the game. Figure 13.5 suggests what is now possible: Information from several screens, even screens from different systems, can be consolidated.

The great challenges in this approach are twofold: How can we use the power of our client devices to get the most possible information from this

FIGURE 13.4 Navigationally oriented user interface.

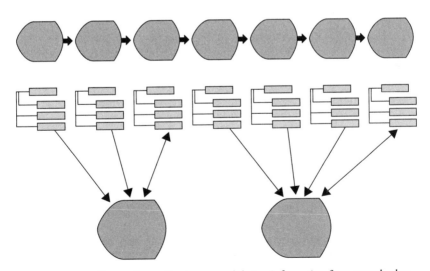

FIGURE 13.5 Composite applications consolidating information from several other systems.

type of architecture, and how we can manage context in this type of application?

Rich Client Interfaces

The thin client interface has been a remarkably successful paradigm for several years, but it is extremely limited. In many ways it is like the old mainframe interfaces, except with better artwork. The thin client interface owes much of its popularity to its ubiquity: Everyone can get at it from anywhere. It also doesn't have the configuration management problems of the "fat client," as client/server became known in the waning years of its existence.

There was some useful functionality in the fat client interfaces, though, if only they could be restored with the ease of distribution of the thin client. This is where "rich client" interfaces come in and how they relate to composite applications.

The goal of rich client interfaces is to allow some user interface interaction to be processed entirely on the client. A simple example is a "show/hide" feature to allow users to collapse some information they are not interested in, in the interest of getting the rest of the information on the screen at the same time for decision making.

Establishing Context

More advanced capabilities include using the actual content to change context and modify behavior. For example, a user may select an item from one panel in one part of the screen. The user may want to drag and drop it to another panel (in this case one that was populated from another system). The rich client allows this, but it's the semantic layer behind it that makes it work.

This behavior, which is very useful, could be hard coded, although this doesn't scale well. So there could be some code (Java applets, or .net-managed applications) that download to enable the interaction.

A more powerful approach would be to tag each of the messages from the legacy systems to a shared semantic representation (similar to what we discussed in Chapter 12). We then have a single set of code that establishes context based on the semantic objects (such that when a patient is dropped onto the scheduling panel, for example, the client would treat that as if it were natively keyed in).

Composite applications are primarily going to be an answer to the "wrap and extend" strategy for legacy systems, although I can also see mixing and matching composite applications built from internal components with those that are being used from third parties on the Web. This brings up the next topic: finding a service.

Finding a Service

Thousands of Web Services are available already, and we have barely scratched the surface.

Design-Time Searching

The current state of the practice for finding Web Services is to go to a site such as SoapClient (shown in Figure 13.6), or XMethods, SalCentral, IBM, or Microsoft, and do a keyword search.

My first search for the local temperature yielded a Web Service that nicely returned the local temperature, but as it was in Celsius, I wanted a conversion service. Although this is useful, my second search came up empty, despite the fact that there were services available that would convert Celsius to Fahrenheit.

This is pretty much exactly the same shoal the object-oriented and component industries washed up on. The absolute number and variety of components from which you could pick exceeded the ability of most developers to find and use. We need to learn from industries that have solved this problem, such as the electronic component industry, and bring some of their best practices to bear.

This is going to involve an ontology and some directed search to help developers gradually close in on what they are looking for.

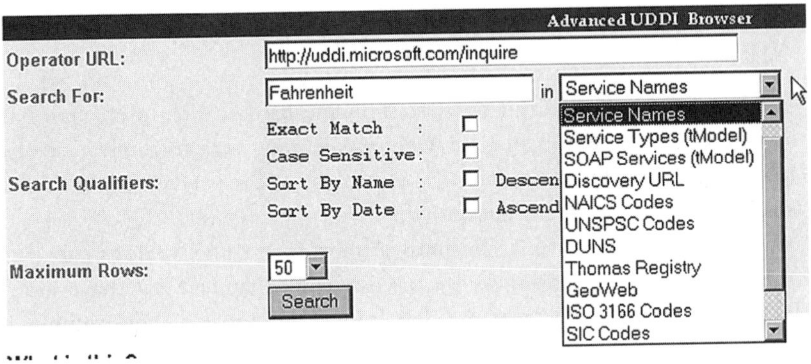

FIGURE 13.6 A UDDI search for a Web Service.

Run-Time Searching

Meanwhile, the longer-term intent is to use these technologies to do selection of Web Services on the fly while the system is being used. Most information systems professionals would, at this point, say "No way." There are so many impediments to this that it almost doesn't seem worth pursuing.

However, I know of at least one example that is close enough to make this plausible. Several years ago I met the head of a firm that had become successful dispatching overseas phone calls. The firm's customers were all the major long distance voice companies and all the major undersea cable operators (some of whom were also long distance voice companies). This company kept real-time data on quality of service (number of drops, noise on the line, etc.), capacity, and real-time pricing per channel or cable. Each overseas call was routed to a switch that selected a circuit and completed that portion of the call. This dispatch was done in milliseconds. Each long distance phone company got the best possible rate for each call. The cable operators, through dynamic pricing, could maximize the utilization of their fixed assets, and the end user got a higher-quality call.

I think this provides an "existence proof" for the concept of run-time service selection. However, we need to keep in mind that this example was in a highly circumscribed domain. Essentially there was only one message type, everyone subscribed to the same protocol, and all participants were known ahead of time.

This is where dynamic selection of Web Services will get its start: selecting from a known list of providers. Eventually, as we'll describe later, this may branch out to include heterogeneous (but compatible) WSDLs and inclusion of newly discovered providers.

Work Flow and Collaboration

Web Services are atomic and stateless. This means that each interaction has to stand on its own. You make a Web Service request; you receive a reply, either synchronously or asynchronously; and you're done. That is, you're done as far as the Web Service is concerned.

But that's not how it is in business. Almost everything we do is part of a longer-duration transaction. As we discussed in Chapter 8, we have long-duration business transactions that last from hours to years. For example, a purchase order is a transaction that may take hours to days, or even weeks, just to research and obtain quotes and approval, and it may be weeks or months until the order is completely satisfied (i.e., received and paid for).

Another set of standards has grown up along with Web Services to deal with this. As with some of the other standards, there was a period when many standards were created and proposed, but the industry has settled on one (at least for now). The standards considered, but subsequently dropped, included business process specification schema (BPSS) from ebXML, XLANG from Microsoft, WSFL from IBM, and BMPL from the Business Process Management Initiative.

The standards currently used are business process execution language for Web Services (BPEL4WS) and Web Service choreography interface (WSCI). BPEL4WS is a joint proposal from IBM, Microsoft, and BEA. BPEL4WS creates a shared stateful context for a number of partners to cooperate on completing a long-duration business transaction. WSCI is from Sun, SAP, BEA, and Intalio.

Work Flow

Historically, work flow was the documentation of the sequence of steps that manual forms went through as they were routed from person to person within an organization. Many work flow initiatives still follow this basic paradigm. Work flow associated with document imaging followed this basic paradigm, but by scanning the paper forms and letters, the organization was able to route the paper more rapidly, including to remote locations, and documents were never lost. Over time organizations gradually phased out the serial approval processes that were a holdover from paper-based days, and they performed more work in parallel.

At the core of all work flow systems are templates that describe users, work queues, and the routing that a particular type of transaction is meant to take. More sophisticated, and high volume, work flow systems allow work to be routed to abstract queues and then assigned to individuals based on their current workload and other considerations.

Orchestration and Choreography

Orchestration and *choreography*, which are used almost interchangeably, are terms for the level at which the templates for the work flow are created. The difference between orchestration or choreography and work flow is that the former is meant to be more proactive. That is, an orchestrated environment is meant to anticipate exceptions and unusual routing of work flow and have resources ready to address them.

In the Web Services world, BizTalk is Microsoft's orchestration environment; a WSCI equivalent is SunOne's WSCI editor.

Collaboration

Collaboration comes in two flavors: serial collaboration and simultaneous collaboration. For the most part, serial collaboration is just the participation in the work flow coordination of tasks that was laid out in the orchestration of a multicompany process.

Simultaneous collaboration involves having multiple people interact on the same work products at the same time. In the trivial case it is electronic whiteboarding. (I suppose the truly trivial, and often most effective, case is old-fashioned whiteboarding.) More sophisticated environments exist, however, such as those in which many engineers can modify the design of a three-dimensional part at the same time, referencing the same model.

So far none of the Web Services has addressed simultaneous collaboration.

Service Contracts

The barrier between Web Services as they currently exist and the promised future of run-time discovery lies primarily in the absence of contracts for the services. In this case the contract that is needed follows from Bertrand Meyer's work on design by contract and concerns low-level contracts between components in an object-oriented environment.[104]

Design by Contract

The contracts we need for Web Services lie somewhere between the method-level assertions of design by contract and the high-level contracts that businesses enter into to do business with each other. As we described in Chapter 2, it is possible and desirable for a traditional contract to be expressed in semantic terms, and in so doing it becomes simpler to construct, less ambiguous, and easier to interpret.

However, the template that these contracts need to flow from has a different set of primitives than the intellectual property transfer contract that we looked at in Chapter 2. The key semantic concepts that must be defined to a level that a system could interpret include the following:

---

104. Bertrand Meyer, *Object Oriented Software Construction.* New Jersey: Prentice Hall, 1988, p 115.

- **Security**—The security contract provisions will concern items such as assurance that information will be encrypted when transported, and the provisions will describe what level of authentication is needed and which categories of authorized users will be allowed access to what data. The security contract may also specify what information that was transported as part of the service invocation will be maintained by the producer and what rights the producer has to that information.

- **Auditability**—This set of provisions will concern whose responsibility it is to ensure that detailed records are kept of all interactions and whether these records need to be at the level of detail to support billing arrangements, security audit, quality-of-service audit, financial audit, or any other requirement.

- **Service level agreements/quality of service**—The provider will establish a set of quality-of-service metrics that will include such factors as capacity (in terms of number of messages by type to be handled per unit of time), response time (average time from message receipt to message reply), and availability (number of minutes of uptime guaranteed over particular windows: daytime, weekend, graveyard, etc.).

- **Billing**—Each service will potentially carry a billing component, typically a cost per handled request. The billing contract will also specify mode of payment (automatic deduct from bank, invoice, etc.) and frequency.

- **Assertions and guarantees**—These are on the content of the messages. For example, the service that provided arithmetic division might assert that the divisor must be nonzero. An inbound message with a zero as the divisor will obviate the service of any obligation other than that of posting an exception. For all messages with valid dividend and divisors, the service guarantees that the result when multiplied by the divisor will yield the dividend (within a set level of precision).

- **Warrantees**—In the event that a guarantee has been violated, this provision specifies the remedy (e.g., payment). Note that there will be warrantees on the Web Service, as well as warrantees on any referenced real-world service. For example, a wholesaler might warrantee that the site will be available 24/7 and credit a month's worth of transactions for any month where availability was less than 99.99%. The wholesaler might also have a warrantee that any item it claimed was available to promise was indeed available to promise, and that a credit of x or x% would be allowed for every violation.

- **Handling exceptions**—This section spells out what actions each participant will take to detect exceptions and what each participant will do (in terms of messages to the other party) in the event of an exception.

For run-time discovery to work, these items (as well as others) will be needed and must be reduced to functions that can be evaluated by the system.

Web Service Management

If we are to rely on an infrastructure of Web Services, whether managed by ourselves or by others, we will need tools and approaches to managing them.

Maintaining the Agreements

First we will need to set up a repository to maintain the agreements we have entered into. This repository will be structured somewhat along the lines of the contracts described in the previous section, but of course will also have to include the WSDL description of the messages themselves. If we are using multiple suppliers for the same service, this will have to be captured, as well as any minimum required usage or maximum or rate-change levels.

Monitoring

The second aspect is monitoring the services on a real-time basis. This monitoring will need to provide statistics to support the service level agreement and other provisions, as well as information to support billing. The requirement for real-time or near–real-time monitoring is to ensure that there is a real-time escalation in the event of a service disruption.

Billing

Third, the Web Services management function should provide the support for and the actual invoicing or transfer of funds as per the contract.

Voting

One last thought in the world of Web Services, and that concerns voting. For the foreseeable future one of the tempting options for Web Services will be those that are provided free of charge. As mentioned earlier, there may be many motivations for providers to provide a service on a free basis.

A concern is that you will not be able to establish a contract with many of the free services, yet they may be so enticing that you will not want to pass them by. Your business may become dependent on them, without you being able to ensure that they are always available, reliable, and accurate.

To address this, I propose that firms build into the service-oriented architecture a voting service. This service would find at least two and preferably three or four providers that provide the same or equivalent services. For example, say that you find a service that provides routing information for your truck fleet. You give it two addresses and it gives you the total mileage for the preferred truck route between the two locations.

You find two more such services and send each request to all three. How you process this information will depend on whether the originating call was synchronous or asynchronous (this is another argument for the asynchronous approach).

For an asynchronous call you wait for all three services to respond (or wait some reasonable time frame, such as 2 minutes) and assume that one of them is off line if they don't respond in that time frame. If all three respond with the same answer (within some preset interval), you pass the information on. Two out of three you might pass on or throw an exception, depending on the importance of the answer. If all three are different you throw an exception. In any case you mark the outliers, return to them later, and review any services that are consistently not agreeing and either cull them or investigate (they might be right even though they don't agree).

For a synchronous call, you send back the first result you get. You keep it, and if both of the other two disagree with the first one, you throw an exception that will stop the originating transaction. If one of the others disagrees, you flag it for follow-up later.

Conclusion

Web Services are "top of the toybox" right now and are receiving a great deal of hype. However, just because they are being hyped doesn't mean there is no substance. Just the opposite: There are huge advantages in deploying Web Services.

Much of this chapter is intended to promote the idea that the advantages of Web Services will not come automatically just because we begin to use the technology. The technology must be mastered, and there is a fair bit of it, but the core issue is to build it into a service-oriented architecture.

There are semantic issues to be resolved in almost every aspect of this architecture, including how, semantically, we identify a Web Service such that it can be found and invoked properly. What are the semantics of a contract between the provider and user of a service? How can a semantic representation aid us in the process of building composite applications from Web Services?

These issues must be resolved. They may be resolved in the context of Web Services; or, as we take up in Chapter 14, we may have to wait for the Semantic Web to resolve them.

The Semantic Web

Tim Berners-Lee invented the World Wide Web and many of the standards we now take for granted, such as hypertext transfer protocol (HTTP), hypertext markup language (HTML), and universal resource locators (URLs). So when Berners-Lee says the Semantic Web is the next big thing, many people take notice.

Several of the foundational technologies behind the Semantic Web have been funded by the Defense Advanced Research Projects Agency (DARPA)[105] under the aegis of the World Wide Web Consortium (W3C). The W3C describes the Semantic Web as "an extension of the current web in which information is given well-defined meaning, better enabling computers and people to work in cooperation."[106] That sounds pretty good. But unless you are deeply involved in this technology, trying to find out a bit more is a challenge. Most of the material on the Web,[107–109] and the few books written on the subject,[110] focus on the technologies needed to make this happen.

---

105. The Defense Advanced Research Projects Agency was one of the key sponsors of Internet.

106. Tim Berners-Lee, James Hendler, Ora Lassila, "The Semantic Web," *Scientific American,* May 2001.

107. A good place to get started is *www.semanticweb.org/* (the community portal).

108. "The Next Web," *Business Week,* March 4, 2002. Available at *www.businessweek.com:/print/magazine/content/02_09/b3772108.htm?mz.*

109. See the official W3C Semantic Web site: *www.w3.org/2001/sw/.*

110. Johan Hjelm, *Creating the Semantic Web with RDF.* New York: Wiley Computer Publishing, 2001.

Although these are essential, this has led to a perception that the Semantic Web is an academic exercise.

In this chapter I'd like to paint the Semantic Web as the logical extension of what I believe is a tidal shift in the emphasis in information processing. We will describe the proposed technology, because not to do so would leave us with nothing but arm waving and blue sky projections. I will try to make the technology understandable by focusing on a few key aspects and building up an example that I think is reasonable and reflects the potential power of this approach.

Let's start, though, with what would you use a Semantic Web for, if you had one.

Killer Apps for the Semantic Web

A "killer app" (application) is the one tool or usage that propels a platform forward. It is the usage that compels the early adopters to use a platform. In the early days of personal computers (PCs), killer apps were actually applications. Since then the term has become generic, meaning any compelling reason to adopt a new platform technology. Once a platform is established, more mainstream users are brought in (largely through word of mouth from the early adopters), and many other uses are found. Visicalc was the killer app for the early PCs in that many of the early adopters bought PCs just to run the spreadsheet. File sharing was the killer app that brought local area networks (LANs) and Novel into the mainstream. Universal (not just within your own company) email was the killer app for the Internet, and academic research (hypertext and search) was the killer app for the Web.

I believe that there are two killer apps for the Semantic Web: better query and agents. (*Disclaimer:* Killer apps are always easy to spot retrospectively, but they are very iffy prospectively.)

Better Query

The big payoff for the Semantic Web will be the ability to execute a conceptual query over the entire Web.

There are two kinds of queries in the world now: structured and unstructured. Structured query language (SQL) and Google are, respectively, the best known exemplars of each. SQL yields precise results for small domains in individual databases if you know the schema; Google yields broad and expansive results over the domain of reachable indexable text on the Internet.

However, neither is adequate, either now or (more important) in the future. They both rely too much on humans. The structured query relies on the human who is doing the requesting knowing three things: where to go (which database), what to ask for (in the vocabulary of the database schema), and how to ask (the query syntax). Although some of this can be hidden with user interfaces, most of these problems are still present.

The unstructured queries require us to be clever about what we ask for and to sift through what we get. While searching for a paper by Uche Ogbuji, I was pleasantly surprised to discover that he has what appears to be a globally unique name—all 257 entries that come up on a search refer to the same person (who, by the way, has written many excellent articles about XML and the Semantic Web). However, a search for something by Roger Smith requires far more sifting on the back end.

Try finding an article written by Hillary Clinton instead of one written about her. And we haven't even gotten to complex queries (e.g., find homes within a quarter mile of a fault line, or find a used car that gets 35 miles per gallon). There just isn't enough cleverness to construct keywords that will have the right amount of proximity and not exclude many good entries. Try finding something that the author of a Web page didn't know, or using terms the author didn't use (that's what our example later in the chapter will cover).

Agents

The Web is a big place, and it's getting bigger all the time. We are incredibly fortunate to have Google, which has managed to keep a centralized copy of all the statically reachable parts of the Web. We have to keep in mind, though, that Google has 10,000 servers dedicated to this task. We also have to keep in mind that a huge percentage of the potentially available information is in databases that are attached to the Web, but are not indexable by Google (or anyone else). You must go to those sites with your specific query, expressed in their language, or fill in their form (supplying your ID and password) to see if they have anything that matches your request.

Agent An agent is a program to which an individual delegates some authority to act on the individual's behalf and the releases to act autonomously.

I believe we will see a lot more of agents in the near future. In the early days of the Internet we were much more aware of them; gopher, archie, and veronica were often used as agents to find things on the Internet, before there were comprehensive indexes. But even now agents (spider, bots, and the like) are crawling the Web as we speak, updating indexes and looking for stuff.

The Semantic Web promises to make possible end-user, task-specific agents. At one level, agents could be long-duration distributed queries. They could also transact on your behalf.

We'll discuss the challenges and the "enables" to getting agents into the hands of everyday users in the section on adoption.

What Is the Semantic Web?

One of the confusions, and also a source of perceived instability on the Semantic Web front, is the number of seemingly overlapping initiatives and their rapid ascendancy and decline. If you examine this more closely, though, it is more encouraging. First, the acronyms are changing faster than the underlying concepts. Second, many of these standards are not contradictory, but operate at different levels. Third, as someone once said, "With death there is hope." The marketplace is winnowing out these ideas and settling on a few useful ones.

Figure 14.1 shows some of the key Semantic Web technologies and their interrelationships. I will describe most of them briefly and focus on resource description framework/notation3 because it is the base technology of the Semantic Web:

- **Knowledge interchange format (KIF)**—This is the interface format that knowledge engineers and those in the artificial intelligence (AI) community use to exchange rules.

- **Dublin Core**—The Dublin Core (from the not so romantic Dublin, Ohio) is metadata for authored materials. It covers books, music, articles, Web pages, and the like. As such, it represents a large portion of what the Web deals with, and it has been widely adopted as the ontology of choice for things such as authorship, title, publish date, copy-

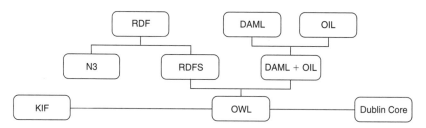

FIGURE 14.1 Some key Semantic Web technologies (the lines represent "begats" relationships).

right holder, and so on. By convention, Dublin Core tags are preceded by *dc:*.

- **DARPA agent markup language (DAML)**—DAML is a schema language that was developed by the U.S. Defense Department. It was often combined with OIL (DAML+OIL), but is now being superseded by OWL.

- **Ontology inference layer (OIL)**—OIL primarily adds inferencing to a schema.

- **Resource description framework (RDF)**—Described below.

- **Notation3**—An abbreviated format for RDF, described below.

- **RDF schema (RDFS)**—An extension to RDF to cover schema concepts such as class, subclass, and so on.

- **Web ontology language (OWL)**—The heir apparent to RDF, DAML+OIL, and RDFS.

Resource Description Framework and Notation3

RDF is the base technology for the Semantic Web. It is a modeling language, and it models a world (the so-called real world or any world of concepts, documents, and ideas). The model is conceptually simple and sound, because it is based on the mathematics of model theory. The model should look familiar by now: two ovals connected by an arrow (Figure 14.2). The RDF model is structurally similar to entity/attribute/value or term/fact/term; what makes it different is that each part of the triplet (either the subject, the property [predicate], or the object) can be a direct reference to the resource that describes this item. The resources are coded as universal resource identifiers (URIs) so that a single unambiguous definition can be found.

For example, we can model fairly concrete things such as the fact that Tim Bray wrote an article titled "What Is RDF?"[111] Figure 14.3 shows this

FIGURE 14.2 Basic RDF model.

---

111. Tim Bray, "What Is RDF?" Available at *www.xml.com/pub/a/2001/01/24/rdf.html*.

FIGURE 14.3 Tim Bray and RDF.

conceptually; however, in RDF terms we should convert each of the terms to resources, as in Figure 14.4 and the equivalent listing in Figure 14.5.

I pulled this example from an article that is almost 5 years old. Several things about the syntax and how we think about RDF have changed over this period. However, I think this example illustrates both what RDF is meant to do and some of the issues that people have when they first come to it. (The diagram was not in the original article. I annotated the word "author" with the prefix "dc:" because it is more in line with current usage, as the meaning of the word "author" would have been defined in the Dublin Core ontology.)

The first part of this makes a lot of sense, and I think it shows where the real strength of RDF lies. In other modeling disciplines we would talk about the article "What Is RDF?" However, the article is a document. It is stored on a computer. We can just point at it. We don't have to talk about it. This is potentially brilliant.

Except that it already underscores some problems. I read this article from a hard copy, so I went to the URL/URI shown—and it wasn't there. I was redirected to the XML.com site, but not to this specific document; I was redirected to the home page. I had to find the document again. This is a separate but related problem that we have had with the current Web since its inception. I can almost hear Tim Berners-Lee,[112] as well as Jacob Neilsen,

FIGURE 14.4 Tim Bray and RDF as resources.

```
<rdf:Description about='http://www.textuality.com/RDF/Why-RDF.html'>
<Author> Tim Bray </Author>
<Home-Page rdf:resource='http://www.textuality.com'/>
</rdf:Description>
```

FIGURE 14.5 Tim Bray and RDF as resources.

112. Tim Berners-Lee, "Cool URI's Don't Change," 1998. Available at *www.w3.org/Provider/Style/URI.html.*

harping on the "URLs must stay active forever" theme.[113] Because once we start building our knowledge lattices on top of explicit references to specific URIs, if the URI changes, the system doesn't work.

It's the other end of the graph that is of real interest. Physical, real-world objects, which are the easiest to model in traditional modeling, are suddenly difficult. What should we find at the end of this link? We should find Tim Bray, but of course that's not possible; he is flesh and blood. What we do find is a home page that sort of has something to do with him, and a link to a page that has some more information, including how to contact him (phone and email). But this hardly seems satisfactory. This isn't Tim Bray. This is how to contact Tim Bray. The specifications and current state of this technology are not very precise about what we should find at the final terminus for a reference to a person, but the person's home page hardly seems definitive, and it is only useful in a limited number of cases.

RDF isn't limited to this type of simplistic association. We can relate concepts to concepts and things to concepts. At the risk of overload, let me introduce the alternative notation for RDF, called Notation3, and show a part of the example I will introduce later.

Figure 14.6 was extracted from a sample genealogy ontology.[114] The first two lines refer to the ontologies used (there were more ontologies in this example). In each case, the link shows where the ontology resides (note to the Semantic Web: we're going to need a more sophisticated versioning system than what was used here—file folders with dates), and the prefix to use in the rest of this document when referring to that ontology. For example, the OWL ("owl:") ontology is where we will find the definition of "inverseOf."

The second half of the listing contains two examples of the Notation3 (n3) notation. Each line is an RDF triple (subject, predicate, object). This is much more concise and easy to read.

```
@prefix owl: <http://www.w3.org/2002/07/owl#>.
@prefix gc: <http://www.daml.org/2001/01/gedcom/gedcom#>.
gc:parent owl:inverseOf gc:child.
gc:grandparent owl:inverseOf gc:grandchild
```

FIGURE 14.6 A snippet of a genealogy ontology in Notation3.

---

113. Jakob Nielsen, "Web Pages Must Live Forever," Nov 29, 1998. Available at *http://useit.com/alertbox/981129.html.*

114. Jos De Roo, *www.agfa.com/w3c/euler/gedcom-relations.n3.*

A Brief Example

I'm going to introduce a more complex example, with some inference. I won't explain how all the inference works; see the references in Appendix B if you're interested. The example is from the same source as the aforementioned genealogy ontology.

Let's take a look at how we can infer new knowledge using the inference rules in Figure 14.7. The letters after the question marks are local variables, local to that rule. In formal semantics they are usually *x* and *y*, but here they are letters that are mnemonic for the domain. In rule 1 we assert that if a child *c* is in family *f*, and a parent *p* is a spouse in the same family *f*, then we can logically infer that *c*'s parent is *p*. Because of the inverse declared previously, we now already know that *c* is *p*'s child. (I realize it seems obvious to a human, but this is hard for a computer to work out.)

In a similar form, rule 6 tells us that if child *c* has a parent *p*, who in turn has a parent *gp*, then *c*'s grandparent is *gp*. Rule 7 tells us that if the grandparent is male, he is also a grandfather to the child.

Armed with the two dozen or so rules in this particular ontology, we could infer just about anything from a database of an extended family as long as we knew the members of each immediate family. We could pose and get sensible answers to questions such as "Who is Billy's uncle?" and "Are Sarah and Irving cousins?" even though the family database does not explicitly specify these relationships.

Semantic Web Adoption

As Malcolm Gladwell would put it, the question is, "Will the Semantic Web 'tip,' and if so, when?"[115] "Tipping" is that transition that turns a disease into

```
(: rule1. ?c gc:childIn ?f. ?p gc:spouseIn ?f) log:implies
(?cgc:parent ?p).
...
(: rule6. ?c gc:parent ?p. ?p gc:parent ?gp) log:implies
(?c gc:grandparent ?gp).
(: rule7. ?c gc:grandparent ?gp. ?gp gc:sex :M) log:implies
(?c gc:grandfather ?gp).
```

FIGURE 14.7 Inference rules in the genealogy ontology.

---

115. Malcolm Gladwell, *The Tipping Point.* Little, Brown, 2002.

an epidemic or a fashion into a fad. For the Semantic Web, the questions are, "What needs to happen as a prerequisite?" and "What might hold it up?" In this section we'll examine some "accelerators" and "inhibitors" to the Semantic Web reaching escape velocity.

Inhibitors

Some of the inhibitors, such as the complexity of the environments and the lack of good examples, may be overcome simply by the presence of a few good books and some Web sites with some good examples as to how to put this technology to use. These items are currently missing, but I don't see any reason why they would be permanently missing.

A bigger inhibitor is the inertia of getting people to mark up their pages with this additional markup language. As of right now, this is a deterrent. Expecting the average Web site owner to correctly tag the content on his or her site, given the current support for this activity, is expecting too much. However, as we mention in the section on accelerators, motivated merchants (and others) will find a way to get this done, and an industry will sprout up to help them.

Cory Doctorow has a fun and provocative, if cynical, view of the problems. It attempts to rely on what people coding this type of information correctly will run into.[116] One of his seven points is that people will not be objective about this coding if their incomes are at stake. The seven points read like the seven deadly sins.

Lack of reliable and useful ontologies is an inhibitor. People have to "commit" to a particular ontology or group of ontologies. There isn't much out there that most people would feel comfortable committing to. With a few exceptions in the medical and scientific fields, most of the ontologies I've seen are experiments and prototypes, and they do not have any commercial backing that would comfort those who would participate.

Another inhibitor is the fact that many end users are not competent to define semantic queries and to program software agents to do their bidding on the Internet. As things stand now, these are nonstarters. However, this could easily change with the right tools.

The final inhibitor is performance issues, or perceived performance issues. In the early 1990s the conventional wisdom was that user interfaces had to be tuned to subsecond response time to get maximum productivity for

---

116. Cory Doctorow, "Metacrap: Putting the Torch to Seven Straw-men of the Meta-utopia," Aug 2001. Available at *www.well.com/~doctorow/metacrap.htm*.

knowledge workers. Along came the Internet, and it was found that people were willing to trade the 5- to 10-second delays for access to information. The Semantic Web will go the same way: Performance will be a block until there is something worth the wait.

Accelerators

Merchants, as well as other purveyors of information and services, want to be found. They want to be found even more than the consumers want to find them. We now take for granted something that we wouldn't have believed 10 years ago: that the average cabinet maker, corner restaurant, and bed and breakfast would willingly code up a description of their offering in an arcane language called HTML, build an application behind that to allow strangers to transact with them, and pay "positioners" fees to help them climb in the search engine rankings. The tools have improved and no one codes in raw HTML anymore, but the fact remains that with their businesses at stake, businesspeople will do some strange things.

In that vein, all it would take would be a search engine that began using semantic tags for relevance, and Web sites would have semantic tags. The more popular the search engine, the more rapidly this would happen. It appears that Google has no current plans to use semantic tags.[117] Google's owners may feel that this would level the playing field at a time when they don't want it leveled.

General Magic, the company that built an early personal digital assistant (PDA), also had an architecture for agent-based software before the Web. General Magic was ahead of its time, but time has a way of recycling good ideas. One of the issues General Magic wrestled with and seems to have solved was the problem of how John Q. Public programs his software agent if he can't program his VCR. The programming language turns out to be "I want," as in "I want a cheap vacation in Mexico." Now, where we would go with this, given that we have (or will have) ontologies and other useful tools at our disposal, would be an informed dialog with John. "When do you want to go?" "Is any area of Mexico more interesting than any other?" "What do you consider to be cheap?" And so on. Armed with this, and perhaps a few more questions the agent may uncover after its first few laps around the Internet, the agent goes out to do John's bidding.

This is far more than Priceline. This is not some prearranged deal. The agent can make any sort of offer you want, and it can be legally binding or

---

117. David M. Ewalt, "The Next Web," *Information Week*, Oct 14, 2002, p 40.

not. But what is far more interesting than the usefulness of this to the consumer is the usefulness to the companies being visited. These companies will keep track of the agent's requests. Over time they will say, "You know, that is the twentieth request for an Aztec pottery trek we've had in the last month. Let's put one on." This is much more valuable than market research. These are real offers, or at least inquiries, that in many cases will have been dollarized.

The final accelerator will be a tool that would allow Web site developers to easily and accurately semantically tag their Web site. Tools that do most of the hard parts of this are already available from companies such as Applied Semantics, Inxight, and Semigix.

Everyone Doesn't Have to Agree to the Same "Über-Ontology"

One of the things that dissuades some people is the belief that for this to work, we all have to subscribe to the same ontology. Anyone who has tried to describe the operation of their entire company on a single database (schema) knows by extension how impossible this is. And yet people want to try.

The "Upper Ontology"

Some groups are working on what is called the "upper ontology." Sometimes this looks like a small veneer to describe the rest of the ontologies, and if that is the case, full speed ahead. But just as often the ontologies become bigger when they should be getting smaller and broader when they should be getting narrower.

Some Very Big Ontologies

Cyc, from Cycorp, is the granddaddy of the big ontologies.[118] To be fair, they haven't set out to create an upper ontology; they set out to build a commonsense database that would allow a computer to reason in a way that is analogous to the way humans reason, in the presence of unstructured data (natural language). This is an ambitious goal. Maybe they've achieved it. Maybe they're close. The problem is that they have seduced many ontologists

---

118. See *www.cyc.com* for further information.

into using this as a starting point, and it is just too unwieldy to be used in practice.

WordNet is similarly a large ontology.[119] It is a dictionary of the English language with which systems can do some limited reasoning. It is useful for dealing with English generically, but it isn't set up to be the source authority on anything. For example, WordNet has information on eight types of mushrooms. Other sites have information on thousands, with far more data.

The issue is not that there is anything wrong with large ontologies. They are useful for some things. But we shouldn't let their success in breadth allow us to believe that with a bit more depth they could handle our semantic integration needs. Just the opposite: As they become larger, and especially as they have more constituents, their size will prevent them from being able to specialize. What we need are a manageable number of moderately sized ontologies.

Six Degrees of Separation

If every business and every person had their own ontology (the idiolect issue again), communication would be chaos. But we also don't think it wise to try to force everyone to subscribe to a common ontology. How are we going to communicate? How will we do commerce?

I think we'll do it in a manner similar to how we do it now. Each specialty and subspecialty will rally around some sort of standard bearer, some institution they believe has best captured their collective knowledge. Urologists will reference a few urology ontologies. Brake pad manufacturers will reference industrial materials ontologies and manufacturing methods ontologies. Each of these in turn will reference more general ontologies in which they express their schema. The urology ontology will be expressed in medical terms (not legal terms, despite current trends) from a more general (not a more comprehensive) medical ontology. The medical ontology in turn will be expressed in a few even more general ontologies, perhaps general anatomy, general etiology, and general activity. All the ontologies will be interlinked, but not all to the same set of ontologies. My guess is that as this system matures, the distance between any two ontologies will be on the order of six degrees.

How Many Types of Entities Are There in the World?

If you observe a typical corporation and look at its production databases, you will find, for a company of any size, at least a thousand database tables and

---

119. The WordNet database is available from many sites, including *www.cogsci.princeton.edu/~wn/*.

tens of thousands of elements (attributes, properties, and relationships, as well as the table entities). From personal observation there seems to be about 10 for every employee in a company. (A company of 1,000 employees could be expected to have 10,000 elements; a company of 100,000 would have a million. These aren't scientific numbers, but I don't think they are too far off.) With a hundred million workers in the United States, we should expect to have about a billion elements floating around our corporate infospace. (Of course many of them are the same, but we have no way of knowing this.)

How may elements are there likely to be in all of commerce? From our discussion on vocabularies, I could easily imagine hundreds of thousands. Maybe even millions. But keep in mind that every distinction we make is not necessarily a new element. Blue pens and red pens are different SKUs, but I don't set up new columns in my database. Where it becomes interesting (and where the question of cross-domain interaction becomes interesting) is, What is the smallest ontology you need to be able to communicate with your trading partners?

A Core Ontology Would Be Helpful

Rather than trying to build an ontology that tries to include everything, we should be looking at ontologies that allow us to describe anything. I don't think this would have to be very large. Elegant, yes. Large, no. I think a few hundred concepts would do it.

A More Elaborate Example

Let's delve into the realm of mushroom harvesting to make this more tangible (or fungible, if you can pardon a bad pun).

Al's Organic Mushrooms

Al harvests and farms wild and domestic organic mushrooms. He has a Web site and sells his mushrooms. Al is a dedicated mycophagist (mushroom eater), and he is committed to the mycologic ontology as shown in Figure 14.8. (Mycology is the branch of botany that studies fungi.) The mycologic ontology has a wealth of knowledge about mushrooms, but Al uses it only to get the names right. So Al can refer to his mushrooms as porcino, with the knowledge that he is synched up with the mycologic ontology entry for *Boletus edulis*.

Al also is committed to the California Produce Growers ontology, which helps him categorize his produce as fresh or dried and organic or nonorganic. It also specifies what restrictions there might be on transporting it.

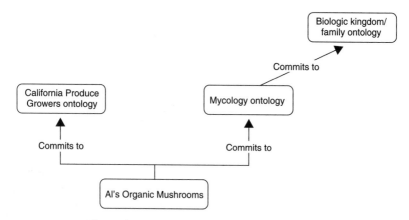

FIGURE 14.8 Al's ontology commitment.

Genus, Species, Family, Order, and Phylum

The mycology ontology has a wealth of data on mushrooms, but only for the fungi kingdom. The mycology ontology in turn commits to a more general biologic ontology that ensures it is using the standard nomenclature for the scientific naming of the many species.

The mycology ontology has information about whether each mushroom is poisonous or could cause hallucinations. It has a wealth of data to help identify what species a given mushroom is. Some of the tests are quite specific.

Conceivably someone could query Al's offering, when joined with the mycology page, and determine if any of the produce was poisonous, even if Al didn't know. If another mycology site committed to the same biologic ontology and knew (or suspected) that a particular species was poisonous, it could reveal that, even if the mycology ontology didn't know.

Food-Drug Interactions

It doesn't have to stop there. We did some work with Multum,[120] a company that has a comprehensive drug reaction database. Not only does it list drug–drug contraindications (which drugs should not be taken with which other drugs), but also drug–food and drug or food and biologic function (i.e.,

---

120. See *www.multum.com/* for further information.

whether a drug or food will have an adverse reaction in some people based on their body chemistry).

Multum is going to commit to HCPCS (Figure 14.9) or an equivalent standards organization for identifying drugs, as well as to unambiguously identify the food substances that people might be allergic to. They commit to the biologic ontology and we're on our way. Now we can traverse the ontologies and determine that the drug warfarin is contraindicated for *Boletus edulis*. (I'm just making this up, so you warfarin takers need not panic, just yet.)

This is just data, until we link your medical record, kept in this example at St. Jude's Hospital, to both the drug ontology (which all hospitals commit to) and the Multum database. Now we can connect your medical record, the drug warfarin, and *Boletus edulis*. Connect to Al's site, and it may have saved your life.

I've made it sound easier than it really is, currently (by about an order of magnitude or two). But this is conceivably possible, and this is where this technology is headed. The only drawback is that the process might be slow, which is why you are far more likely to have an agent do this research than a query.

My motivation in going through this example is to show how each local participant, committing only to a few ontologies, could be completely interlinked, and information could be deduced without anyone in the chain having the whole picture.

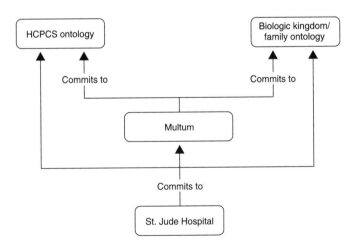

FIGURE 14.9 A hospital and a drug interaction database.

What Else Is Needed

We're not there yet. This section outlines some of the other capabilities we need to have in place to make this a reality.

Security

Much of what we are talking about is highly valued intellectual property. At a minimum it needs to be secured, or it will be guarded and its full value might never be realized. Agents need to be secured so that they do not conduct unauthorized activity on your behalf.

Trust, Veracity, and Bozos

Just as we do implicitly in the real world, we need ways of keeping track of which sources are reliable (i.e., which ontologies have reliable information, as far as we are concerned). The flip side is a more robust version of a "bozo filter." If the mushrooms from Al tasted terrible, despite rave reviews from a dozen mycophagists, you put those dozen reviewers on a "bozo list." The scope of the bozo list is at least mushrooms, perhaps all cuisine, and perhaps any opinions. The next time you look at reviews for food, their opinions and votes will be excluded.

Free Markup

As James Hendler has pointed out, another source of semantic tagging is the tools that support the authoring process.[121] When you select the image of a giraffe from a clip art source and include it in your document, it will be genus and species identified.

Semiautomated Tag Assignment

We require at least semiautomated support for semantic tagging of content. Some of these tools, such as those from Applied Semantics* and Verity, already exist at the high end, and it may only be a matter of packaging them or something similar for mass use.

---

121. James Hendler, "Agents on the Semantic Web." Available at
www.cs.umd.edu/users/hendler/AgentWeb.html.

*Applied Semantics has been acquired by Google.

Grammar Checker for Your Tag Assignment

A variation on semiautomated tag assignment would be to have a special kind of agent that uses the ontologies you are committed to and evaluates the fidelity of your assignments based on other attributes available. For example, you may have tagged your Studebaker as a new car. The agent could tell, either from the model year or from the fact that Studebaker stopped making cars 40 years ago, that you had mistagged this content. It should be able to work similar to the grammar checker in a word processor, comparing a specific instance of a sentence with a number of rules about words and grammar.

Version Management

Ontologies will change and evolve over time. We need to be able to know when the change is *accretive* (forward compatible for sites committed to it) and when it is *evulsive* (when something is torn out or otherwise changed so as not to be backward compatible). Version management of ontologies, in at least some cases, also needs to be able to answer questions such as "In the year 2002, what was our knowledge about the lethality of *Boletus edulis?*"

The Interlocutor

We like to believe that we will have natural language interpreters that will figure out all the fine points of what we mean from our utterances. However, even if that is possible (and I'm not convinced it is), we have the problem that what we say may be incomplete relative to what we needed to say, and we will need a software conversationalist that can intermediate between us and an ontology and help us refine what we are saying.

Summary

I can't say whether or when the Semantic Web will arrive. I believe that if it does arrive it will appear to have come about all of a sudden (as in the performing arts, sports, and politics, "overnight success" takes on average 10 years to achieve). We will be scrambling around trying to make our sites, interfaces, and applications "semantic" so we won't get left out of this brave new world.

In this chapter we reviewed the key enabling technologies of the Semantic Web and worked through several examples that show the strengths and some of the limitations of this technology as it has been implemented to date. In particular we outlined a moderately complex example, because most practitioners would do well to move beyond the toy applications that are used for demonstrations and begin to explore how this will work when it starts to scale to real applications.

Rather than wait for the last minute, as we did with the Internet (where there were many winners and losers once the dust had settled), I suggest that we begin adopting these technologies now, at a measured pace. The technology works. You don't have to wait for it to reach critical mass to use it. You can use it internally, experiment with it, and learn its capabilities. In doing so you will learn much more about your current systems, improve them, and be ready for the next wave as a bonus.

Speaking of getting ready, Chapter 15 is about what to do next.

Getting Started

So what should you do on Monday morning?

I suppose that after the last two chapters, the natural thing to do would be to start handicapping which technology is going to win: Web Services or the Semantic Web. Don't worry about that. Who wins (unless you happen to be a vendor serving one of those two ecologies) will not matter nearly as much as how much the industry shifts toward a semantic focus on systems development and interoperation. To the extent that this shift happens, your ability to take advantage of changes will be directly proportional to the effort you've put into your semantic makeover, rather than which technology you selected.

In the early days of relational databases or object-oriented programming, it mattered less which technology you picked (although in each case there were significant "religious wars" over the technologies). The important thing was that you moved in that direction and learned what you needed to learn, individually and corporately, to apply these paradigms to your systems.

Chapter 15 is intentionally brief. It is meant to help you put together your own action plan in terms of what you do with this information.

Build Skills

This book only scratches the surface of each of the areas it covers. Appendix B lists some resources where you can pursue any of the areas brought up here in much more depth. I've organized the resources by topic, because there are certain to be some areas you're more interested in than others, and I've annotated the references so you can direct your search more effectively.

Some areas of semantics are changing rapidly. (What we think the ancient Greeks thought about semantics isn't changing very fast, but standards in the upper level of the Semantic Web stack are turning over on a quarterly basis.) As such I will attempt to keep this information current and provide live links at *www.semanticsinbusiness.com.* The reference material includes books, conferences, discussion groups, and Web sites that will help you take these concepts further.

Experiment

Most of what I've described in this book is experiential, in that you learn by doing. You can read about any of these technologies, but until you try to put them into practice you will be missing about two thirds of the learning opportunity. Because this technology will be new to you, and some of it is new to just about everyone, I recommend that you set up an environment where you can experiment safely. Don't commit a mission-critical project with a tight deadline to these new technologies, at least until you've had time to experiment with them on a prototype.

At this point you should be experimenting with OWL and RDF, Web Services, and message brokers, if you haven't already done so. You should also be experimenting with some of the more abstract concepts brought up here, such as semantically inspired elicitation and data profiling as a means to find meaning.

Rethink Everything that Is in Flight

Everyone has some projects in progress. These are your best and most immediate opportunities to take these ideas for a spin. Following are some ideas organized by the type of initiatives you might have going.

Application Development

- Rethink the boundary and the scope from the standpoint of how they fit in with the rest of the enterprise.
- Perform a set of semantic modeling sessions to determine if there are any constructive changes you could make to your data model.
- Ask yourself whether there are any unstructured data interpretation needs that could be met by a package or a tool.

- Have you looked at the areas of your application most likely to change, and considered applying metadata design techniques to those areas?

Selecting Packaged Applications

- Add to the requirements items such as the need for an XML or Web Services interface.
- Go one step further and examine whether the interfaces are really what you need to fit the rest of your architecture.
- Select a package that can be partitioned and decommissioned in pieces if need be.

Implementing an Application Package

- If you're in the middle of implementing a package, ask yourself whether you really understand the semantics of the package you're implementing.
- If you understand the semantics, are they well documented? Can you express the semantics of the interfaces?
- If you don't understand the semantics of the system you're implementing, now would be a good time to learn them. Try a semantic modeling session with the vendor.

Systems Integration

- Build a message model as the basis for your integration efforts.
- Make sure you can express any of your interfaces in XML and potentially RDF, even if for performance or other reasons you aren't doing that now.
- Do data profiling on the data you will be integrating; make sure it means what you think it means.

Middleware Upgrade

- If you are in the middle of upgrading your middleware, check that it will support a message-oriented style of interaction.
- Make sure you are building to a message broker style of architecture to overcome the exponential explosion of interfaces.

- If appropriate, determine whether a semantic broker would fit in with the new middleware.

- Make sure that the way you are implementing the middleware doesn't cause you to become too closely tied to a particular vendor or a point-to-point style of interfacing.

Knowledge- or Content-Related Initiatives

- If you have any initiatives that deal with knowledge or content, have you looked at a knowledge base or a rules repository?

- If so, do you have a good semantically based ontology on which to express the knowledge or the rules?

- Have you looked at the use of codes and categories throughout your application systems and considered centralizing them under the purview of an ontology-based repository?

- Do you have a consistent way to identify real-world items (partners, products, locations, etc.) and intellectual property (official versions of documents, code sets, etc.)?

Business-to-Business and eCommerce Initiatives

- Do you have a common vocabulary or taxonomy that you can use to avoid having to reimplement your mappings for all your trading partners?

- Do you have an enterprise solution for business-to-business (B2B) or are you allowing this to be done on a project-by-project basis?

- Are your eCommerce initiatives integrated with your transaction systems, or are they stand-alone systems?

Web Site Upgrades

- If you are in the midst of a Web site upgrade, have you considered converting the content to a format that would allow more reuse, such as XML instead of HTML or pdf?

- Have you made arrangements to repurpose your content to alternative devices, such as handheld devices, cell phones, voice interfaces, or tablets?

- Are Web site transactions integrated with your broader work flow initiatives?

Platform Rationalization

- If you are in the midst of rationalizing your platforms (consolidating some old hardware, databases, operating systems, etc.), it is a good time to ask yourself what the motivation for the consolidation is.
- If some of the platforms have become obsolete, that's a good reason to rationalize.
- If the rationale is to get all the platforms to talk to each other, or to make interoperability easier, you may want to rethink this. It may be more effective to wrap the platform with an adaptor and replace it later at your leisure or when it truly becomes obsolete (whichever occurs first).

Software Maintenance

- Almost everyone is involved in software maintenance. In the midst of this, though, you might ask whether your current systems are unwieldy to maintain (most are).
- If your current systems are unwieldy to maintain, can you use your maintenance requests as an opportunity to begin refactoring your application into partitions that are more cohesive, easier to maintain, and possible to replace?
- Instill a step for all maintenance work to explicitly capture the semantics of the portion of the database that the maintenance request touched. (This will require a repository of some sort to maintain this information as you gather it.)

Application Architecture

- If you do not have a project underway to define or redefine your application architecture, you need one before you do any more implementation projects ("first do no [more] harm").
- Determine your need for shared services, and conduct a requirements study.
- Begin to think how you will make data accessible in a transparent and unambiguous manner.
- Identify message-based interfaces for your shared services that are specific enough to be useful and generic enough to be shared.

This should give you some food for thought, as well as areas where you can start applying semantics to the work you're already doing. I hope that, after looking at this list and reflecting on the content of the book, you will realize that semantics, far from an arcane specialty, is at the heart of everything we do as information system professionals.

Concluding Thoughts

The good news is that you really can't make any mistakes here. Any effort you make to better understand your current systems, to consider the semantics of new systems or your integration efforts, to adopt new technology that will allow looser coupling, or to tag your current content with semantic tags, no matter what ontology or technology you use, will have short-term and long-term benefits. As we've discussed in each chapter along the way, your short-term efforts will yield immediate payback if you scrutinize them from a semantic standpoint. The long-term payoff comes because you will never be done upgrading your systems, but each upgrade from now on will be easier to the extent that your semantics have been captured and expressed. As mentioned previously, I have set up a Web site to explore ideas from this book more thoroughly and provide more up-to-date information. The Web site is *www.semantics.bz.*

Congratulations

I want to thank you and congratulate you on making it all the way through this book. Regardless of your background, there must have been sections that were unfamiliar, challenging, or perhaps just obtuse. So I thank you for hanging in there, and I trust you stuck with it because you found something of value. Now that you have made it all the way through I'd like to make three requests of you.

Request Number 1

While this is still fresh in your mind, would you drop me a line with feedback on the content of this book? If you found it directly useful to your work and would like to leave a testimonial that I could put on my Web site or on a future dust jacket, please email me at this address:

testimonial@semanticarts.com

Please let me know if I can use your name, your company name, or both.

Request Number 2

I hope to prepare a second edition of this book. I intend to update it with new information and new companies that have entered any of the spaces I have discussed. Most of all, I'm interested in your comments that would make this book more useful for other readers. Please send comments or suggestions concerning any parts of the book that are inaccurate, misleading, or hard to follow. I will attempt to incorporate as many of your suggestions as I can. Please email me at the following address:

SiBS@semanticarts.com

The most substantive comments will be acknowledged in the acknowledgments section, so please let me know how (or if) you would like your name and affiliation presented.

Request Number 3

Finally, and this is just a pet peeve of mine, perhaps you could help me by committing to remove this saying from your idiolect:

"It's just semantics!"

Quick Reference

This appendix is meant to provide a quick reference to some of the more important topics covered in this book.

Semantics

Semantics is the study of meaning. It is of interest to us here because as we automate our business processes we cannot help but deal with the meaning of the information we are capturing and processing.

Semantics in business systems has been very informal up to this point. We "capture" requirements, expressed in "terms" that we define, yet the meaning of these terms is not very rigorous. As a result, systems are much more complex than they need to be, they are inflexible, and they tend to be difficult to integrate with other systems, because each system deals with similar but not identical semantic definitions for related terms.

Our best hope for dealing with our semantic overload is to spend more time understanding the meaning of the information we are dealing with. There are many techniques for doing this, and this book is just an introduction to these techniques. Some of the key approaches described herein include the following:

- **Reference ontologies**—An ontology is an organized description of the meaning of concepts and terms in a given domain. One of the first approaches that leads to shared meaning is to commit to a known or accepted ontology.

- **Semantic primitives**—Linguists and anthropologists have concluded that there are a small number of "semantic primitives" that are so fundamental that they are found in all languages and cultures, and are so basic that they defy definition in other terms. We postulate that there is a comparable small subset of semantic primitives that form the basis of all definable business objects. Such a set of semantic primitives, once well understood, would allow systems to communicate even if one system didn't know all the terms used by the other system. A full treatment of this topic is beyond the scope of this book; the concept is introduced in Chapter 9.

- **Formal methods**—There has been a great deal of work, mostly academic, using formal methods to create provably correct inferences from given starting points. This work is encouraging for the implications it will have on large-scale use of semantics and ontologies.

Business Process

A business process is a set of activities an organization performs on a repetitive basis as part of its strategy to implement its mission. Business processes typically deal with physical goods, services performed on physical goods, or services that deal entirely with information. There are six major types of business processes based on the relationship between the materials, services, and information being manipulated:

- **Extractive processes**—These processes deal with removing physical goods from the environment, such as mining, oil and gas, and forestry and agriculture. These processes deal with tradeoffs between effectiveness of the extraction process and the use of resources, as well as side effects to the environment.

- **Conversion processes**—These processes deal with converting physical materials from one form to another. This includes all the traditional manufacturing processes such as smelting, casting, milling, extruding, cutting, bending, welding, plating, and so on. It also includes construction processes and most power generation processes (the conversion of material to energy).

- **Transportation processes**—These processes involve the physical movement of physical items (goods as well as people). This includes the traditional macrolevel transportation activities (airlines, trucking, railroad, shipping), as well as intraplant transportation, such as conveyor belts and cranes.

- **Facility services**—These are services performed on a facility to make it of continuing use to an enterprise or the public, including janitorial services, maintenance, and repair.

- **Personal services**—These are services performed on people, including health care, grooming (haircutting, manicure), and entertainment.
- **Information processes**—These processes involve the manipulation of information. This includes processes that are not currently automated, such as engineering, law, and medicine (other than specific interventions), as well as most administrative and clerical tasks.

Business processes are end-to-end strategies for dealing with a particular type of event, and they encompass many different specific processes. The reason for separating them is that each has different characteristics in terms of the way it consumes resources and the effect of capital investment on the improvement of throughput and resource usage.

Most businesses are involved in a Darwinian struggle with their peers to deliver the best end result with the least use of resources. How they do this depends on how they constitute their business processes. One strategy is to reconfigure their processes to use less valuable resources. A more common strategy is to automate the most frequently occurring processes. In the case of manufacturing, automation is the process of replacing manual labor with machine-powered labor.

Much of this book concerns how making capital investments in information processes can yield high returns, but only if we learn the lessons of flexible versus rigid automation, as has been discovered in the world of manufacturing.

Ontology

As Tom Gruber puts it, "An ontology is a specification of a conceptualization."* This means that an ontology is a way of specifying what the concepts behind a set of terms mean. Ontologies are the evolution of other approaches to organizing meaning, specifically glossary, vocabulary, and taxonomy:

- **Glossary**—A glossary is a collection of terms used in a domain, with their definitions. It is not meant to be comprehensive or precise, but to inform a human reader of enough of the meaning of a term to comprehend the sentence.
- **Vocabulary**—A vocabulary, or sometimes a "controlled vocabulary," is an exhaustive list of all the terms for a given domain or subdomain. Often a vocabulary has definitions associated with it, but this is not essential.

---

*http://www-ksl.stanford.edu/kst/what-is-an-ontology.html

- **Taxonomy**—A taxonomy is an organized set of terms. The organization is almost always a hierarchy. In a rigorous taxonomy the meaning of the hierarchic relationship is the same throughout. For example, the biologic classification of species into genus, family, order, and phylum is a rigorous taxonomy in that each hierarchic relationship means "is a type of." Many other taxonomies are far less consistent, with the result that the taxonomy becomes more of a grouping mechanism that is intended to help people find similar terms.

Before saying any more about ontologies, let's briefly discuss dictionaries, thesauri, and encyclopedias.

- **Dictionary**—The purpose of a dictionary is to define terms. Defining a term should concentrate on making sure the reader knows the general type of thing that the term refers to and then distinguishing the term from any other closely related terms. Dictionaries occasionally do this, but they devote a surprising amount of space to "encyclopedia-style" definitions, as well as circular definitions (terms defined in terms of other terms, which eventually are defined in terms of the first term*).

- **Thesaurus**—A thesaurus is a network of related meanings. However, with a few exceptions (e.g., WordNet) the relationships don't mean anything and are not consistent. There are no definitions in a thesaurus; the assumption is that you know what the word means, and you're looking for a similar word. The organization of a thesaurus, such as *Roget's Thesaurus,* is a rich taxonomy of concepts in the English language.

- **Encyclopedia**—An encyclopedia is meant to tell you a great deal about a concept, once you know the concept. You might refer to a dictionary to find out what a badger is, but you would refer to an encyclopedia to find out as much as you can about badgers (their habits and ranges, their diet, etc.).

An ontology is an organized body of knowledge. It is a graph (as opposed to a hierarchy) of concepts. The concepts have terms associated with them, because that is how we know and communicate concepts. The ontology helps us refine the identification of a concept (such as "rule in" and "rule out" criteria for membership) so that we can find similar terms and express everything we know about a concept. In that way an ontology is a combination of a dictionary, a thesaurus, and an encyclopedia, expressed more precisely.

---

*Possibly a record for the most times the word "term" was used in a single sentence.

Metadata

Metadata is data about data. Data, by itself, doesn't mean anything. One of the primary ways we ascribe meaning to data is by associating it with "metadata" that specifically tells us something about the instance in question. Typically the metadata is stored in data dictionaries or classes or somewhere where it need not be repeated for every instance of the data. We might store dozens of types of data about a datum, including the following:

- Physical representation information (stored as an "int" or a "float")
- Precision information (stored as a "float" or "double")
- Validation (validation that this item has already passed, such as "must be >50")
- Source (where the data came from, including program and user)
- Owner (who owns the data; e.g., who has which rights in its duplication)
- Temporal data (when the data was captured and posted)
- Display information (default display characteristic of this item; two decimal places)
- Name of the term (what the datum is called)
- Metadata type (attribute, entity, relationship)
- Semantic type (measurement, category, etc.)

Traditionally, metadata is static; we set it up in the data dictionaries and programs, and each instance takes on the metadata it had when it was created. But a metadata-inspired design recognizes that certain types of routine changes require changes to the static parts of the metadata (database definition, classes, programs, etc.). By shifting some of the metadata from the static realm to the dynamic realm, the design can be made much more flexible and reliable at the same time. Chapter 6 provides a detailed description and case study.

Data Modeling

Data modeling is the art and science of arranging the structure and relationship of data to be stored in such a way as to optimize certain characteristics of the use of the data. In the early days of data processing, one of the main goals of data modeling was to optimize the storage of data. Later it became optimizing the access of the data. Relational theory brought with it a style of data modeling that emphasized integrity management and ensuring consistency in the presence of updates.

Object-oriented design is a form of data modeling, although practitioners typically don't think of it that way. They don't think of it that way partially because they still often store their data in relational databases and because they concentrate on modeling the behavior of the system, with the data being secondary. However, data modeling is going on in any object-oriented system. It is optimized either for reuse (classes inherit from other classes in a way that allows them to reuse, as much as possible, the shared attributes in a parent class) or for polymorphism (any of a number of different objects can be treated similarly, but they still preserve their difference where appropriate).

Data modeling also proceeds from high-level abstract models, through logical models, to physical models, and on to implementation. At each level, constraints about the target implementation are introduced. What should happen, but rarely does, is that the conceptual and logical models should be preserved and cross-referenced to their physical counterparts. System changes should be introduced at the conceptual level and rippled through, maintaining the correlations all the way through. However, this is rarely done. Once a system is implemented, maintainers know that they will be making their changes to the implemented model, and they see little benefit in maintaining the upper levels.

This is unfortunate, because many of the problems of systems integration and intercompany commerce can only be addressed at the higher levels.

Semantic modeling is a type of conceptual modeling that focuses on the meaning of the information. Further, it focuses on describing the meaning in such a way that similarities are uncovered and there is much more opportunity for shared functionality.

Integration and Enterprise Application Integration

Enterprise application integration (EAI) refers to a set of tools, technologies, methodologies, and infrastructure intended to "integrate" the data and functionality in the many applications that exist with an enterprise.

Most businesses now have dozens to hundreds, and in some cases thousands, of applications that they use to run their businesses. Each has its own definition of what the data in these applications mean. They spend between

30% and 60% of their development and maintenance budgets on building and maintaining integration between their applications.

There are several approaches to integrating systems, each with its own advantages and disadvantages:

- **Manual**—Still the most common way to integrate two systems is to have a human read information from one system and enter it into another. This has the advantage of flexibility and low capital cost, and it provides a way to handle data anomalies, but it is by far the most expensive way to do integration.

- **Shared database**—Having two applications share a single database ensures that they are dealing with a consistent data definition. The main drawback to this approach is that as we add more applications to a database we are essentially creating larger and larger applications. Applications do not scale, and as they get larger they become less economical to build and maintain. In addition, the popularity of packaged software has marginalized this approach.

- **Point-to-point interfaces**—There are many ways to write an interface from one application to another: You can call a routine in the other application, you can write out a record specifically for the other system to process, or you can write records directly to the other system's database. They all suffer from a scale problem: If you only have a few applications to integrate, this works fairly well; if you have dozens or hundreds of applications, however, the number of interconnections goes up geometrically while the number of applications only increases arithmetically.

- **Messages and intermediaries**—Most of the attention of late has been on approaches that would create some sort of intermediary so that each application would not need to know about every other application. By knowing only about the "hub" or "broker," the number of interconnections can be reduced dramatically. Messages also help with this approach by creating a more flexible structure that can survive many changes without requiring changes on the part of the receiving application.

Almost every company has a combination of all these approaches in place, with most current efforts being directed toward the messages and intermediaries approach.

What makes EAI so difficult and time consuming is that each application has a definition of the terms it uses. Often this definition is not explicit, but it is in use in the organization. Integrators look at the definition of the terms and often assume that the definition is what was implemented. They figure out how the data must be converted to make it compatible, and then they write programs to do those transformations. However, in test, or sometimes in production, it is occasionally discovered that a particular field is used for some purpose other than what it is documented as.

The application of semantics in this area enables us to find what the data in each of the applications really means, both what it is purported to be and how the extant data is being used. Semantic modeling in connection with data profiling is very helpful for this.

Business Rules

The goal of business rules is to extract business logic from the procedural application code, where it currently resides, and store it in a place and format where it can be reasoned about and changed much more easily. Currently the business logic of an application is marbled throughout the procedural code, which is often millions of lines of code. Because of the way the code is structured and divided into modules, the same logic often must be applied and reapplied, creating many opportunities for inconsistency. In the business rules approach, the rules are expressed as declarative statements that do not embody procedural concerns or flow of control. These rules can be stored in a database in such a way that tools can reason about their completeness and potential inconsistencies (in other words, are these two rules likely to contradict each other in some circumstances?).

Separating the business rules from the rest of the code involves two nontrivial operations:

- Determining the rules and expressing them consistently
- Ensuring that the rules execute when they should

There are many sources for determining what the business rules are. The existing code is one set of validated rules; however, extracting the rules from the legacy code is no mean feat. There are tools that will help with this, but they can only uncover the rules that were implemented, using the terms that were used in the data model. Another good source are the requirements of the applications, starting with the imposed requirements: laws and regulations. Laws and regulations play a role in more and more applications, and they are amenable to being reduced to rule expression. The other sources are the strategy of the enterprise and interviews with key users.

Ensuring that the rules execute (or "fire") when needed is also a nontrivial problem. The two most common approaches to date have been to fire as a side effect on a database update (any time the order table is updated, fire these rules) or to have the applications know when they must explicitly call the rules engine (this works well for things such as pricing or scheduling where the applications cannot do the operation on their own and know they need to call something to get the function completed). However, neither of these approaches is ideal. A more likely successor will be a business rules engine that operates on message traffic. Work flow routing systems already exist that do this, and it seems a logical extension to extend this to more general rule processing.

The connection between business rules and semantics exists at two levels:

- Business rules are expressed in terms of "terms." If we accept all the terms that we find in all the applications and regulations, we end up with a rule base nearly as complicated as the code base it was meant to augment. We end up with a large number of rules just to describe which terms are synonyms or near synonyms. A rich semantic model and ontology provides an elegant base on which to express the rules.

- The rules themselves are instances of classes that each have specific semantic meaning. Each business rule taxonomy works approximately the same: To replace procedural logic, the business rule environment creates a number of parametric rule types. These rule types are arranged in a hierarchy. The whole structure is a semantic model of business rules, and it is the elegance of the model that makes it possible to build relatively simple tools to evaluate the rule base or (on the execution side) to determine which rules to fire at run time.

Extensible Markup Language

Extensible markup language (XML) has rapidly become the "lingua franca" for content representation and system integration. It is likely to become a standard on which much else will be built.

XML is a tagged markup language. Unlike HTML, which is also a tagged language, XML does not have a fixed set of tags. The XML tags can be defined by users, or more often by consortia or internal standards groups. Unlike SGML, from which it descended, XML is much simpler to parse and it is much easier to create tools to manipulate it.

Soon after XML was proposed, the popular press reported that the difference between HTML and XML was that the former was a presentation markup language whereas the latter was a "semantic" markup language. Although there is a grain of truth in that, it has caused a great deal of confusion. XML's tag structure allows you to define your own semantics for a message or a document, but there is nothing about the spec or the language that helps you ascribe any semantic meaning to the tags.

One of the interesting side effects of the ubiquity of XML is that two domains that had previously been distinct, the domain of messages (or transactions) and the domain of documents, can now be expressed in the same syntax. Previously messages or transactions were described in "fixed field" formatted records, electronic data interchange (EDI) between companies, and various proprietary schemes within companies. Documents were described in markup languages such as SGML, if at all. XML wakes us up to the possibility that messages and documents are not really fundamentally different, and a message can be thought of as a small, special-purpose document.

The structure and syntax of the allowable tag combinations in an XML document are defined in its schema. DTD, a carryover from SGML, was the most popular schema language initially. Recently, schemas expressed in XML have become more popular, the most common being XSD.

The presence and popularity of XML have created a torrent of tools and standards that are expressed in XML. Virtually every conceivable industry group has formed consortia and used them to promote an XML-based definition of the standard terms and transactions in its industry. There are hundreds, perhaps thousands, of these industry-led standards in existence already. Additionally, many tool and software package vendors now allow their tools to be parametrically applied via XML and their packages interfaced via XML. Perhaps the most significant development in this area is Web Services.

Web Services

Web Services are a standard way to invoke functionality remotely, potentially from anywhere on the Web, and to express the interchange in terms of XML messages. Riding on the coattails of XML, Web Services have also sprung into almost uniform adoption, primarily because of a need to execute functionality remotely without getting tied into proprietary protocols for interchange.

Before Web Services, developers had to adopt a proprietary protocol to call functionality remotely. In many cases this meant CORBA or Microsoft's DCOM. But there were many problems with these, mostly related to their nonuniform availability. The other issue is that developers are becoming more and more aware of the advantages of mixing synchronous and asynchronous messaging to get the most optimal solutions. Most of the distributed programming interfaces greatly encouraged synchronous messaging.

Synchronous messaging means the calling program will block further execution and wait for a response. This is much more familiar for developers because it makes the remote invocation seem much like a subroutine call. However, there are several problems with this approach, especially as you start to scale up. First, as you begin to rely on more and more remote sources for functionality, you have to deal with the possibility that the service is not available, or is perhaps slow, due to a heavy load. Even if you are dealing only with local services, a synchronous interchange means that all the components and communication channels must be sized to meet peek demands, not average demands, which can often be an order of magnitude different. In asynchronous processing the calling program sends the message, but it does not wait for the reply. The reply (if there is one) will be received later, perhaps on a different channel. Web Services are highly flexible in this regard.

The way Web Services actually work, of course, involves another suite of XML-inspired acronyms. Start with the concept that there is a producer of the service and a consumer of the service. The consumer would like to invoke the producer's service. Here is how it works:

- The producer defines the interface in an XML language called WSDL.

- The producer registers the service in a UDDI registry.

- The potential consumer searches through the UDDI registry for a compatible service, finds the producer's service, and downloads the WSDL definition of how to invoke the service and what if anything to expect back.

- The consumer also gets the location of the producer's service.

- The consumer marshals his or her parameters into the format prescribed by the WSDL request schema, encloses the request in a SOAP envelope (another XML dialect; this one can reach a service destination even through a firewall), and sends the request to the location provided.

- The consumer is informed whether the request will be handled synchronously or not and either waits for the response or arranges to get a response later.

- When the response arrives, the consumer uses the other half of the WSDL definition to figure out what to do with all the tags in the response.

There are a host of issues with Web Services that deal with semantics. For example, for two companies to agree on what the tags in the WSDL messages mean, they will have to agree on the semantics of those tags. If this is to be done without human intervention (a long-term goal), there is an even greater need for a precise semantic definition.

Semantic Web

The Semantic Web is a vision of Tim Berners-Lee, the original architect of the World Wide Web, which enables computers and users to cooperate in processing data on a global basis. The premise of the Semantic Web is that the current World Wide Web does a great job of indexing documents, but that there is very little opportunity for systems to help us digest this information.

With the Semantic Web in place, a user could ask a question and the Web would cooperate to find a meaningful answer. The search would not be limited to finding keywords or to known schema, but the query would understand the concepts behind the question and could compare them at a conceptual level to concepts encoded on Web sites.

For this to work, several technologies must be developed and deployed. Many of these are under development in academic and research groups.

Resource description framework (RDF) is the cornerstone technology. RDF is a way to express models of data or knowledge. It is a simple "triplet" of information, consisting of a subject, a property or predicate, and an object. What makes it unique is that any of these three can be a universal resource identifier (URI), which grounds the model in a definitive definition of the thing modeled.

RDFS adds a few modeling primitives to RDF to allow object-oriented modeling. OWL, which is the official successor to DAML + OIL, adds the expressive power needed to model ontologies in the RDF syntax. (See Chapter 14 for definitions of these acronyms.) With OWL we now have a way to express ontologies in a standard format. Many products and tools are being marketed to help with the process of building ontologies in OWL (and other) formats, such as Protégé from Stanford.

It is understood that there won't be one overarching standard ontology on which everyone will agree; instead, there will be many ontologies, each for a specific domain or perspective. Each site then will determine which ontologies the site will use to express its semantics, and it will "commit" to those ontologies.

Perhaps the largest hurdle is marking up Web sites and databases in these new languages and expressing them in terms of the ontologies that they have committed to. This is a major area of research and commercial activity, but at present there is no clear winner in terms of approach or tools.

Finally, query tools will need to evolve to capture the intent of a query and traverse the various sites that have committed to the same ontology or others that are reachable transitively.

Resources for Further Investigation

This appendix contains resources you may find useful if you wish to pursue further any of the topics covered in this volume. I've organized this reference section into 14 major categories. There are overlaps with each of these areas, but this should get you started. *Note:* If there was not an apparent creation date, the date listed for Web articles (e.g., 5-Oct-02) indicates the date on which the article was accessed or downloaded.

Philosophy

Books

Coffa, J. Alberto. *The Semantic Tradition from Kant to Carnap to the Vienna Station.* New York: Cambridge University Press, 1991. Semantics underwent a major transition in philosophy from the late nineteenth to early twentieth century. However, I found very little related to business systems.

Copleston, Frederick S. J. *A History of Philosophy.* New York: Image Books, 1985. One good volume that covers a lot of philosophy.

Ogden, C. K., Richards, I. A. *The Meaning of Meaning.* New York: Harcourt, Brace & Co., 1956.

Rousseau, Jean Jacques. *The Social Contract.* New York: Hafner Publishing Co., 1947. Where do our obligations come from?

Simons, Peter. *Study in Ontology.* Oxford: Oxford University Press, 1987. Study of the relationship of parts to wholes: When do we consider the collection and when do we deal with the members?

Magazine and Web Articles

Kant, Immanuel. 18-June-01. Metaphysics. Web article: *http://www.utm.edu/research/iep/k/kantmeta.htm.*

Sellars, Wilfred. 9-May-56. Is There a Synthetic A Priori? In Hook, Sidney. American Philosophers at Work: The Philosophic Science in the United States, New York: Criterion, 1956, pp 135–159. Web article: *www.ditext.com/sellars/itsa.html.* Comments on Kant analysis.

van Cleave, Kent B. 20-Jun-98. Metaphysical Functionalism. Web article: *http://ourworld.compuserve.com/homepages/KVC/philbg.htm.*

Zajicek, G. 2-Jan-01. Cancer and Metaphysics. *Cancer Journal*, pp 243–248. Web article: *www.what-is-cancer.com/papers/cancerandmetaphysics200.html.*

27-Dec-01. The Origins of Western Thought. Web article: *www.philosophypages.com/hy/2b.htm.*

27-Dec-01. Socrates: Philosophical Life. Web article: *www.philosohypages.com/hy/2d.htm.*

27-Dec-01. Plato: Immortality and the Forms. Web article: *www.philosophypages.com/hy/2f.htm.*

27-Dec-01. Aristotle: Forms and Souls. Web article: *www.philosophypages.com/hy/2p.htm.*

27-Dec-01. Aristotle: Logical Methods. Web article: *www.philosophypages.com/hy/2n.htm.*

27-Dec-02. Prediction an Ontology: The Categories. Web article: *http://faculty.washington.edu/smcohen/320/cats320.htm.*

5-Dec-01. Prediction, Homonymy, and The Categories. Web article: *http://aristotle.tamu.edu/~rasmith/courses/ancient/prediction.html.*

5-Dec-03. Logic. Web article: *www.newadvent.org/cathen/09324a.htm.*

27-Dec-01. Kant: Experience and Reality. Web article: *www.philosophypages.com/hy/5g.htm.*

27-Dec-01. Leibniz: Logic and Harmony. Web article: *www.philosophypages.com/hy/4j.htm.*

27-Dec-01. Descartes: A New Approach. Web article: *www.philosophypages.com/hy/4b.htm.*

27-Dec-01. Kant: Synthetic A Priori Judgments. Web article: *www.philsophypages.com/hy/5f.htm.*

10-Nov-02. Skepticism—Sources of Knowledge. Web article: *www.philosophyonline.co.uk/tok/scepticism2.htm.*

3-Aug-02. Stanford Encyclopedia of Philosophy Abridged Table of Contents. Web article: *http://plato.stanford.edu/contents.html.* Good index of the breadth of philosophical topic areas.

Semantics

Books

Arnheim, Rudolf. *Visual Thinking.* Berkeley: University of California Press, 1969. Indications that we needn't think exclusively in words.

Epstein, Richard L. *The Semantic Foundations of Logic: Predicate Logic.* Oxford: Oxford University Press, 1994. Formal semantics.

Goddard, Cliff. *Semantic Analysis: A Practical Introduction.* Oxford: Oxford University Press, 1998.

Kempson, Ruth M. *Semantic Theory.* Oxford: Cambridge University Press, 1977.

Saeed, John I. *Semantics.* Oxford: Blackwell Publishers, 1997. Excellent introductory book on semantics in everyday life.

Semantic Analysis of Virtual Classes and Tested Classes Ole Lehrmann Madsen (OOPLA '99). Notes from Conference on Object-Oriented Programming, Systems, Languages, and Applications. Denver, November 1–5, 1999.

Magazine and Web Articles

Dawes, Milton. 5-Oct-02. General Semantics: A Critical and Meta-Critical System. Web article: *www.general-semantics.org/Basics/MD_meta.shtml.*

Kenyon, Ralph E. 21-Aug-92. On "Similarity of Structure." Web article: *www.xenodochy.org/gs/similar.html.*

Kenyon, Ralph E. 5-Oct-02. What is "knowledge" (a la Korzybski)? Web article: *www.xenodochy.org/gs/knowledge.html.*

Kenyon, Ralph E. 5-Oct-02. General Semantics. Web article: *http://ww.xenodochy.org/gs/*.

Kenyon, Ralph E. 5-Oct-84. Popper's Philosophy of Science. Web article: *www.xenodocy.org/article/popper.html*.

Kenyon, Ralph E. 5-Oct-02. Genetic Epistemology. Web article: *www.xenodochy.org/gs/gesum.html*.

Kenyon, Ralph E. 5-Oct-02. Levels or Perspectives on the Use of Language. Web article: *www.xenodocy.org/gs/gslevels.html*.

Korzybski, Alfred. 1-Apr-95. Science and Sanity: An Introduction to Non-Aristotelian Systems and General Semantics. Web article: *www.amazon.com/exec/obidos/tg/detail/-/0937298018/ref=pd_bxgy_text_1/103-051*.

Mayper, Stuart A. 5-Oct-02. The Place of Aristotelian Logic in Non-Aristotelian Evaluation: Einstein, Korzybski, and Popper. Web article: *www.general-semantics.org/basics/SM_logic.shtml*.

Pula, Robert P. 5-Oct-02. Some Notes on the Human Brain. Web article: *www.general-semantics.org/Basics/RPP_brain.shtml*.

Linguistics

Books

Allen, J. P. B., Van Buren, Paul. *Chomsky: Selected Readings*. Oxford: Oxford University Press, 1971.

Baker, Mark C. *The Atoms of Language: The Mind's Hidden Rules of Grammar*. New York: Basic Books, 2001. Component parts of language.

Brown, Cecil H. *Language and Living Things. Uniformities in Folk Classification and Naming*. New Brunswick: Rutgers University Press, 1984.

Feibaum, Christina. *Introduction to WordNet: An On-line Lexical Database*. Cambridge, MA: MIT Press, 1998. WordNet has nearly half a million terms lexically analyzed and freely available.

Jurafsky, Daniel, Martin, James H. *Speech and Language Processing: An Introduction to Natural Language Processing, Computational Learning, and Speech Recognition.* New Jersey: Prentice Hall, 2000. How humans generate and interpret speech. Contains much information on phonemes.

Kodish, Susan Presby, Kodish, Bruce I. *Drive Yourself Sane Using the Uncommon Sense of General Semantics.* Pasadena: Extensional Publishing, 2001. How words affect our thoughts.

Lakoff, George, Núñez, Rafael E. *Where Mathematics Comes From: How the Embodied Mind Brings Mathematics into Being.* New York: Basic Books, 2000. Lakoff's theory that our ability to process mathematics is based on our physical being (not our 10 fingers, but more basic).

Maher, John, Groves, Judy. *Introducing Chomsky.* New York: Totem Books, 1996.

Pinker, Steven. *Words and Rules: The Ingredients of Language.* New York: Basic Books, 1999. Author of *How the Brain Works* takes on how we process language. Much great information on the interplay of what parts of language we have to memorize and what we compose.

Trask, R. L. *Key Concepts in Language and Linguistics.* London: Routledge, 1999.

Wardhaugh, Ronald. *Introduction to Linguistics.* New York: McGraw-Hill, 1972. Good introductory text.

Wierzbicka, Anna. *Semantic Primes and Universals.* Oxford: Oxford University Press, 1996. One of the pioneers of the semantic prime theory, which states that there are a small number of concepts (about 50) that are too basic to be defined and that we know everything else in terms of these concepts.

Magazine and Web Articles

Harvey, Kaolin R. 12-Dec-01. Bloomfield, Korzybski, and the Meaning of Language Science: A Tale of Two Scholars. Thesis. Available at *www.plaza.powersurfr.com/krh/writing/korz0.html.*

Richards, I. A. 6-Oct-02. The Meaning of Meaning. Web article: *www.colorado.edu/communication/meta-discourses/Theory/ richards/sld001.htm.*

Prototype and Category Theory

Books

Goddard, Cliff. *Semantic Analysis, Semantic Primes and Universal Grammar.* Oxford: Oxford University Press, 1998. One of the seminal works on semantic primes.

Horwich, Paul. *Meaning.* Oxford: Clarendon Press, 1998. *www.oup.co.uk/isbn/0-19-823824-X.*

Lakoff, George. *Women, Fire and Dangerous Things.* New York: Basic Books, 1990. Prototype theory: how we form categories from exemplars.

Pierce, Benjamin C. *Basic Category Theory for Computer Scientists.* Cambridge: Massachusetts Institute of Technology, 1993.

Taylor, John R. *Linguistic Categorization: Prototypes in Linguistic Theory, Second Edition.* Oxford: Clarendon Press, 1995. *www.oup.co.uk/isbn/0-19-870012-1.*

Magazine and Web Articles

Atran, Scott. 3-Dec-01. Folk Biology and the Anthropology of Science: Cognitive Universals and Cultural Particulars. Web article: *http://www.bbsonline.org/Preprints/OldArchive/bbs.atran.html.* Folk biology studies the way everyday people construct their own taxonomies of living things, and what that reveals about our innate categorizing.

Goddard, Cliff. Jun-03. The Natural Semantic Metalanguage Homepage. Web article: *www.une.edu.au/arts/LCL/disciplines/linguistics/nsmpage.htm.* This is where the semantic primes of language are recorded.

Green, Stuart P. 19-Jan-01. Prototype Theory and the Classification of Offenses in a Revised Model Penal Code: A General Approach to the Special Part. Web article: *http://wings.buffalo.edu/law/bclc/bclr.htm.* Use of prototype theory.

Hofstede, A. H. M., Lippe, E. A Category Theory Approach to Conceptual Data Modeling. *RAIRO Theoretical Informatics and Applications* 30(1):31–79, August 1996.

Holt, Jim. Whose Idea Is It, Anyway? *Lingua Franca* Sept/Oct 1994. Available at *www.linguafranca.com/Archive/whose.html*.

Humphreys, Rebecca. 23-May-96. Categorisation and Prototypes. Web article: *http://www.ecs.soton.ac.uk/~harnad/Hypermail/Explaining. Mind96/0180.html*. More on prototype theory.

Hunn, Eugene S. 3-Dec-01. Evidence for the Precocious Acquisition of Plant Knowledge by Zapotec Children. Web article: *http://faculty.washington.edu/hunn/MZPA.htm*.

Kripke, Saul. 5-Dec-01. About the Author of Wittenstein on Rules and Private Language. Web article: *http://krypton.mankato.msus.edu/~`witt.kauthor.html*.

Kripke, Saul. 5-Dec-01. Phil2100 Lecture 7. Web article: *http://krypton.mnsu.edu/~witt/kauthor.html*.

Rae, Amadeo M. 25-Nov-98. Folk Mammalogy of the Northern Pimans. Web article: *www.uapress.arizona.edu/samples/sam1206.htm*. More folk biology.

Richards, I. A. Spring 1998. Proper meaning Web article: *www.colorado.edu/comunication/meta-discourses/Paper/ App_Papers/Cahill.htm*.

Wittgenstein, Ludwig. 5-Dec-01. Tractatus Logico Philosophicus. Web article: *www.kfs.org/~jonathan/witt/tlph.html*.

Zitzen, Michaela. 4-Dec-01. On the Efficiency of Prototype Theoretical Semantics. Web article: *http://ang3-11.phil-fak.uni-duesseldorf.de/~ang3/ LANA/Zitzen.html*.

27-Dec-01. Ladwig Wittgenstein: Analysis of Language. Web article: *www.philosophypages.com/hy/6s.htm*.

3-Dec-01. Ethnobiological Classification: Categorization. Lecture 12. Web article: *www.rbgkew.org.uk/peopleplants/regions/ thailand/lecture12.htm*.

6-Oct-02. Basic English Word Lists. Web page: *http://ogden.basic-english.org/bewords.html*. Basic English is a movement to try to find the 600 "basic" concepts in English on which all other concepts are based.

Artificial Intelligence and Knowledge Management

Books

Gardenfors, Peter. *Conceptual Spaces: The Geometry of Thought.* Cambridge, Mass.: MIT Press, 2000. Professor Gardenfors puts forward the notion that there is a way of modeling knowledge that lies between the high-level symbolic models of AI and the low-level "connectionist" models of neural nets. He calls this modeling approach "conceptual spaces." The proposal is that much of what we reason about can be mapped to geometric positions in a hypothetic space, and the relative distance between items is what creates their "similarity."

Sowa, John F. *Knowledge Representation: Logical, Philosophical, and Computational Foundations.* Pacific Grove: Brooks/Cole, 2000. Definitive book on applying formal semantics.

Magazine and Web Articles

Dennett, Daniel. 21-Jan-02. What Kind of System of "Coding" of Semantic Information Does the Brain Use? Web article: *http://www.kurzweilai.net/meme/frame.html?main=/articles/art0381.html?m%3D3.*

Hollander, Dave. 4-Jan-02. Just-in-Time Information Management. KM Essays. Web article: *www.mhxml.com/papers/km-essays.htm.*

Mueller, Erik T. 1-Dec-99. A Database and Lexicon of Scripts for ThoughtTreasure. Web article: *www.signiform.com/tt/htm/script.htm.* ThoughtTreasure.

8-Dec-01. R-Objects Pepper Screen Shot Gallery. Web page: *www.r-objects.com/gallery/.*

9-Apr-00. ThoughtTreasure: A Natural Language/Commonsense Platform. An Overview. Web page: *www.signiform.com/tt/htm/overview.htm.* ThoughtTreasure.

11-Nov-02. ThoughtTreasure FAQ. Web page: *www.signiform.com/tt/htm/faq.htm.* ThoughtTreasure.

6-Mar-01. Press Release: Cycorp. Web article: *www.cyc.com/opencycpressrelease03062001.html.* On the Cyc project.

1996–2002. OpenCyc Selected Vocabulary and Upper Ontology. Web article: *www.cyc.com/cycdoc/vocab/vocab-toc.html*. On the Cyc project.

Business Rules

Books

Ross, Ronald G. *The Business Rule Book: Classifying, Defining and Modeling Rules*. Houston: Business Rule Solutions, LLC, 1997. Dense but thorough. Nearly 100 rule types with multiple examples of each.

Von Halle, Barbara. *Business Rules Applied: Building Better Systems Using the Business Rule Approach*. New York: Wiley, 2002. Focuses on the methodology of applying business rules.

Magazine and Web Articles

Buckley, Alex. 9-Oct-02. Profit from Events and Patterns (Part 2). Web article: *www.brcommunity.com/cgi-bin/x.pl/print/p-b113b.htm*.

Kim, Eugene E. Dec 2001. The Intellectual Foundation of Information Organization. Web Techniques: *http://www.newarchitectmag.com/documents/s=4181/new1013635633/index.html*.

Lin, Nelson. 9-Oct-02. Alternatives for Rule-Based Application Development. Web article: *www.brcommunity.com/cgi-bin/s.pl/resources/n007.htm*.

Schacher, Markus. 9-Oct-02. Business Rules and Prolog. Web article: *www.brcommunity.com/cgi-bin/x.pl/print/p-b118.htm*. Prolog is an older AI language that is not used as widely now.

20-Dec-01. What Is Business Logic? Web article: *wysiwyg://26/www.versata.vjsp?pageid=370*.

11-Apr-02. Leading the Way in the Business Rule Approach. Web article: *www.brsolutions.com*.

7-Jun-03. The Rule Markup Initiative. Web article: *www.dfki.uni-kl.de.ruleml/*. Rules in XML.

29-Oct-01. Model-Driven Development Can Add Years to Business
Applications. Web article: *http://anaystq.ebizq.net/insider/102901.html.*
Some insight as to what aspects of model-based systems can lead to
long-living applications.

Semantic and Conceptual Modeling

Books

Cammarata, Stephanie, Shane, Darrell, Ram, Prasad. *IID: An Intelligent
Information Dictionary for Managing Semantic Metadata.* Santa Monica:
Rand, 1991.

Cárdenas, Alfonso F., McLeod, Dennis. *Research Foundations in Object-
Oriented and Semantic Database Systems.* New Jersey: Prentice Hall,
1990.

de Brock, Bert. *Foundations of Semantic Databases.* New York: Prentice
Hall, 1995.

Dewitz, Sandra, Olson, Michael. *Semantic Object Modeling with Salsa:
A Tutorial.* New York: McGraw-Hill, 1994. Salsa was a semantic
modeling tool from WallData.

Fowler, Martin, Scott, Kendall. *UML Distilled: Applying the Standard
Object Modeling Language.* Reading, Mass.: Addison-Wesley, 1997. Best
introductory book on UML; brief but surprisingly thorough.

Kilov, Haim, Ross, James. *Information Modeling: An Object-Oriented
Approach.* New Jersey: Prentice Hall, 1994.

Lukose, Dickson, et al. *Conceptual Structures: Fulfilling Peirce's Dream.*
Berlin: Springer-Verlag, 1997.

Rishe, Naphtali. *Database Design: The Semantic Modeling Approach.* New
York: McGraw-Hill, 1992.

Teorey, Toby J. *Database Modeling and Design.* San Francisco: Morgan
Kaufmann, 1999.

Warmer, Jos, Kleppe, Anneke. *The Object Constraint Language: Precise
Modeling with UML.* Reading, Mass.: Addison-Wesley, 1999. UML's
underlying constraint language.

Williams, Simon. *The Associative Model of Data.* Bucks, Great Britain: Lazy Software Ltd., 2000. A new model of database design and implementation based on promoting associations to a first-class object. Highly compatible with Semantic Web and business rule approaches.

Wisse, Pieter. *Metapattern Context and Time in Information Models.* Boston: Addison-Wesley, 2001. Complex book with several profound ideas, the primary idea being the central role of context in design and how it can dynamically change over time.

Magazine and Web Articles

Ahmed, Kal. 2-Oct-02. Introducing Topic Maps. *XML Journal,* pp 22–27. Available at *www.xml-journal.com.*

Becker, Scot A. May-98. Common Model Fragments: People and Organizations. Web article: *www.inconcept.com/JCM/May1998/becker.html.* The more common semantic primitives.

Bourdeaux, John Jan. 2002. FatWire Dynamic Content Management. Web article: *www.fatwire.com.* A commercial package for content management.

Brasethvik, Terje. 1-Apr-98. A Semantic Modeling Approach to Metadata. Web article: *www.idi.ntnu.no/~divitini/iiis-98/papers/brase.pdf.* Brief but good.

Bronder, Michael. 1-Oct-02. Demystifying Document Management: Navigating the CMS Software Marketplace. Web article: *www.newarchitectmag.com/documents/s=7576/na1002a/index.html.*

Bry, Francois, Eisinger, Norbert. 23-Mar-00. Data Modeling with Markup Languages (DM2L). Web article: *www.pms.infomatik.uni-muenchen.de/forschung/datamodeling-markup.html.*

D'Souza, Desmond, Wills, Alan. 21-May-99. Types and Classes: A Language-Independent View. Web article: *www.iconcomp.com/papers/Types-and-classes/Col5.frm.html.*

Duvall, Mel. 9-Apr-02. Knowledge Management Vendors Go Vertical II. Web article: *www.intranetjournal.com/articles/200204/km_04_09_02a.html.*

Farley, Jim. 1-Mar-01. Platform Comparison. *Software Development,* pp 37–42. Available at *www.sdmagazine.com.*

Girow, Andrew. 19-Oct-96. Binary Relations Approach to Building Object Database Model. Web article: *www.geocities.com/SiliconValley/Bay/1927/oc9611.html.*

Gonzalez, Angel. 14-Aug-01. Searching for Google's Successor. Web article: *www.wired.com/news/print/0,1294,45905,00.html.*

Jonsson, Jan. 1-Mar-90. Semantic Modeling through Identification and Characterization of Objects. SIGMOD Record. Available at *www.rocq.inria.fr/verso/publications/ sigmod/Jonsson:1990:SMT.html.*

Kelly, George. 30-Jun-02. Webgrid II. Web article: *http://sern.ucalgary.ca/courses/SENG/611/F01/WebGrid97.html.* A tool for building graphic semantic structures.

Liddle, Stephen W., et al. A Summary of the ER'97 Workshop on Behavioral Modeling. Web article: *http://osm7.cs.byu.edu/ER97/workshop4/summary.html.* Behavioral modeling essentially adds methods to ER methodology.

Meek, Brian. 1-Sep-94. A Taxonomy of Datatypes. *Sigplan Notices* 29(9):159–167. Available at *www.kcl.ac.uk/kis/support/cit/staff/brian/taxosn.html.*

Olofson, Carl W. 1-Aug-02. Addressing the Semantic Gap in Databases: Lazy Software and the Associative Model of Data. Web article: *www.lazysoft.com/docs/analysts/idc/27774at.htm.* More on the associative model.

Ort, Ed. 17-Oct-00. Ten Things to Know about Selecting a Content Management System. Web article: *http://deb.sun.com/practices/howtos/selecting_cms.jsp.*

Papazoglou, M. P. 1-Sep-95. Unraveling the Semantics of Conceptual Schemas. *Communications of the ACM* 38(9):94.

Parson, Jeffrey, Wand, Yair. 1-June-97. Choosing Classes in Conceptual Modeling. *Communications of the ACM* 40(6):63–69.

Pepper, Steve. 24-Dec-02. The Tao of Topic Maps. Web page: *www.ontopia.net/topicmaps/materials/tao.html.*

Shaw, Mildred L. G., Gaines, Brian R. 1-Oct-92. Kelly's "Geometry of Psychological Space" and Its Significance for Cognitive Modeling. *New Psychologist,* pp 23–31. Available at *http://repgrid.com/reports/PSYCH/NewPsych92/index.html.*

Simmons, Brent. 26-Jul-00. Radio Userland: License. Web article: *http://radio.userland.com/discuss/msgReaders$19?mode=day.*

Tardiveau, Max. 1-Jun-99. The Meta Object Facility: The Final Frontier of Modeling. *Journal of Object Oriented Programming.* Available at *www.eui.upm.es/biblio/revistas/rev99/115–0399.htm.* UML's metamodel.

Wang, Richard Y. Feb-98. A Product Perspective on Total Data Quality Management. *Communications of the ACM* 41(2):58–65.

10-Nov-02. Some Content Management Systems Try to Do It All. Web image: *http://dcb.sun.com/omages/selecting_cms_content-management.gif.*

1999–2001. Primary Data and Their Structurization Techniques. Web article: *www.comteco.ru/EN/DATAMODE/1structu.htm.*

19-Oct-02. Semantic Introduction to Databases. Web article: *www.hpdrc.fiu.edu/library/books/datades-book/chapters/chapters.html.*

21-Dec-01. Smart Tags Are Stupid. Web article: *www.glassdog.com/smarttags/.*

12-Mar-02. Model Driven Architecture. Architecture Board MDA Drafting Team. OMG's approach to model-driven architecture. Includes metadata representation. Web article: *www.omg.org/mda.*

Application and Technical Architecture Issues

Books

Dennis, Alan, et al. *Systems Analysis and Design: An Object-Oriented Approach with UML.* New York: Wiley, 2002. Good guide to using UML for object-oriented design.

Edwards, W. Keith. *Core JINI.* New Jersey: Prentice Hall, 1999. JINI is Sun's initiative on peer-oriented architectures.

Freeman, Eric, Hupfer, Susan, Arnold, Ken. *JavaSpaces: Principles, Patterns, and Practice.* Boston: Addison-Wesley, 1999.

Meyer, Bertrand. *Object-Oriented Software Construction*. New Jersey: Prentice Hall, 1988. Classic text on object-oriented software development. One of the early treatments of design by contract, with consistent use of preconditions and postconditions.

Rechtin, Eberhardt, Maier, Mark W. *The Art of Systems Architecting*. Florida: CRC Press LLC, 1997.

Rinehart, Martin. *Java Database Development*. Berkeley: McGraw-Hill, 1998. Using Java as a wrapper for relational databases.

Singh, Inderjeet, et al. *Designing Enterprise Applications with the J2EE Platform*. Boston: Addison-Wesley, 2002. J2EE is the Java framework for enterprise architecture.

Sowizral, Henry, et al. *The Java 3D API Specification*. Cambridge: Addison-Wesley, 2000.

Walrath, Kathy, Campione, Mary. *The JFC Swing Tutorial: A Guide to Constructing GUIs*. Boston: Addison-Wesley, 1999. Java's interface-building kit.

Magazine and Web Articles

Berners-Lee, Tim. 1-Sep-98. Web Architecture from 50,000 ft. Web article: *www.w3.org/DesignIssues/Architecture.html*.

Bray, Tim, Guha, R. V. 17-Dec-01. An MCF Tutorial. Web article: *www.w3.org/TR/NOTE-MCF-XML-970624/MCF-tutorial.html*.

Hayes, Brian. May/Jun-02. Terabyte Territory. *American Scientist* 90:212–216. Trends in disk storage.

Hokel, Thomas A. 1993–2000. The Zachman Framework for Enterprise Architecture. Web article: *www.frameworksoft.com/html/body_zf_overview.html*.

Hurst, Walter. 1-May-02. The Critical Role of Application Architecture. *Java Developers Journal*. Available at *www.wakesoft.com/docucenter.html*. Making the case for establishing an architecture rather than just adding on to the existing architecture.

Melnik, Sergey. 13-Jun-01. Generic Interoperability. Web article: *www-diglib.stanford.edu/diglib/ginf/*.

Melnik, Sergey, Decker, Stefan. 4-Sep-00. A Layered Approach to Information Modeling and Interoperability on the Web. Web article: *www-db.standford.edu/~melnik/pub/sw00/.* Excellent article on the layers of metadata and how they need to be architected.

Turner, Roy M. 1-Mar-98. Context-Mediated Behavior for Intelligent Agents. *International Journal of Human-Computer Studies* 48(3):307–330. Available at *http://cdps.umcs.maine.edu/Papers/1998/IJHCS-Context/.* Key role of context.

Zachman, John. 19-Oct-02. Information Systems Architecture—ISA. Web page: *www.istis.unomaha.edu/isqa/vanvliet/arch/isa/isa-rows.htm.*

Zachman, John A. 6-Jul-02. Enterprise Architecture: A Framework. Web article: *www.zifa.com/zifajz02.html.* The Zachman framework is a widely accepted framework for organizing all the aspects of an enterprise's technical infrastructure.

Zachman, John A. 6-Jul-02. Enterprise Architecture: The Issue of the Century. Web article: *http:www.zifa.com/zifajz01.htm.*

Zachman, John A. 13-May-02. Concepts of the Framework for Enterprise Architecture: Background, Description and Utility. Web article: *www.members.ozemail.com.au/`visible/papers/zachman3.html.*

Enterprise Application Integration and B2B

Magazine and Web Articles

Anthes, Gary H. 12-May-02. The Search Is On. *ComputerWorld.* Web article: *www.computerworld.com/databasetopics/data/story/0,10801,70041,00.html.*

Barlas, Demir. 13-Sep-02. Imperial Sugar Line 56. Web article: *www.line56.com/articles/default.asp?ArticlesID=4012.*

Bond, David. 2-Jul-02. When to Use Synchronous EAI Messaging. *eAi Journal,* pp 8–13. Very good article on the pros and cons of asynchronous and synchronous messaging and running synchronous exchanges on asynchronous channels.

Bulter, Martin. 1-Nov-02. What's Better: Applications Integration or Integrated Applications? *eAi Journal,* 37. Basically "big database" versus integration.

Business Resilience Primer. Cisco Executive Education Series 1a–8a. Web article: *www.cisco.com/go/resilience.* Some of the infrastructure issues that will be necessary for Web Services.

Coleman, Patrick. 27-Feb-01. ERP Integration Options. Web article: *http://eai.ebizq.net/erp/coleman_1.html.* Enterprise resource planning (ERP) systems are among the largest and hardest applications to integrate.

Devraj, Sankar. 1-Sep-01. Reengineering Legacy Systems. *Application Development Trends,* pp 43–46. Available at *www.adtmag.com/article.asp?id=4803.* Issues with getting legacy systems integrated.

Ericson, Jim. 10-Jan-02. EDI and the Internet. Web article: *www.line56.com/articles/default.asp?ArticleID=3287&Keywords= EDI++AND+internet.*

Harreld, Heather. 18-Apr-02. Linking up process pieces. *InfoWorld,* issue 16, pp 62–65. Available at *www.infoworld.com.*

Iltis, Susannah. 1-Mar-95. Z39.50: An Overview of Development and the Future. Web article: *www.cqs.washinton.edu/~camel/z/z.html.*

Jovellanos, Chito. Resolving Context and Meaning in Computer-Based Communications. Dama International Symposium, Apr 2–May 2, 2002. Using statistical models on EDI transactions.

Lay, Philip. 2-Aug-02. Back to Basics in e-Business. *Under the Buzz* 3(8), 2002. Web article: *www.chasmgroup.com/underthebuzz_archives.htm.*

McGoveran, David. 2-Oct-02. Enterprise Integrity: Data Integration, Part V. *eAi Journal,* p 6. One of a series of articles on the importance of metadata in developing your EAI strategy.

McGoveran, David. 2-Sep-02. Enterprise Integrity: Data Integration, Part IV. *eAi Journal,* 6.

Meehan, Michael. 12-May-02. Data's Tower of Babel. *ComputerWorld,* pp 38–41.

Morgenthal, J. P. 2-Sep-02. Electronic Business Registries. *eAi Journal,* pp 13–14.

Roedner, Don. 2-Sep-02. The Next Wave of Integration Platforms. *eAi Journal,* pp 16–19.

Simos, Mark A. 1-Apr-01. Synquiry's Information Synthesis Technology: Solving the Hidden Problem of Semantic Integration for B2B Multi-vendor Aggregation. Web article (Synquiry): *www.synquiry.com.*

Stephens, Todd. 1-May-02. Meta Data Success: Service Based Organization. DAMA International Symposium. Guide to setting up a metadata architecture for an enterprise.

Strom, David. 8-Jul-02. Dressing Up Open Systems. VARBusiness, pp 31–40. Available at *www.varsbusiness.com.*

Varlamov, Stan. 2-Sep-02. Security Strategies for EAI. *eAi Journal,* pp 41–44. Security is a major issue at this junction with EAI.

von den Heuvel, William-Jan. 1-Oct-02. Enterprise Application Integrations and Complex Adaptive Systems. *Communications of the ACM* 45(10):59–64.

Web Services: The New Generation of Application Integration. Data Junction Web site: *www.datajunction.com.* Using Web Services for EAI.

Zachman, John A. 1993–1996. Enterprise Architecture and Legacy Systems. Web article: *http://members.ozemail.com.au/`visible/papers/zachman1.htm.*

Ontologies

Books

Fensel, Dieter. *Ontologies: A Silver Bullet for Knowledge Management and Electronic Commerce.* Berlin: Springer-Verlag, 2001. Brief but informative.

Magazine and Web Articles

Economic Classification Policy Committee. 8-Feb-93. Aggregation Structures and Hierarchies Issues. Paper No. 2. Web article: *www.census.gov/epcd/naics/issues2.* Motivation for shifting from SIC to NAICS codes.

Gruber, Tom. 9-Oct-01. What Is an Ontology? Web article: *www.ksl.stanford.edu/kst/what-is-an-ontology.htm.* Classic article on ontologies.

Heflin, Jeff. Fall 2001. The Semantic Web Syllabus. Web article: *www.cse.lehigh.edu/~heflin/courses/se-fall01/.*

Heflin, Jeff. 4-Oct-00. General Ontology (Draft). Web article: *www.cs.umd.edu/projects/plus/SHOE/onts/commerce1.0.html.* SHOE.

Heflin, Jeff. 28-Apr-00. Commerce Ontology (Draft). Web article: *www.cs.umd.edu/projets/plus/SHOE/onts/commerce1.0.html.* SHOE.

Hever, Boo. 5-Oct-02. Testing Vocabulary. Web article: *www.forumeducation.net/servelet/pages/vi/mat/vocarticle.htm.*

Hillmann, Diane. 14-Jun-01. Using Dublin Core. Web article: *http://dublincore.org/documents/usageguide/.* SHOE.

Jeflin, Jeff, et al. 7-Mar-02. Requirements for a Web Ontology Language. Web article: *www.w3.org/TR/2002/WD-webont-reg-20020307/.*

Kingston, John. 1-Sep-02. Ontologies, Multi-Perspective Modeling and Knowledge Auditing Information Research Report. Web article: *www.informatics.ed.ac.uk/publications/report/0053.html.*

Lagoze, Carl. 1-Jan-01. Keeping Dublin Core Simple. D-Lib Magazine 7(1), Jan 2001. Available at *www.dlib.org/dlib/january01/lagoze/01lagoze.html.* Dublin Core is a widely used ontology for authored documents.

Luke, Sean. 6-Dec-01. Adding Semantic Knowledge to an HTML Page Using SHOE. Web article: *www.cs.umd.edu/projects/plus/SHOE/ html-pages.html.* SHOE is an early ontology language.

McGuinness, Deborah L. 14-18-Aug-01. Conceptual Modeling for Distributed Ontology Environments. Web article: *www.ontology.org/main/papers/iccs-dlm.html.*

Noy, Natalya F., McGuinness, Deborah L. 3-Jul-02. Ontology Development 101: A Guide to Creating Your First Ontology. Web article: *http://protege.stanford.edu/publications/ ontology_development_ontology101-noy-mcguiness.html.*

Phytila, Chris. 2-Jul-03. SUMO Ontology Language. Web article: *http://onotology.teknowledge.com/.*

Poli, Roberto. 5-Jul-03. Proposals about the Structure of Ontology. Web article: *www.formalontology.it/section_5.htm.*

Ruedinger, Klein. 3-Dec-01. Daimler Chrysler Use Cases. Web article: *http://list.w3.org/Archives/Public/www-webont-wg/2001Dec/002.htm.*

Taxonomy and Content Classification. Verity Web site: *www.verity.com.* How Verity sets up and uses taxonomies to interpret unstructured data.

Trippe, Bill. 1-Aug-01. Taxonomies and Topic Maps: Categorization Steps Forward. Econtent Web site: *www.econtentmag.com/Articles/Article Reader.aspx?ArticleID=1070&CategoryID=21*. Topic maps are a way of associating content with topics.

Wolff, Christian. 8-Dec-01. What Is Ontology? Ontologia sue Philosophia Prima. Web article: *www.formalontology.it/section_4.htm*. Good definition.

9-Dec-01. Some Ongoing KBS/Ontology Projects and Groups. Web article: *www.cs.utexas.edu/users/mfkb/related.html*.

5-Oct-02. Does Size Matter? Web article: *http://216.239.53.100/search?q+cache:vFfosHVsMzUC:www.english.uiuc. edu/baron/302/*. . .

24-Dec-02. Basics: Classification, Nomenclature, and Key Making. Web article: *www.csdl.tamu.edu/FLORA/tfplab/lab1a.htm*.

18-Aug-02. Participants and Their Position Papers/Talks. Web page: *http://lsdis.cs.uga.edu/SemNSF/SemWebWorkshopParticipants.htm*.

13-Jun-01. Markup Languages and Ontologies. Web page: *www.semanticweb.org/knowmarkup.html*.

12-Feb-03. DCMI Type Vocabulary. Web page: *http://dublincore.org/documents/dcmi-type-vocabulary/*.

23-Nov-02. Model-Theoretic Semantics. Web page: *www.xrefer.com/entry/572261*.

23-Nov-02. Truth Conditions. Web page: *www.xrefer.com/entry.jsp?xrefid=573583*.

9-Dec-01. TOVE Ontologies. Web page: *www.eil.utoronto.ca/tove/toveont.html*.

21-Dec-01. Ontologies by Keyword. Web article: *www.daml.org/ontologies/keyword.html*.

15-Jun-02. About the TGN. Web article: *www.getty.edu/research/tools/vocabulary/tgn/about.html*.

25-Nov-02. Plant and Animal Species Evolution Cruncher. Chapter 11. Web article: *http://evolution-facts.org/c11.htm*. One of many sources for species and genus examples.

4-Nov-02. Inxight Declared "Winner" among Categorization, Taxonomy Generation and Data Visualization Companies by the 451. Insight Press Releases. Web article: *http://inxight.com/news/021104_the451.html*. Hyperbolic trees and unstructured data interpretation.

5-Oct-02. Measuring the Size of Your Vocabulary. Vocabulary Testing. Web article: *www.geocities.com/rnseitz/Vocabulary_Testing.html*. Source of vocabulary size statistics.

7-Feb-99. Dublin Core Metadata Element Set, Version 1.1: Reference Description. Web article: *http://dublincore.org/documents/dces*. Dublin Core.

7-Nov-00. Dublin Core Qualifiers. Web article: *http://dublincore.org/documents/dcmes-qualifiers*. Dublin Core.

6-Dec-01. SHOE Base Ontology. Web article: *www.cs.umd.edu/projects/plus/SHOE/onts/base1.0.html*. SHOE.

2-Jul-99. Dublin Core Metadata Element Set, Version 1.1: Reference Description. Web article: *http://dublincore.org/documents/dces/*. SHOE.

March-98. The Need for Shared Ontology. Web article: *www.ontology.org*. Sets up the need for shared meaning as a basis for B2B eCommerce.

9-Oct-01. Taxonomy of Life. Web article: *www.bartleby.com/61/charts/T00654000.html*. One version of the biologic taxonomy.

5-Oct-02. How Many Words? World Wide Words. Web article: *www.quinion.com/words/articles/howmany.htm*. Another take on how many words have been made up.

Specific Domains as Examples

Books

Barry, Douglas K. *Web Services and Service-Oriented Architectures: The Savvy Manager's Guide.* Amsterdam: Morgan Kaufman, 2003.

Downes, John, Goodman, Jordan Elliot. *Dictionary of Finance and Investment Terms.* New York: Barron's Educational Series, 1998. Comprehensive dictionary of financial terms.

Garner, Bryan A. *Black's Law Dictionary.* St. Paul: West Group, 1999.

Goltra, Peter S. *Medcin: A New Nomenclature for Clinical Medicine.* New York: Springer-Verlag, 1997. Medcin is the vocabulary behind a health care differential diagnosis system.

Magazine and Web Articles

Geerts, Guido L. 3-Apr-98. The Timeless Way of Building Accounting Information Systems: The "Activity" Pattern. Web page: *http://jeffsutherland.org/oopsla97/guido.html.*

McCarthy, William E., Andersen, Arthur. 11-Jun-99. Semantic Modeling in Accounting Education, Practice, and Research: Some Progress and Impediments. Web page: *www.msu.edu/user/mccarth4/chen-con.html.*

McCarthy, William E., et al. 31-Mar-98. The Evolution of Enterprise Information Systems: From Sticks and Jars Past Journals and Ledgers toward Interorganizational Webs of Business Objects and Beyond. Web page: *http://jeffsutherland.com/oopsla96/mccarspot.html.* Semantics of accounting.

Sarin, Sunil K. 1-Apr-98. Object-Oriented Workflow Technology in InConcert. Web page: *www.inconcert.com/prodinfo/sunil.htm.*

Spottiswoode, Christopher. 25-Aug-97. The Emperor's New Clothes: An Outsider's Perspective. Web page: *www.tiac.net/users/jsuth/oopsla96/spottisw.html.* Fresh look at accounting.

Tuttle, Mark S., et al. 30-July-01. The Semantic Web as "Perfection Seeking": A View from Drug Terminology. Web article: *www.apelon.com/news/papers/Tuttle%20Semantic%20Web.pdf.*

Watson, Andrew. 25-Aug-97. Coda: OMG Rationale for Choosing the Classical Object Model. Web page: *www.tiac.net/users/jsuth/oopsla96/watson.html.*

Zellen, Barry. 8-Dec-01. XML-Based Financial Info on the Web. Web page: *www.hpworldmagazine.com/hpworldnews/hpw102/04eser.html.*

13-Jun-01. Towards a Medical Semantic Web. Web article: *www.healtheybermap.semanticweb.org/icd_btm.htm.* How health care will profit from the Semantic Web.

Web Services

Books

Deitel, H. M., et al. *Web Services: A Technical Introduction.* New Jersey: Prentice Hall, 2003. Overview of Web Services, primarily focusing on mechanics.

Magazine and Web Articles

Raybould, Neil. March-02. Creating a Mobile Solution. *XML Journal* 3(2):20–26. Available at *www.xml-journal.com*.

Akireddy, Ravi. March-02. Parsing Filters. *XML Journal* 3(2):28–33. Available at *www.xml-journal.com*.

Apshankar, Kapil. 17-Apr-02. Enterprise Resource Planning and Web Services. Web article: *www.webservicesarchitect.com/content/articles/apshankar01print.asp*.

Arsanjani, Ali. 2-Oct-02. Developing and Integrating Enterprise Components and Services. *Communications of the ACM* 45(10):31–34.

Asaravala, Amit. 2-Nov-02. Can Public Web Services Work? *New Architect Magazine*. Available at *www.newarchitectmag.com*.

Bloomberg, Jason. 23-Mar-02. One Nerd's View of Web Services. Web article: *www.zapthink.com/flashes/03232002rhodes.html*.

Bloomberg, Jason. 15-Apr-02. Insight: How Service-Oriented Development Will Transform the Software Industry. Web article: *www.zapthink.com/reports/ZTI-WS101.html*.

Bloomberg, Jason. 20-Jun-02. Report: XML and Web Services Security. Web article: *www.zapthink.com/reports/ZTR-WS104.html*.

Bloomberg, Jason, Schmelzer, Ronald. 10-Jun-02. Want to Service-Enable your Enterprise? Model First! Web article: *www.zapthink.com/flashes/06102002Flash.html*.

Bloomberg, Jason, Schmelzer, Ronald. 17-May-02. Why "Web Services" Sucks . . . Web article: *www.zapthink.com/flashes/05172002Flash.html*.

Borck, James R. 19-Nov-01. Expressway to Discovery. *InfoWorld* 59. Available at *http://archive.infoworld.com/articles/op/xml/01/11/12/011112opborck.xml*.

Borck, James R. 9-Nov-01. Pop the Top on SODA. *InfoWorld* Web article: *http://staging.infoworld.com/articles/op/xml/01/11/12/011112opborck.xml? Template=/storypages/print*. . . . SODA is service-oriented development architecture.

Box, Don 19-Apr-02. A Brief History of SOAP. XML Web article: *http://webservices.xml.com/pub/a/ws/2001/04/04/soap.html*. SOAP.

Burbeck, Steve. 1-Oct-00. The Tao of e-Business Services: The Evolution of Web Applications into Service-Oriented Components of Web Services. Web article: *www.106-ibm.com/developerworks/webservices/library/ws-tao/*.

Cameron, Bobby. 29-Aug-02. CIOs Should Govern Web Services Now. Web article: *www.ftponline.com/resources/managingdev/becameron_08_29_02/*. . . . If you don't get on top of this it will get out of control.

Carlson, David. 2-Feb-02. Modeling XML Applications with UML. Web article: *www.sdmagazine.com/print/documentID=20887*.

Connell, Brian. 2-Sep-02. The Seven Pillars of Web Services Management. *eAi Journal* 20–23.

Fensel, D., Bussler, C. The Web Service Modeling Framework: WSMF Extended. Abstract. Web article: *http://informatik.uibk.ac.at/users/c70385/wese/wsmf.bis2002.pdf*. Making the case that in order for dynamic lookup to work, we're going to have to model this much more explicitly.

Fernandez, Eduardo B. 2-Sep-02. Web Services Security: Waltzing through Port 80. Web article: *www.sdmagazine.com/print/documentID=28092*. The pluses and minuses of SOAP's ability to operate through firewalls.

Fonseca, Brian, Scannell, Ed. 12-Apr-02. Microsoft plays XML Politics. *InfoWorld*. Available at *www.infoworld.com/article/02/04/12/020415hnsecurity_1.html*. How Microsoft is making nice with open standards.

Fremantle, Paul, et al. 2-Oct-02. Enterprise Services. *Communications of the ACM* 45(10):77–82.

Glass, Graham. 1-Feb-02. Web Services Description Language (WSDL). Web article: *www-106.ibm.com/developerworks/webservices/library/ws-peer4/*. Web Services.

Harbart, Juliane. 25-Jan-02. X-Query: A Universal Query Interface for XML. Web article: *www.softwareag.com/xml/library/harbarth_X-query.htm*. Xquery has since been superceded, but the concepts are quite good.

Holland, Paul. 2-Sep-02. Building Web Services from Existing Applications. *eAi Journal* 45–47. The strategy of "wrapping" your current applications and exposing their API as a Web Service.

Homan, David. 21-Oct-02. Web Services and Integration. *Information Week* 65–70.

Hoobler, Roy. March-02. Apply-Templates Revisited. *XML Journal* 3(2):42–48. Available at *www.xml-journal.com*.

Jaenicke, Coco. March-02. Going Native. XML Journal 3(2):50–52. Available at *www.xml-journal.com*.

Jones, Mark, Harreld, Heather. 2-Aug-02. Office gets its XML Groove. *InfoWorld*. Available at *www.infoworld.com/article/02/08/02/ 020805hnofficetool_1.html*. Microsoft Office will support XML, and how that ties in with the P2P software "Groove."

Khoshaffin, Setrag. 25-Jul-02. Web Services and Virtual Enterprises. Web article: *www.webservicesarchitect.com/content/articles/koshafian01.asp*. Web Services.

Lingingston, Brian. 1-Apr-02. Microsoft's Handset War. *InfoWorld*. Available at *www.infoworld.com*.

McCarthy, James. 1-Jun-02. Reap the Benefits of Document Style Web Services. Web article: *www-106.ibm.com/developerworks/ webservices/library/ws-docstyle.html*. Very good article on making sure the way you implement Web Services builds in flexibility.

McCormick, John. 2-Jun-02. Quick Integration Fix? *Baseline,* pp 22–24.

Morgenthal, J. P. 2-Sep-02. Electronic Business Registries. *eAi Journal,* pp 13–14. UDDI is just one possible form of this.

Muehlbauer, Jen. 2-Apr-02. Orbitz Reaches New Heights. *New Architect Magazine*. Available at *www.newarchitectmag.com*. How Orbitz (the new travel site) got up and running so rapidly with new technology.

Myerson, Judith M. Web Service Architectures. Web article: *www.webservicesarchitect.com/content/articles/myerson01.asp*. Comparison of some of the key alternatives.

Ogbuji, Uche. 1-Nov-00. Using WSDL in SOAP Applications. Web article: *www-106.ibm.com/developerworks/webservices/library/ ws-soap/?dwzone=ws*. How-to article on Web Services description language.

O'Riordan, David. 10-Apr-02. Business Process Standards for Web Services. Web article: *www.webservicesarchitect.com/contetn/articles/oriordan01.asp.*

Radko, John. 25-Jul-02. Web Services: Time for a Reality Check? Web article: *http://news.com.com/2010-1075-946176.html.*

Reitano, John, Marcus, Glen. 2-Sep-02. Special Guide: Web Services Tools. Web article: *www.sdmagazine.com/print/documentID=28093.*

Schemlzer, Ronald. 10-Jun-02. Report: Service-Oriented Integration— Using Web Services and XML to Integrate Systems. Web article: *www.zapthink.com/reports/ZTR-WS103.html.*

Schwartz, Ephraim, Sullivan, Tom. 22-Oct-01. Keeping Secrets. *InfoWorld* 38. Available at *www.infoworld.com.*

Schwartz, Jeffrey. 16-Sep-02. Finding the Right Formula for UDDI. *VARBusiness* 22. Available at *www.varsbusiness.com.*

Seybold, Patricia. 2-Oct-02. An Executive Guide to Web Services: How to Optimize Web Services Investments to Improve your Customer Experience. Web book: *www.psgroup.com/doc/products/2002/6/WEBSERV-EXEC.* Very good executive-level summary of Web Services.

Sherman, Doron. 2-Nov-02. Web Service Orchestration: Blurring the Line between Development and Integration. *eAi Journal,* pp 42–46. Good primer on orchestration (basically a graphic cross-application development tool).

Shirky, Clay. 27-Oct-01. Web Services: It's So Crazy, It Just Might Not Work. Web article: *www.xml.com/1pt/a/2001/10/03/webservices.html.* Pushing back on the hype machine.

Smith, David. 16-May-02. Web Series Architecture: A Four-Platform Framework. Web article: *www4.gartner.com/DisplayDocument?doc_cd=106876.*

Smith, Roger. 16-Sep-02. Modeling in the Service Oriented Architecture. Web article: *www.devx.com/javaSR/articles/smith1/smith1p.asp.*

Speer, James. 6-May-02. SQL 2000. Web article: *www.topxml.com/people/speer/updategrambasics.asp.*

Stal, Michael. Web Services: Beyond Component-Based Computing. *Communications of the ACM* 45(10):71–76, Oct 2002. Helpful in distinguishing services and components.

Sullivan, Tom. 8-Oct-02. Itxpp: Gartner Grades the Web Services Standards. InfoWorld. Available at *www.infoworld.com/article/02/01/08/021008hnwsgrade_1.html.* Some perspective on which standards are stable and which aren't.

van Eyle, Ben. 1-Aug-02. Web Services: A Business Perspective Platform Choice. Web article: *www.theserverside.com/resources/article.jsp?1=WebServices.*

Varlamov, Stan. 2-Sep-02. Security Strategies for EAI. *eAi Journal,* pp 41–44. Security is a major theme in EAI.

Whittington, Ken. 1-Oct-02. XDBMS: The New Kid in Town. *eAi Journal,* pp 26–33. Relational database support of XML.

Wilkes, Lawrence. 2-Oct-02. WestGlobal mScape 2.0—Web Services Management. *CBDI Journal,* pp 22–26. Issues in setting up the infrastructure to manage Web Services.

Williams, Kevin. 1-Jan-02. XML Structures for Existing Databases. Web article: *www-106.ibm.com/developerworks/xml/library/x-struct/.*

Worthen, Ben. 1-Sep-02. Web Services: Still Not Ready for Prime Time. *CIO Magazine.* Available at *www.cio.com/archive/090102/prime.html.* Bucking the trend, some reasons for cautious adoption.

Yager, Tom. 4-Mar-02. Talking the Biz Talk. *InfoWorld* 35. Available at *www.infoworld.com.*

Yang, Andy. 2-Sep-02. Web Services Security. *eAi Journal,* pp 33–37. Security.

XML

Books

Ahmed, Kal, Ancha, Sudhir, Cioroianu, Andrei. *Professional Java XML.* Birmingham, UK: Wrox Press Ltd, 2001.

Daum, Berthold, Merten, Udo. *System Architecture with XML*. San Francisco: Morgan Kaufmann, 2003. Excellent work on the many areas of application architecture where XML should be playing a role.

Dick, Kevin, Taylor, David A. *XML: A Manager's Guide*. Boston: Addison-Wesley, 2000. Brief management-level introduction to XML.

Goldfarb, Charles F., Prescod, Paul. *The XML Handbook*. New Jersey: Prentice Hall, 2000.

Graves, Mark. *Designing XML Databases*. New Jersey: Prentice Hall, 2002.

Kotok, Alan, Webber, David R. R. *ebXML: The New Global Standard for Doing Business over the Internet*. Indianapolis: New Riders Publishing, 2002.

McGrath, Sean. *XML by Example: Building e-Commerce Applications*. New Jersey: Prentice Hall, 1998. Good introductory book for XML.

Morgenthal, J. P., la Forge, Bill. *Enterprise Application Integration with XML and Java*. New Jersey: Prentice Hall, 2001. How XML fits in with the Java architectures.

Pitts-Moultis, Natanya, Kirk, Cheryl. *XML Black Book*. Scottsdale, Ariz.: The Coriolis Group, 1999.

Schmelzer, Ron, et al. *XML and Web Services Unleashed*. Indianapolis: Sams Publishing, 2002.

St. Laurent, Simon, Johnson, Joe, Dumbill, Edd. *Programming Web Services with XML-RPC*. Sebastopol, Calif.: O'Reilly & Associates, Inc., 2001. XML-RPC was the predecessor to SOAP.

Thuraisingham, Bhavani. *XML Databases and the Semantic Web*. Florida: CRC Press LLC, 2002. Several vendors now offer native XML databases. This book categorizes many of the concerns.

Tittel, Ed, Boumphrey, Frank. *XML for Dummies*. Foster City, Calif.: IDG Books Worldwide, Inc., 2000. Good introductory book for XML.

Magazine and Web Articles

Ahonen, Helena et al. 16-Dec-01. Improving the Accessibility of SGML Documents. Web article: *www.infoloom.com/gcaconfs/WEB/barcelona97/heinon28.HTM*.

Aun, Fred. 30-Apr-01. "X" Marks the Spot. *Smart Partner,* pp 24–25. Available at *www.smartpartnermag.com.*

Berlind, David. 9-Oct-01. How XML Could Bring an End to All Your Troubles. Web article: *www.zdnet.com/anchordest/stories/story/0,10738,2830958,00.html.*

Box, Don. 1-Sep-99. Lessons from the Component Wars: An XML Manifesto. Web article: *http://msdn.microsoft.com/xml/articles/xmlmanifesto.asp.*

Cagle, Kurt. 2-Nov-02. eXcelon Stylus. *New Architect Magazine* 46. Available at *www.newarchitectmag.com.* eXcelon is an XML database company.

Cagle, Kurt. 25-Sep-02. XSLT 2.0 Sweetens Application Efficacy. Web article: *www.fawcette.com/xmlmag/2002_06/magazine/columns/practice/kcagle/.*

Chahuneau, Francois. 16-Dec-01. SGML and Schemas: From SGML DTDs to XML-DATA. Web article: *http://infoloom.com/gcaconfs/WEB/paris98/chahunea/HTM.* SGML.

Champion, Michael. 17-May-01. Daring to Do Less with XML. Web article: *www.xml.com/1pt/a/2001/05/02/champion.html.*

Channell, Charles, Lehrer, Nancy. 19-Jun-05. OEM User's Guide. Web page: *www.cacs.louisana.edu/~jyoon/grad/vldb/oem/oem_user.html.*

Chelsom, John. 16-Dec-01. The Marriage of XML and Databases. Web article: *www.infoloom.com/gcaconfs/WEB/granada99/che.htm.*

Chen, Anne. 7-Aug-00. Getting to XML. *eWeek,* pp 55–60. Available at *www.eweek.com.*

Cover, Robin. 23-Oct-98. XML and Semantic Transparency. Web article: *www.oasis-open.org/cover/sgml-xml.html.* The "Cover Pages" are among the most comprehensive sources for XML information on the Web.

Cowan, John, Tobin, Richard. 24-Oct-01. XML Information Set. Web article: *www.w3.org/TR/2001/REC-xml-infoset-20011024.*

Craig, Bob. 6-Oct-02. Theory communication. Web article: *www.colorado.edu/communication/meta-discourses/index.htm.*

Decker, Stefan. 13-Dec-01. WebOnt Use-Case Area: Web Services. Web article: *www-db.stanford.edu/~stefan/webont/121301/.*

Finkelstein, Clive. 1-Sep-99. The Impact of Technology. Web article: *www.tdan.com/i011hy02.htm.* Excerpt from *Building Corporate Portals with XML,* by Clive Finkelstein and Peter Aiken (McGraw-Hill, 1999).

Freese, Eric. 16-Dec-01. Using Topic Maps. Web article: *www.infoloom.com/gcaconsfs/WEB/paris200/S22-01.HTM.* Topic maps.

Guha, R. V., Bray, Tim. 17-Dec-01. Meta Content Framework Using XML. Web article: *www.textuality.com/mcf/NOTE-MCF-XML.html.*

Holland, Roberta. 7-Aug-00. XML Takes on Graphics. *eWeek* 18. Available at *www.eweek.com.* Scalar vector graphics in XML.

Leon, Mark. 2-Apr-01. Where's the XML? *InfoWorld,* pp 36–37. Available at *www.infoworld.com.*

Mertz, David. 1-Dec-02. XML Tip: Using CSS2 to Display XML Documents. Web article: *www-106.ibm.com.co. . .s/xml/library/x-tipcss2/index.html.* Different approach to styling XML.

Shohoud, Yasser. XML's Grand Schema. *XML Magazine,* pp 38–44, Summer 2000. Available at *www.xmlmag.com.*

Udell, Jon. 11-Nov-02. Jean Paoli on XML in Office 11. Web article: *www.infoworld.com/articles/op/xml/02/11/14/021114opwebserv.xml.* Where Microsoft is going with XML.

van der Vlist, Eric. 21-Nov-01. XSLT and Xquery: A Difference of Culture. Web article: *http://xmlhack.com/read.php?item=1463.* XSLT is a declarative way to transform XML documents.

Wayne, Rick. 2-Nov-02. The Moth Thing Again. *Software Development* 20.

The Semantic Web

Books

Cruz, Isabel F., et al. *Proceedings of SWWS'01: The First Semantic Web Working Symposium.* Stanford, 2001. Papers from the Semantic Web Workshop at Stanford in 2001.

Fensel, Dieter, et al. *Spinning the Semantic Web.* MIT Press, 2003. A series of articles by many of the guiding lights on the Semantic Web vision.

Geroimenko, Vladimir, Chen, Chaomei (editors). *Visualizing the Semantic Web*. Springer-Verlag, 2003. A collection of articles on advanced 3D and other tools for visualizing complex structures such as the ontologies on which the Semantic Web is to be built.

Hjelm, Johan. *Creating the Semantic Web with RDF.* New York: Wiley Computer Publishing, 2001. One of the few books available on RDF.

Magazine and Web Articles

Allen, Joshua. 3-Jul-02. Making a Semantic Web. Web article: *www.netcrucible.com/semantic.html.* Semantic Web.

Bechhofer, Sean, et al. 28-Nov-00. An Informal Description of Standard OIL and Instance OIL. Web article: *www.ontoknowledge.org/oil/.* Ontology inference layer.

Beckett, David. 6-Sep-01. Refactoring RDF/XML Syntax. Web article: *www.w3.org/TR/Rdf-syntax-grammar/.*

Berners-Lee, Tim. 1-Sep-98. Web Architecture from 50,000 ft. Web article: *www.w3.org/DesignIssues/RDFnot.html.*

Berners-Lee, Tim. 1-Sep-98. Semantic Web Road Map. Web article: *www.w3.org/DesignIssues/Semantic.html.* Semantic Web.

Berners-Lee, Tim. 1999. Axioms of Web Architecture: The Meaning of a Document. Web article: *www.w3.org/DesignIssues/Meaning.html.* Semantic Web.

Berners-Lee, Tim, et al. 1-May-01. The Semantic Web. *Scientific American*, pp 35–43. Available at *www.sciam.com* The classic mainstream article on the Semantic Web.

Berners-Lee, Tim, Miller, Eric. 11-Nov-02. The Semantic Web Lifts off. Web article: *www.ercim.org/publication/Ercim_News/enw51/ berners-lee.html.* Semantic Web.

Bray, Tim. 3-Jul-02. What is RDF? Web article: *www.xml.com/1pt/a/2001/01/24/rdf.html.*

Brickley, Dan, Guha, R. V. 27-Mar-00. Resource Description Framework (RDF) Schema Specification 1.0. Web article: *www.w3.org/TR/2000/CR-rdf-schema-20000327/.*

Cherry, Steven M. 2-Sep-02. Weaving a Web of Ideas. *IEEE Spectrum.*

Dumbill, Edd. 3-Jul-02. The Semantic Web: A Primer. Web article: *www.xml.com/1pt/a/2000/11/01/semanticweb/index.html.* Semantic Web.

Ernst, Johannes. 2-Jul-02. Semantic Web Business Special Interest Group. Web article: *http://business.semanticweb.org.* People interested in promoting the use of the Semantic Web in business.

Ewalt, David E. 14-Oct-02. Next Web. *Information Week,* pp 35–44. Available at *www.informationweek.com.* Nice introduction to the Semantic Web.

Fillies, Christian. 18-Aug-02. SemTalk: A RDFS Editor for Visio 2000. Web article: *www.semtalk.com/pub/swws.htm.* RDF.

Frauenfelder, Mark. 1-Nov-02. A Smarter Web. Web article: *www.techreview.com/magazine/nov01/frauenfelder.asp.* Semantic Web.

Gil, Yolanda, Ratnakar, Varun. 11-Nov-02. Markup Languages: Comparison and Examples. Web article: *http://trellis.semanticweb.org/expect/web/semanticweb/comparison.html.*

Hayes, Patrick. 25-Sep-01. RDF Model Theory. Web article: *www.w3.org/TR/CCPP-struct-vocab/.* RDF.

Heflin, Jeff, Hendler, James. 22-Jun-05. Semantic Interoperability on the Web. Web article: *www.cs.umd.edu/projects/plus/SHOE/pubs/extreme2000.pdf.* Excellent article on how the Semantic Web is intended to work.

Helflin, Jeffrey Douglas. 23-Jun-05. Towards the Semantic Web: Knowledge Representation in a Dynamic, Distributed Environment. Abstract. Available at *www.cse.lehigh.edu/~heflin/pubs/ heflin-thesis-orig.pdf.*

Hendler, James, Parsia, Bijan. 2-Oct-02. XML and the Semantic Web. *XML Journal,* pp 30–34. Available at *www.xml-journal.com.*

Horrocks, I. 29-Nov-00. A Denotational Semantics for Standard OIL and Instance Oil. Web article: *www.ontoknowledge.org/oil/downl/semantics.pdf.* Ontology interchange layer.

Horrocks, I. 9-Dec-01. Commands. Web page: *www.cs.man.ac.uk/`horrocks/DAML-OIL/daml-oil.rdf.*

Kannan, Robert, et al. 12-Nov-02. Semantic Web for Collaborative Software Processes. Web article: *http://bluehawk.monmouth.edu/academic/dna/weti96ff.htm*. Semantic Web.

Klyne, Graham, et al. 15-Mar-01. Composite Capability/Preference Profiles (CC/PP): Structure and Vocabularies. Web article: *www.w3.org/TR/CCPP-struct-vocab/*.

Koivunes, Marja-Riitta. 12-Dec-01. SW Principles 3: Web of Trust. Web page: *www.w3.org/Talks/2001/1102-semweb-fin/slide14-0.html*.

Lassila, Ora, Swick, Ralph R. 22-Feb-99. Resource Description Framework (RDF): Model and Syntax Specification. Web article: *www.w3.org/TR/REC-rdf-syntax/*. RDF.

McBride, Brian. 8-Nov-02. Resource Description Framework (RDF): Concepts and Abstract Syntax. Web article: *www.w3.org/TR/2002/WD-rdf-concepts-20021108/*. RDF.

McBride, Brian. 24-Nov-02. RDF Semantics. Web article: *www.w3.org/TF/rdf-mt/*.

Ogbuji, Uche. 2-Jun-02. The Language of the Semantic Web. *New Architect Magazine*, pp 30–33. Available at *www.newarchitectmag.com*. Good overview of RDF.

Patel, Manjula. Harvesting RDF. Metadata PowerPoint presentation: *www.ukoln.ac.uk/*.

Robie, Jonathan. The Syntactic Web. Web article: *www.idealliance.org/papers/xml2001/papers/html/03-01-04.html*. Makes the case that XML by itself is not semantic.

Uschold, Michael. Where are the Semantic in the Semantic Web? Web article: *lsdis.cs.uga.edu/events/Uschold-talk.htm*. Great material on some key semantic distinctions, such as the explicit/tacit dichotomy.

Weinberger, David. 14-Jun-02. The Semantic Argument. Web article: *www.darwinmag.com/read/swiftkick/column.html?ArtilcleID=421*.

Glossary

Term	Context or *Acronym Expansion*	Definition
A2A	*application to application*	Integration between two applications without human intervention.
A2H	*application to human*	One-way interaction, application to human, as in flight monitors or "push" technology.
abduction	logic	To create hypotheses about probable causes from patterns observed. This is the primary source of new knowledge. Data mining is essentially an abductive process. See also *induction* and *deduction.*
abstract	class or ontology design	More generalized representation (e.g., *animal* is more abstract than *bear*).
accidental	problem/solution	The complexity of a solution that is introduced by the tools and methods of solving the problem. See *essential.*
accretive	changes, especially to a system	Changes that add on gradually, without disruption, similar to the way a river changes its contour by silting up at the bends. Antonym: evulsive.
acronym	lexical	Word formed from the initial letters of a compound word or phrase.
acyclic	hierarchy, graph, network	Does not loop recursively. If you were one of your own ancestors, you would have a cyclic family tree.

Term	Context or Acronym Expansion	Definition
adapters	software	Small software components that bind an interface to an existing application.
agent	software	Autonomous software program acting on a user's behalf.
aggregate	model	Type of relationship that implies ownership.
agile methods	methodology	Approach to software development that relies on the design and the requirements emerging from the process of building and interacting with the sponsors of the project. See *XP*.
algorithm	software	Procedural, step-by-step method to solve a given problem.
aliases	vocabulary	Synonym.
ambiguity	vocabulary	Definition or identification that leaves uncertainty as to the specific assignment of referent to thing.
anonymizing	software	Property of hiding identity from one software module to reduce its specific dependency on one implementation.
antonymy	vocabulary	Opposite (e.g., "good" is an antonym of "bad").
API	*Application Processing Interface*	A published interface to an application or module that allows the programs to call or invoke services.
applets	software	Small units of an application.
application	software	Group of software functionalities implemented together to solve a business problem.
application server	infrastructure	Middle tier in a three-tier architecture, where business logic is performed.
architecture	software	Overall arrangement of the components out of which applications are built and delivered. More than just the selection of tools.
artificial intelligence (AI)	software	Software that performs some function that we had previously ascribed to humans only, such as natural language processing.

Term	Context or Acronym Expansion	Definition
ASCII	*American Standard Code for Information Interchange*	Character set used by most PCs. As opposed to EBCDIC (the mainframe character set) and Unicode (the internationalized character set).
assert	logic programming	Establish a fact (e.g., assert that Robert Jones is employee 1234).
association	modeling	Type of relationship that does not imply ownership.
associative database	modeling	Style of database design that uses sentences to describe associations.
asynchronous	software	Style of message or RPC invocation where the sender does not wait for a response from the receiver.
atomic	database	Smallest whole unit of work. An atomic transaction is one that must complete or fail in its entirety.
attribute	modeling	A property of an entity, other than a relationship. Usually single valued.
auditability	process	Capability of a process to be reviewed by a third party after the fact. Generally requires nonalterable log, identification of users, etc.
authentication	software	Verifying that persons or agents are who they claim to be.
available	software	Property of a system that is operable and can be accessed by the users or agents who need it. Often measured in the percent of potential time it is actually available (as in 99.999% availability).
axiom	logic	Description of self-evident truth.
B2B	*business to business*	Integration between businesses (as opposed to business to consumer) characterized by the potential for more investment in the interaction and potentially higher volume of transactions.

Term	Context or Acronym Expansion	Definition
B2C	*business to consumer*	Merchandizing directly to consumers, typically through a Web site.
behavior	object-oriented software	Methods that execute code.
bill of material	model	Hierarchic structure of parts; can be "to be" (the ordered parts list to build a car) or "as is" (the specific parts that went into this car).
binary	relationship	Two-way relationship. A relationship with an inverse.
bind	software	Attaching a request to an implementation. Implementations are in specific technologies, and to invoke them one has to attach an often abstract description of a request to the specific module that will invoke it. Adaptors bind to applications.
bit	software	Single binary unit of data (a 1 or a 0).
Biztalk	product	Microsoft's message orchestration product.
blocking	software	To wait for a reply after a request has been made. A blocking request makes the interaction synchronous for the requestor.
BNF	*Bakus-Naur form*	Language for expressing the grammar of a programming language.
bootstrapping	software	Process of bringing up a software environment. Software has the problem of having to exist in some context. Often the context in which software was created is not available on another machine. By convention, there is a small number of instructions that all environments understand; the bootstrap process defines more and more elaborate contexts, in sequence, to create the context in which the complete systems will run. Note similarity to the ontology problem.
bots	software robots	Agents.

Term	Context or Acronym Expansion	Definition
bozo	people	Person whose opinions you distrust. From Bozo the Clown. Bozo filters are put on email clients or discussions to screen out known bozos.
BPEL4WS	*business process execution language for Web Services*	Standards for the definition of multiple-step Web service–mediated process flow.
BPSS	*business process specification schema*	The ebXML work flow specification.
broker	software	A go-between. A message broker is a piece of software that you send your message to instead of its final destination. This frees the sender from having to know about the final recipient.
bursty	communication	Communication or message that does not come at a uniform rate; it comes in "bursts."
byte	software	Single character, 8 bits. Base unit of storage size.
cache	software	A storage of data either nearer to the end use or in a form that is easier to use. Intended to reduce latency at time of use.
canonical	message/model	An accepted standard. In message modeling, it is the process of declaring a standard for message content rather than allowing each project to define its own.
capital	software economics	A one-time investment in a process that is expected to reduce operating costs over time.
cardinality	modeling	Constraint on the number of successors on a relationship. The cardinality for the relationship "biologic mother" is 1; for "biologic child" it is 0 or greater.

Term	Context or Acronym Expansion	Definition
categorize	modeling	To ascribe an instance to a knowledge-level group, for the purpose of inferring additional information about the instance.
causation	modeling	Relationship with teleologic attribute. For example, travel causes displacement/motion.
CDATA	XML/HTML	Character data that is meant to be ignored by the parser (e.g., images). See also *PCDATA*.
ChemXL	XML	Standard XML vocabulary for the chemical industry.
choreography	messaging	Prespecifying the sequence of operations in a standard work flow. Same as *orchestration*.
class	object-oriented development	Definition of attributes and behaviors for a type of instance. Basic modules for object-oriented development (OO). In OO, *class* and *type* are nearly synonyms, but the slight difference causes considerable problems.
client	software	Requestor. Also the user interface tier in a three-tier architecture.
coarse grain	service	Service that does a large unit of work. Collecting an overdue receivable would be a coarse-grain service.
CODASYL	*Conference on Data Systems Languages;* database	Prerelational database standard that used a network model in which database navigation followed predefined pointers.
cohesion	software design	Property of a module in which all the parts belong together. In a cohesive module all the parts are closely related; there are no extraneous parts.
column	database	Attribute for relational databases.
COM	*component object model*	Microsoft standard for binding local components.

Term	Context or *Acronym Expansion*	Definition
combinatorial	system	Complexity increases more than proportionally with number of interacting parts.
commitment to ontology	Semantic Web	Declaration that a domain or document makes in terms of using and agreeing with the meaning of terms from a particular ontology. Key to different documents being able to intercommunicate.
compiled	software	Source code converted to machine-specific instructions (which bind the source code to the machine instruction set).
composite application	software	Combination of more than one "back-end" system into one unit of work. Often combined into one user interface.
compound	words	Group of individual words whose meaning can only be known in combination (e.g., World Series).
conceptual model	modeling	Model independent of implementation.
conceptualization	ontology	Abstract, simplified view of the world that we wish to represent for some purpose.
configurable	architecture	Style of development in which independent components can be configured into new combinations. Promotes flexibility. Distinct from *customization,* which, in changing a particular configuration, makes it rigid.
configurable	application package	Data-driven parameters that can be set at implementation time to achieve different behaviors from the system.
conjunction	logic	And.
ConnectBy	database	Oracle-specific SQL extension for bill of material processing in relational database.
consortium	vocabulary	Group of companies.
constraints	database	Predicates that must be true or else transactions will not be committed.

Term	Context or Acronym Expansion	Definition
content	data	Intellectual property. Often documents or messages.
contracts	software design	Style of design that sets up contracts between calling and called routines. Can be evaluated at run time.
contracts	legal	Intentionally obscured agreements between parties for the purpose of requiring more human interpretation.
copybooks	software	Early form of "include" statements that would copy standard code or data definitions from a library.
CORBA	*common object request broker architecture*	Middleware developed under OMG. Platform-neutral way for programs to call other programs.
cosmology	philosophy	Subdiscipline of metaphysics concerned with the nature of being.
coupling	design	Linking two software components such that they are dependent on each other.
cowpaths	architecture	Initial way something is done, which, if mindlessly repeated, will become doctrine.
customization	software	Changing a software package source code to more closely match a particular set of requirements. Increases maintenance effort, makes upgrades difficult, and often invalidates warranties.
CWMI	*common warehouse metadata interchange*	Standard for expressing metadata between data warehouse products.
cXML	*Commerce XML*	Standards for eProcurement.
cyclomatic	design	Measure of the complexity of control structure of a procedural program.
DAG	*directed acylic graph*	Graph (network) in which all the nodes are connected and prevented from looping.

Term	Context or Acronym Expansion	Definition
DAML	*DARPA agent markup language*	Extensions to RDF to create ontologies for the Semantic Web.
DAML+OIL	ontology	DAML and OIL are used together often enough that the combination is referred to as DAML+OIL.
DARPA	*Defense Advanced Research Projects Agency*	Funding source for early Internet and currently the Semantic Web.
database	computer systems	Place to persistently store data
DCOM	*distributed component object model*	Microsoft's standard for binding to distributed components.
DDL	*data definition language*	The language used to describe the data definitions (metadata) in relational systems.
declarative	software	Type of language in which code writer does not control the flow of control at execution time.
decomposition, functional	design	Style of breaking a problem down into its constituent parts along functional lines.
decoupling	design	Process of separating software modules that had previously been coupled, for the purpose of improving the flexibility and ability to change the parts independently.
deduction	logic	To infer knowledge of an instance from its membership in a category or type. The process of using knowledge but not of creating it.
default	user interface	Property values that are true often enough that they are provided as a time-saving aid to a data entry operator.
default	database	Property values for a category or class that are generally held to be true for all members, but can be distinguished from those that have been declared to be true for the instance.

Term	Context or Acronym Expansion	Definition
definition	vocabulary	Description of what something means; often sufficient for humans, rarely sufficient for software agents.
delegation	software design	Act of turning over to another module the specific implementation of some feature. The delegator need not know how the delegatee implements the function.
delimiters	messages	Separators in a message that allow a parser to know where one element starts and ends.
dependency	software design	Recognition that one software component will be adversely affected if another one changes. Most software has dependencies on its operating system, but will also have dependencies of an often deep stack of other software components.
deployment	software implementation	Act of getting software functionality into the field.
design by contract	message architecture	Style of message design or service architecture in which "contracts" are established between applications and services regarding allowed calling conventions and service to be provided.
design by contract	object-oriented design	Style of development in which "contracts" are established between classes in an object-oriented design. Contracts are instantiated as preconditions and postconditions or assertions.
design time	software	Refers to things that must be changed when the software is being designed (or modified). For example, a scheduling algorithm is normally a design-time choice. However, it is possible to design an architecture in which the algorithm is a run-time option that could be selected by a user or another software component
developers	people	People who create software.

Term	Context or Acronym Expansion	Definition
dialect	language	Subset of a language agreed to by a group of people. Similar to an ontology, with the members of the group who share the dialect being committed to the ontology.
dictionary	database	Place where metadata for the definition of tables, columns, and so on are stored.
dictionary	language	Collection of word definitions, with the purpose of distinguishing closely related words. Most dictionaries contain considerable encyclopedia functionality, which obscures their distinction function.
dimension	general	Aspect or element from which you can regard something.
dimension	data warehousing	One of the axes in a data warehouse that can be used to query or summarize the facts in the warehouse.
directed	model	In a network model the property that says whether the arcs have "arrows." A project plan is "directed" in that the precedent relationships go in a particular direction. A thesaurus is undirected in that the definitions are only related, without having a direction to them.
directed graph	model	Graph in which the arcs are directed.
disambiguate	vocabulary	Process of selecting between alternative, ambiguous, interpretations. Conversationally, people do this by asking, "Do you mean x or y?"
dispatch	message architecture	To send a request to its final destination. A broker *dispatches* messages.
distinction	vocabulary	To set up rules for disambiguating closely related concepts.
DML	*data manipulation language*	Language that allows agents to access or change data in a database. SQL is by far the most common DML.

Term	Context or Acronym Expansion	Definition
DMOZ	*directory Mozilla*	Group of volunteers who categorize Web sites.
DNS	*Domain Name Server*	Designated node that assigns or tracks names and their relation to devices (e.g., jones.com is at IP 198.243.127.19).
document	data	The content in a message or other intellectual property. May be encoded in XML, but needn't be.
document	paper	Physical object in the real world. Lawyers refer to the "wet ink" as being the physical document that has the original signature.
DOM	*document object model*	API that allows programmers to access nodes in an XML document. Operates in memory, so not appropriate for extremely large documents. See *SAX*.
domain	general	Area under consideration (e.g., the *domain* of eCommerce or manufacturing).
domain	relational	Set of all possible values for an attribute. See also *range (relational)*.
domain	ontology	A constraint on the classes on which a property can be used.
DSD	*document structure description*	Early XML schema language.
DTD	*document-type definition*	Schema language for SGML and XML.
Dublin Core	ontology	Standard ontology for documents.
dynamic	design	Characterized as being able to change at run time.
EAI	*enterprise application integration*	Industry and products involved in making the interfacing of applications more economical.
EBCDIC	*extended binary coded decimal interchange code*	Mainframe character set. See *ASCII*.

Term	Context or Acronym Expansion	Definition
ebXML	*electronic business XML*	United Nations–sponsored standards for eCommerce.
eCommerce	*electronic commerce*	Doing business through computers (without human intermediaries).
EDI	*electronic data interchange*	Standards for high-volume B2B transactional exchange.
EER	*extended entity relationship*	Entity relationship design with inheritance.
effectivity	versioning	Versioning scheme in which portions of a structure become available or unavailable as of certain dates. A manufacturer may make a model change "date effective," meaning that after a certain date it will manufacture the model in a different way.
element	XML	Atomic unit of meaning in XML.
elicit	process	To draw out; especially to draw out the meaning of something from a group of users.
eMarketplace	eCommerce	Place where people or agents go to meet others involved in trade.
empiricists	philosophy	Group of eighteenth-century philosophers who believed that most of what we know comes from our senses.
encrypting	software	Process of obscuring data such that unauthorized users cannot understand it.
encyclopedia	vocabulary	A description of what is known about a concept. This is distinct from distinguishing one concept from another, closely related, concept.
entailment	logic	Semantic implication within a context; for example, buying *entails* paying.
enterprise	organization	General term for businesses, government organizations, and nonprofit organizations.
entity	database	Basic element used to construct relational designs.

Term	Context or Acronym Expansion	Definition
epistemology	philosophy	Branch of philosophy that studies the nature of knowledge.
eProcurement	software	Act of buying over the Internet.
equivalent	logic	Two representations of the same thing.
ER	*entity relationship*	Style of design focused on entities and their relationships to each other.
ERP	*enterprise resource planning*	Originally *manufacturing resource planning,* but generalized for nonmanufacturing companies. Has become synonymous with *large-scale integrated applications.*
essential	problem/solution	That which is necessary. Fred Brooks, in *The Mythical Man-Month: Essays on Software Engineering* (Addison-Wesley, 1975), distinguished between "essence" and "accident" as the two sources of complexity in software systems. The essential part was that which had to do with the problem and could not be gotten rid of. The accidental part was that which we introduced to the problem in attempting to solve it.
ETL	*extract, transform, and load*	A data warehouse architecture that separates the population of a data warehouse into three stages: *extracting* data from the source; *transforming* it into a form suitable for update; and *loading* it, which is an efficient posting process.
evulsive	changes, especially to a system	Rapid, discontinuous change (e.g., a change to a data structure that breaks dependent modules).
exabyte	data storage	One billion gigabytes (1,000,000,000,000,000,000 bytes).
exception	process flow	A non-normal control flow; often an error generated by an environmental issue (e.g., disk full).
explicit	semantic	Formal expression of knowledge.

Term	Context or Acronym Expansion	Definition
extensible	database or model	Capable of being added to accretively. An extensible data structure is one to which additive changes can easily be made. Relational databases are extensible at the table level, in that columns can be added to tables without requiring programs to be rewritten.
extensional	model	A set defined by a specific list. The states of the United States is an *extensional* set. See *intensional*.
extract	data warehousing	Select and copy data from a source to be used for subsequent processing.
fan in/out	modeling	Cardinality of relationship. If an object refers to many other objects, we say it has a high degree of fan out. If it is referred to by many other objects, we say it has a high degree of fan in.
fat client	architecture	Architecture in which user interface and business logic are on the desktop tier. Drawback is that every change to the system potentially involves complex deployment and rollout to make the changes to all the affected desktops.
field	data	Legacy system equivalent of a column.
fine grain	service	Service that does a small unit of work. An example of an extremely fine-grain service would be one that added two numbers together.
finite autonoma	software	State machine with a finite number of states and transitions.
firewall	architecture	Component, usually hardware and software, intended to enforce policies of access control to an intranet.
FOAF	*friend of a friend*	Ontology about people and their properties.
folk genera	linguistics	Nonscientific creation of categories for dealing with nature. Deals with the way people make and use categories.

Term	Context or Acronym Expansion	Definition
GAAP	*generally accepted accounting practices*	Rules about what the categories in financial statements mean; rules about other accounting treatments.
generalize	ontology	To create a more abstract definition or category.
geospatial	ontology	Pertaining to locations and regions on the earth. Can be located and reasoned about in terms of area.
gigabyte	data storage	One billion bytes.
glossary	vocabulary	Dictionary.
grain	service	See *coarse grain* and *fine grain*.
grammar	language	Set of rules for ordering vocabulary items. In computer science may be expressed formally (e.g., in a BNF).
granularity	service	Size of the service; see *coarse grain* and *fine grain*.
graph	model	A model of entities (nodes) connected to relationships (arcs).
grounding	semantics	Connection of implication to empirical data. How we connect pure thought to the real world.
GUI	*graphic user interface*	Presentation of an interface for use by a human, on a graphic screen with a pointing device.
H2A	*human to application*	Interface in which a human supplies information to an application. Data entry.
H2A2H	*human to application to human*	Traditional application that combines aspects of the application supplying data to the person and vice versa.
H2H	*human to human*	A computer application in which the application makes no semantic distinctions and simply passes along uninterpreted information. Email is H2H, except for the header data.

Term	Context or Acronym Expansion	Definition
hiding, data	software design	Design principle in which more maintainable code is promoted by hiding much of the detail of the implementation from the invoker. This allows the called routine to change some details without considering how it will affect other programs. Greatly reduces dependency.
hierarchy	ontology	Tree-style arrangement of terms or classes in which each child has only one parent (single inheritance).
histogram	data	Statistics on the frequency of occurrence of keywords by an optimizing routine to make searches faster.
homonym	linguistics	Two different meanings sharing the same word and the same spelling (e.g., *mogul* the emperor versus *mogul* the ski bump).
HTML	*hypertext markup language*	Tag language on which the World Wide Web is based. Markup is for presentation only.
HTTP	*hypertext transfer protocol*	Standard request to Web servers. Protocol on which much of the World Wide Web is based.
hype	marketing	Attempt to gain market share by promoting a product as revolutionary or a breakthrough. To substantiate such claims, vendors often craft claims that obfuscate the real capability of products. This can lead to Gartner's "trough of disillusionment."*
hyperbolic	visualization	Style of presenting hierarchic data that recenters the view on a selected item, which allows a user to navigate a complex space more easily.
hyperlink	document	A one-way reference from one document to another. Originally promoted by Ted Nelson, hyperlinks became implemented in the World Wide Web as the navigational links followed from one Web page to another.

*Ted Nelson, Literary Machines. San Antonio: Project Xanadu, 1987.

Term	Context or Acronym Expansion	Definition
hypernymy	ontology	Word of a more specific meaning; for example, "Arabian" is a kind of "horse."
hyponymy	lexical	Inverse of *hypernymy*; for example, "mammal" is a more general type than "horse."
idealism	philosophy	Belief that the categories we deduce from observation are imperfect forms of a generalized ideal.
identify	semantics	To associate the description of an entity with its real-world counterpart.
identity	semantics	That which we perceive to be permanent about a perceived real-world entity; the identity of a person or an organization
idiolect	language	Dialect spoken by an individual.
implementation	software	Instantiation of and conversion to a software application.
induction	logic	Process of creating categories from instances. Probabilistic reasoning.
inference	semantics	Reasoning from known propositions.
infrastructure	software	The environment that must be present for an application to operate.
inheritance	software	The accretion of properties and behaviors from a hyponym.
input	software	Act of supplying information to an application.
instances	software or data	Specific individual groups of data, usually created from some sort of template. In object-oriented systems, calling "new()" on a class creates an object that is of the type of the class. In a database system, inserting a row in a table creates an instance of that entity.
instantiate	software	The act of creating an instance.

Term	Context or *Acronym Expansion*	Definition
integrator	person, organization	Humans who build interfaces between applications.
intellectual property	semantics	Property created by humans; not necessarily tangible. Includes documents, ideas, patents, songs, movies, brands, trade secrets, software, content, databases, and knowledge.
intensional	model	A set defined by rules. Each time the rules are executed you may get a different set. The set of customers with overdue balances is an intentional set. Opposite of extensional.
interface	software	Subset of a component's functionality that is presented for other programs to access. Could be a data interface or a behavioral interface. *See data hiding.*
interface, user	H2A or A2H	See *GUI.*
interfacing	integration	A style of integration that relies on programmed point-to-point interfaces.
intermediary	eCommerce	One (usually a person or company) who acts as a go-between in eCommerce; attempts to disintermediate (take out) as many intermediaries as possible.
intermediate	integration	A common representation that allows many interfaces to be written to the common interface instead of to each other. Reduces combinatorial explosion.
Internet	network	Set of computers that address each other through DNS and URLs, use HTTP for the primary access protocol, and display information in HTML. Global in scope, traveling over public networks, as opposed to intranets.
interpret	language	Process of making sense out of the world or spoken language.

Term	Context or Acronym Expansion	Definition
interpret	software	To compile source instructions one at a time as needed. This delays binding to machine instructions until run time.
intranet	network	Use of Internet technologies and tools in a private network.
inverse of	model	For bidirectional relationships, the one that "goes the other way" ("child" is the inverse of "parent").
invoked	software	Called, or executed.
isa	model	Shorthand for the specialization/ generalization relationship. Basis for inheritance in object-oriented design. See also *subsumption*.
iterative	method	Method that approaches a problem by successive reapplications of the same process. Distinct from waterfall style, which attempts to do the design and build processes once.
J2EE	*Java 2 Platform Enterprise Edition*	Java-based framework for middleware, particularly at the application server level.
jargon	language	Words in a dialect intended to keep the nonmembers from knowing what's going on.
join	relational database	In relational databases, process whereby two tables are combined into one based on their sharing of key values.
junction	database design	Entity whose role it is to resolve many-to-many cardinality relationships. For example, for there to be a relationship between students and classes in a relational design, there must be a junction record.
key	database design	An attribute or attributes that are designated to identify a particular entity. Social Security number is often used as a key for a "person" entity.

Term	Context or Acronym Expansion	Definition
keyword	content	To find content, we extract some of the less common words from a document and index them back to their location in the document.
KIF	*knowledge interchange format*	Standard format for exchanging rules between AI systems.
knowledge	model	An agent has knowledge of a scenario or context to the extent that it has a model that provides some degree of predictability.
knowledge level	AI, modeling	Part of a model in which you reason about the behavior of the system rather than its implementation.
languages	human	The spoken and written utterances that humans use to communicate (e.g., English and Chinese). Each has its own vocabulary, grammar, and ontology.
languages	computer	Utterances intended to be readable by humans that can be translated into an equivalent set of instructions that can be processed by a computer. Each has its own vocabulary, grammar, and ontology.
latency	network	The time delay between a request and a reply. *Latency* is affected by network congestion, the number and type of intermediaries, and the processing done at the receiving site.
layers	architectures	Separation of an architecture into components, each of which deals with information at different levels of abstraction. The ISO seven-layer protocol for communication is a classic example. Also often referred to as "stack."
LDBT	*long-duration business transaction*	Basis for most business processes. LDBTs are events that usually originate from a stimulus outside the company, and take human-scale time to complete. For example, procuring a part could take hours to months,

Term	Context or *Acronym Expansion*	Definition
		especially to completely close it out by receiving it and paying for it.
legacy	system	An older application. May frustrate sponsors because it is difficult to change, no one knows exactly what it does, or components on which it is dependent are becoming obsolete.
lexical	language	Pertaining to words, as in a lexical analysis of text.
lexicographer	language	Person who writes dictionaries.
lexicon	vocabulary	Computer-readable dictionary of attributes.
linguistic	language	Pertaining to language.
literal	data	Constant variable (sounds like an oxymoron).
loose coupling	architecture	Arrangement whereby components are attached in a way that makes them easier to detach and reattach at run time, promoting easier change.
lumpers	categorizers	A category of categorizers who tend to group things into fewer, larger categories.
made item	semantic	Physically discrete item, with persistent identity, that was manufactured.
magnitude	semantic	Measurement on one of these dimensions: distance, mass, or time.
mainframe	architecture	Older-style centralized computer architecture, still supporting a huge number of legacy applications.
maintainability	software	Property of an application that makes it easier to change; includes desirable features such as high cohesion, loose coupling, literate programming, low cyclomatic complexity, and good documentation.
mandatory	model	In a relationship, a constraint that a particular relationship must have at least one successor.

Term	Context or *Acronym Expansion*	Definition
Markov	algorithm	Statistical algorithm for finding patterns and predicting similarity in unstructured documents.
markup	language	Annotating documents by inserting matching tags to offset certain sections.
marshal	communication	To serialize a set of data for transmission.
mereology	semantics	Study of part/whole relationships.
meronomy	semantics	Terms related through a part/whole relationship (sometimes called *metonymy*).
message	architecture	A request or reply expressed in data; often expressed as an XML document.
message	object-oriented design	Object-oriented design refers to a method call as a message, even though it is a function call.
message broker	software	A software intermediary that dispatches messages to their correct site.
message-oriented middleware	architecture	Style of architecture that features intercomponent communication through messages and message routing through a message broker.
meta	general	To transcend or go above. For most of computer science it means "about," as in "*metadata* is data about data."
metadata	data	Data about data. Includes data that describes how data is stored, where it is stored, how it is validated, and what it means.
metametadata	data	Data about metadata (usually at a high level of abstraction).
metapattern	architecture	An architecture that takes context as one of its central premises.

Term	Context or Acronym Expansion	Definition
metaphysics	philosophy	Branch of philosophy that deals with understanding the fundamental nature of everything, particularly the relationship of mind to matter.
method	object-oriented design	Function bound to a class.
middleware	software	Non–application-specific software that performs infrastructure tasks.
model-theoretic semantics	semantics	An account of meaning in which sentences are interpreted in terms of a model of, or an abstract formal structure representing, an actual or possible state of the world.
MOM	*message-oriented middleware*	See *message-oriented middleware*.
MRP	*manufacturing resource planning*	Application that manages most of the functions of a manufacturing company.
multiple inheritance	software/ ontologies	Framework that allows classes to inherit from more than one parent.
MVC	*model view controller*	Design paradigm for GUI applications that separates the underlying *model* (what is being manipulated) from the *view* (the presentation of the model) and from the *controller* (the set of events that are allowed to be performed by the user). By overlaying the controller functions on the view, it creates the illusion of direct manipulation.
mycophagist	food	Someone who eats mushrooms.
N3	*Notation3*	Shorthand way of writing RDF.
NAICS	*North American Industrial Classification System*	Revised taxonomy of business classification; replaces Standard Industrial Code (SIC).
n-airty	relation	See *valence*.
namespace	semantics	Domain within which a name is guaranteed to be unique and findable.

Term	Context or Acronym Expansion	Definition
navigational	data model, UI	Refers to following a series of links or pointers to accomplish a task. A navigational user interface has users go from screen to screen to accomplish a task (as opposed to a composite application). A navigational data model relies on a programmer traversing pointers to get to additional data.
net (.net)	software	Microsoft's XML-based framework.
network	computer system	Topologic arrangement of hardware and connections to allow access to shared components.
network	model	Graph where nodes can have more than one entrance arc, as distinct from a hierarchy that allows only one inbound link.
NIAM	*Nijssen's information analysis method*	Predecessor to ORM.
NLP	*natural language processing*	Branch of artificial intelligence that deals with interpreting and generating humanlike speech.
NLP	*neurolinguistic programming*	Discipline within therapy that deals with how language reveals impoverished mental models that prevent people from accomplishing their goals.
nomenclature	vocabulary	Set of names for terms in a given domain.
nominalization	linguistics	To convert a verb to a noun. Used in software programs to create a handle for a method.
normalization	database	Arrangement of attributes to tables in a relational design so as to avoid update anomalies. Ensuring that each property is dependent only on the primary keys of its table.
Notation3	semantics	Shorthand way of writing RDF.
OCR	*optical character recognition*	Applications that can read typed or handwritten characters and convert to ASCII text.

Term	Context or Acronym Expansion	Definition
ODBC	*open database connectivity*	Standard to allow programmers to write to an abstract relational database layer and delay binding until run time.
OIL	*ontology inference layer*	Standard for defining ontologies.
OMG	*object management group*	Nonprofit organization that promotes open systems standards.
ontology	semantics	Specification of a conceptualization.
OO	*object oriented*	A style of software development organized around classes of objects, in which the code encapsulates the data. Promotes data hiding and cohesion. Class inheritance implements typing, as well as code reuse.
open systems	computer systems	Computer systems where at least the interfaces and very often the implementation is publically available and not controlled by a single entity.
orchestration	work flow	Preset direction of flow of activity. Synonymous with *choreography*.
ORM	*object role modeling*	Conceptual design notation focused on role modeling. Enables good modeling, especially for relationships of higher valence.
orthogonal	categorization	Literally "at right angles." Refers to finding aspects of categorization that are as independent of each other as possible.
OWL	*Web ontology language*	Successor to DAML + OIL; a proposed W3C standard. Note: Dyslexic acronym is attributed to the owl in Winnie the Pooh who spelled his name WOL.
package	application	Predeveloped generic application; an application software package.
package	software development	Unit of deployment for software, usually consisting of many OO classes.

Term	Context or Acronym Expansion	Definition
parse	software	To separate an incoming stream of data into its constituent parts based on a grammar and various delimiters.
PCDATA	XML/HTML	"Parse-able" character data; refers to text that can be parsed. See also *CDATA*.
PDA	*personal digital assistant*	Handheld computer typically for contact lists, calendar, and to-do lists.
perception	mind	Process whereby humans discern order in a complex world.
phenomenology	philosophy	Philosophy that reality consists of objects and events as perceived by human consciousness. Similar to the philosophy of the sophists.
platform	computers	Standard environment in which an application operates. Typically a family of compatible hardware and operating systems defines a platform; database management systems may also define a platform, as may the Internet protocols.
polymorphism	object-oriented design	Literally "to take many forms." In object-oriented design, subclasses of a class implement the public interface to the parent class in such a way that a message sent to a collection of parents and children would be responded to by each appropriately, without the caller knowing.
polysemous	linguistics	Word with multiple related meanings (e.g., *mouth*, the anatomic opening, and *mouth*, the opening of a cave).
portal	UI	Composite application presented through a Web front end. Often an attempt to bring all the interfaces available to a particular group of users to one point.
pragmatism	philosophy	Philosophy that holds that both the meaning and the truth of any idea is a function of its practical outome.

Term	Context or Acronym Expansion	Definition
precision, semantic	semantics	The degree of refinement or specificity applied to a particular semantic categorization. For example, *car repair manual* is a more semantically precise term than *document*, even though both may be equally accurate.
precompiler	software	A processor that runs before the primary compiler; may expand copybooks, "includes," and so on.
preconditions	software design	Assertions in design by contract that are enforced to be true prior to method executing.
predicate	logic	A statement you can make about something that can be evaluated later as true or false.
primary key	relational design	The unique identifier for instances of an entity. For example, in a customer table, we might declare that CustomerID is to be the primary key and therefore the unique identifier.
primitive	semantics	Types that are atomic and have no supertypes. Some maintain that there are a few semantic primitives from which all business-related applications can be built.
procedural	programming	Coding style in which flow of control is explicitly expressed by the programmer.
procedure	software	A coherent grouping of code.
procedure	work flow	Instructions for human users of computer systems that augment the built-in work flow.
processes	work flow	Higher-level abstractions of end-to-end business processes.
production	implementation	Area where the versions of applications that are approved for use by end users are kept.
program	software (verb)	To reduce an algorithm to code, usually procedural code.
program	software (noun)	A compilable unit of code.

Term	Context or Acronym Expansion	Definition
projection	database	The set of return values desired from a query.
property	semantic	That which is subject to ownership. Can be tangible or intellectual.
property	model	In object-oriented design, either an attribute or a relationship.
proprietary	software	Infrastructure in which the public interface is controlled by a single company or a small number of companies. Sometimes refers to single-company implementations of an open interface.
protocol	communications	Rules governing transmitting and receiving data.
prototypes	linguistics	A way of defining categories around exemplar representatives (e.g., a robin may be a prototype for the category "bird").
prototypes	software	Artifact in iterative development in which a disposable version of a user interface is presented to users and sponsors to allow them to clarify their requirements.
publish	message	At the occurrence of a predefined event, message is sent to all components that have indicated an interest by previously subscribing.
publish/subscribe	architecture	Style of interaction in which the consumers of information indicate that they are interested in certain types of changes from certain sources. When the change occurs they are notified via a message. This is instead of either continual polling, asking for the information when you need it (but it may not be available), or batching interfaces.
QOS	*quality of service*	Measure of the goodness of a communication channel (dropped packets, etc.).

Term	Context or Acronym Expansion	Definition
query	database (noun)	A declarative statement describing the data set that a user or program wants to obtain from a database.
query	application (verb)	To request information from a data store.
queue	infrastructure	Temporary storage for unprocessed messages; allows called process to operate more efficiently and ensures that all messages are processed.
range	relational	A restricted set of the domain of values to which an attribute can belong.
range	ontology	Restriction on the values of which a property must be a member.
RDF	*resource description framework*	Basic model for expressing knowledge in the Semantic Web.
RDFS	*RDF schema*	Adds schema properties to RDF, such as "subclass" and "inverse."
reachable	network	The set of all nodes in a graph that can be arrived at by traversing arcs.
recursive	programming	Flow of control in which a module calls a new instance of itself an indefinite number of times.
reference	model	To establish a one-way relationship to an object (point to).
referential integrity	database	Property of database management system that allows it to manage the relationship of instances in different tables such that a change or deletion in one table does not invalidate information in another. Referential integrity would prevent the deletion of a customer if there were still orders outstanding for that customer.
reify	semantics	To treat an abstraction as if it were real. Marriage is the reification of a relationship, as are most entities in most databases.

Term	Context or Acronym Expansion	Definition
relational	database	Database characterized by implementation of relationships by matching key values in different tables.
relationship	model	Named link between two objects that defines the kind of relationship instances might have. In business rules, a *relationship* is a fact.
relationship	instance	Set of pointers to other objects that a particular object is associated with via a named relationship.
repartitioning	architecture	Intentional effort to redefine the boundaries of a set of applications to achieve better cohesion at the application level, as well as potentially looser coupling.
repeaters	data structures	Parts of a data structure that occur more than once. May be a fixed number of repeaters. The number may be defined in a header record, or it may be undefined until a particular delimiter is encountered. Common in EDI and older data structures.
repository	metadata	Place to persistently store metadata. A database for metadata.
request	message	Type of message intended to solicit information; reply is called a *response*.
resource	RDF	In RDF terms, a URI or a literal.
response	message	Reply to request containing information.
rich client	architecture	Generalized client that is able to mimic much of the behavior of a fat client interface, allowing the user interface to be more responsive without having application specific client side code.
rights	semantic	Ownership primitives that indicate what an owner can do with owned property.
rigidity	architecture	Property of a system that makes it hard to change, generally due to overimplementation of dependencies.

Term	Context or Acronym Expansion	Definition
RMI	*remote method invocation*	J2EE method of invoking behavior on remote components.
robust	architecture	Designed in a way that is resilient to adverse events in the environment.
routing	middleware	Dynamic determination of destination of a message.
RozettaNet	eCommerce	Standards for supply chain eCommerce.
RPC	*remote procedure call*	Mechanism for invoking a component on another platform. Usually requires binding to the specific RPC technology.
RuleML	XML	XML standard for expressing rules.
run time	software	Refers to things that can change when the program is running as opposed to those things that must be changed when the program is being designed (or compiled). Shifting things (e.g., hardware, software, data) from design time to run time can make the system much more flexible.
RUP	*rational unified process*	Methodology promoted by Rational Corporation; uses UML and promotes iterative development.
SAML	*security assertions markup language*	Standard way to indicate authorizations.
SAX	*simple API for XML*	Programmable interface for an XML document that doesn't require it all be in memory.
scale	architecture	Ability to process larger volumes of work. Often requires an architecture that allows replication of processing units without a bottleneck.
schema	XML	Allowable tags and their sequencing, usually expressed in DTD or XSD.
schema	database	Data definition for tables.

Term	Context or Acronym Expansion	Definition
SCM	*supply chain management*	Application, or integration effort, to allow a company to have more oversight of the parts vendors, all the way through the chain of suppliers to the extractive vendors.
scope	application	Size or boundary. Scope may be described in terms of functions to be automated, or it may be defined in terms of degree of semantic precision required.
SDM	*semantic data modeling*	Conceptual database modeling based on semantics.
semantic	philosophy	Concerned with the study of meaning (often the meaning of words). In business systems we are concerned with making the meaning of data explicit (structuring unstructured data), as well as making it explicit enough that an agent could reason about it.
Semantic Web	network	Next-generation Internet in which all the content is tagged with semantic tags and committed to ontologies. An interlinking of ontologies will allow agents to reason about information only tangentially connected (and not previously connected by their creators).
semiotics	philosophy	Branch of linguistic study primarily concerned with human use of signs, symbols, syntax, and semantics.
sentient	mind	Capable of reasoning. Alternative definition includes being capable of feeling, but that has no applicability for business systems.
service	software (noun)	A software component that is accessed via a message. Typically the component executes on its own platform in its own environment, and only the result is sent back to the caller. Most non–service-based architectures involve the component executing in the caller's environment.

Term	Context or Acronym Expansion	Definition
SGML	*standard generalized markup language*	Early tagged document markup language. Was popular for complex document creation, but complexity of language led to it being largely superceded by HTML and XML.
SHOE	*simple HTML ontology extension*	An early project to extend HTML with semantic tags.
shredding	XML	Parsing an XML document into its constituent parts to be stored atomically in a relational database.
similarity	semantics	Lexical relations of words with related meaning. For example, "gluttonous" is similar to "greedy."
SKU	*stock-keeping unit*	Level of semantic precision used by inventory control systems. If red and blue widgets are interchangeable at the point of use, they will be identified by the same SKU number.
SOA	*service-oriented architecture*	Application architecture organized around the use of services, including Web Services.
SOAP	*simple object access protocol*	Wrapper for Web Service requests that allows them to be invoked across the Internet, including through firewalls.
SODA	*service-oriented development architecture*	See *SOA*.
software	computer systems	Intellectual property that imposes semantic meaning on input from humans or devices to which it is attached.
SOI	*service-oriented integration*	Performing EAI using service-based technologies.
sophists	philosophy	Group of philosophers who believed that the world existed only to the extent it was perceived. "Man is the measure of all things" was a saying of the sophists.
source	messaging	Point of origination of a request. May be important for auditability and security.

Term	Context or Acronym Expansion	Definition
source code	software	Human-readable procedural or declarative statements that can be compiled into equivalent machine-executable code.
specialization	ontology	Increasing semantic precision by subtyping. Almost an exact antonym to generalization, but there are a few obscure conditions where generalization and specialization are not inverses.
specs (specifications)	software	Reduction of requirements or design into a document to be used to direct further development.
splitters	ontology	People who are inclined to create new categories whenever new distinctions come up.
SQL	*Structured Query Language*	Declarative language for expressing queries and updates to relational databases.
state	object-oriented development	The values of all the properties of an object at a specific time.
state	software	A special type of category that allows the item being referenced to dynamically change properties as it changes state. Historically implemented in code or in a finite-state machine.
stateless	service	Property of a service that allows it to scale. The service does not maintain state (object-oriented style state) between invocations, so the next time a request is made it need not go back to the previous service.
static	object-oriented development	Methods that operate at the class level and do not need an instance to function.
static	software	Fixed binding or linkage. Not dynamic. Static linking cannot change at run time, as opposed to dynamic linking, which can.
status	category	Same as state (category), usually referring to the state of physical items or long-duration business transactions (e.g., "What is the status of this order?").

Term	Context or Acronym Expansion	Definition
store	database	To record data in a nonvolatile medium (the data will be retained even if the power is turned off or a program crashes).
STP	*straight-through processing*	Early acronym for what is now called Real Time Enterprise (RTE).
stub	software	Small bit of software. Sometimes refers to the start of a program generated by a case tool. May also refer to the bit of code that binds a request to a platform and API.
style sheet	declarative	Set of structured hints to be applied to a family of documents to create a particular type of display.
subroutines	software	Software modules usually compiled at the same time, and linked in with the calling program, but still obeying the rules of data hiding by only referring to shared data through the defined calling interface.
subscribe	message	Indicate to potential publisher of messages that a component is interested in receiving notification in the event of a change.
substance	philosophy	Physical material (e.g., "lumber" consists of the substance "wood").
subsumption	ontology	To classify, include, or incorporate in a more comprehensive category or under a general principle. The "isa" relationship.
subtypes	ontology	A proper subtype "is" one of its parent types, more specifically a specialization of that type.
Swetsville Zoo	place	Private park in Fort Collins where you can visit creatures made from surplus parts.
syllogism	philosophy	Style of inductive logic that starts with a generalization (all men are mortal), includes a categorization (Socrates is a man), and concludes with a semantic entailment or the instance taking on an attribute of the category (Socrates is mortal).

Term	Context or Acronym Expansion	Definition
symbolic	AI or formal semantics	Semantic reasoning with variables substituted for semantically known objects. Conclusions drawn at this level are universally true.
synchronous	messaging	Message style in which the requestor blocks and waits for a reply.
synonymy	ontology	Two terms that mean the same thing. As pointed out by John Saeed, there are few true synonyms.*
syntactic	semiotics	Concerning the grammar order or special characters in a document or message.
table	relational	Storage place for entities in a relational database. All entities are stored in tables, with each column representing an attribute.
tacit	semantics	That which has not been expressed in formal terms. Tacit knowledge may be knowledge we have without knowing that we have it.
tag	markup	Delimiters that also contain information. Most common type are matched tags such as ⟨t⟩42⟨/t⟩, which is the number 42 tagged by the tag "t."
taxonomy	semantics	A vocabulary ordered into a hierarchy, generally to find terms easily, and also to subtype the terms.
TBL	*Tim Berners-Lee*	WWW inventor; often goes by his initials.
technology	semantics	Application of knowledge to a problem area to improve performance or reduce use of resources. Clothing is a technology for conserving body heat. Vendors of software products would have you believe that their product is a technology for conserving something or performing something better.
templates	software	Preexisting outline that allows for the generation of new data conforming to the

*John Saeed, Semantics. Oxford, UK: Blackwell, 1997.

Term	Context or Acronym Expansion	Definition
		patten of the template. In object-oriented development a class is the template for the creation of a new object, but much more complex templates are possible.
temporal	semantic	Pertaining to time. Events and plans are temporal entities.
terabyte	storage	One thousand gigabytes. Data warehouses with a terabyte of information are now common.
term	business rule	Semantic object. Vocabulary item. The basic building block of facts and rules.
term	ontology	A label on a concept.
text	semantics	A portion of a document expressed in characters (as opposed to sound or graphics).
thing	semantics	Often the top of a generalization tree. This is the top object in the Cyc ontology. Some ontologies restrict "thing" to tangible real-world items with persistence.
tier	architecture	Original computer architectures were monolithic in that all processing occurred on a single machine. Over time, separation of concerns led to more flexible architectures by separating processing into different tiers. Two-tier systems typically had a fat client processing user interface and business logic on one tier (the desktop) and persistence on another tier (the database server). Three-tier architectures added a third layer in the middle (the application server) where most of the business logic migrated to. Current architectures are n tiered, where n is some positive integer.
time now	temporal	Concept of "now" implemented in systems. Should be expressed in Universal time (Greenwich Mean Time) to prevent issues with servers in different time zones recording

Term	Context or Acronym Expansion	Definition
		the same fact differently. Many temporal functions should be expressed in terms of *time now* (e.g., a task planned to start at some time before "time now" is probably late if there is no actual start time).
tipping point	fashion and epidemiology	A characteristic of complex systems that a particular phenomenon can exist for a long time until conditions are right for it to reach epidemic proportions. The inflexion point has been referred to by Malcolm Gladwell as the *tipping point*.
token	parsing	The unit to which a parser divides text for subsequent processing. For a tagged markup such as an XML document, this is the data between the tags (recursively).
topology	network	The spatial layout and interconnectedness of any type of network. We may speak of the topology of the hardware network, but we could also speak of the topology of an ontology (e.g., how much fan in/fan out exists).
traffic	network	Number of packets traversing a network.
transaction	database	An atomic unit of work that either succeeds or fails.
tree	model	A directed graph in which nodes are not referred to by more than one node (children do not have more than one parent).
trigger	database	Routine attached to a database table that is guaranteed to fire (execute) in the event of a prespecified occurrence (e.g., the updating of a particular attribute). The trigger will typically send a message, or side effect, that may update other tables in the database. Similar in structure to a publish/subscribe in which the publishers and subscribers are tables instead of programs and the database management system is managing the subscriptions.

Term	Context or Acronym Expansion	Definition
triple	RDF	Knowledge expressed in a three-part grammar, which has been called "subject, predicate, object," as well as "resource, property, values."
truth conditions	semantics	The conditions under which a sentence or a proposition expressed by it is true; for example, the statement "I have red hair" is true under the condition that the speaker has, in fact, red hair. It is not true in the abstract, but only when grounded.
Turing test	AI	Litmus test of artificial intelligence: Can a program fool enough people into believing that it is human that we should ascribe "intelligence" to it?
UDDI	*universal description, discovery, and integration*	Standard for a registry or yellow pages for finding services.
UML	*unified modeling language*	Modeling language for object-oriented development popularized by Rational Corporation.
UMLS	*unified medical language system*	Ontology of medical terms used for searching medical literature.
unambiguous	semantic	Refers to specific item or category in requisite level of semantic precision.
unary	relation	One-way relation; pointer. Most relations are *binary*, which means they are automatically maintained both ways and can be traversed both ways.
Unicode	character set	Character set rich enough to represent non–Latin-based languages, such as Chinese and Burmese.
unique	constraint	There cannot be more than one equivalent item of this type within the scope indicated. We may say that customer numbers must be *unique* (within our organization or database) or we may say that there can only be one

Term	Context or Acronym Expansion	Definition
		successor on a relationship, meaning there can't be more than one of that type in that set.
unstructured data	documents	Data (textual, video, sound, graphics) that has not been interpreted, tagged, or structured.
URI	*uniform resource identifier*	Unambiguous location of a resource in RDF.
URL	*uniform resource locator*	A resolvable location on the reachable Internet.
user	software	The role of a person relative to a particular application. For agents it is the person on whom the agent is working. Note that in both cases the user's identity is what confers security and authority.
valence	relation	Number of type of successors to a relationship. Also called the "*n*-arity." Most relationships have a valence of 2 (binary relationships), but relationships with a valence of 3 or 4 are not uncommon.
validation	XML/HTML	Determination that a document obeys all the rules set out in its schema.
veracity	semantics	Degree to which we believe something to be true. High veracity = high degree in belief in the truth of the assertion.
version	software, semantics	Modification of a basic instance that shares the same identifier. We can have different versions of a document that all contain the same basic document identifier. We can have different versions of an ontology, perhaps with date effectivity.
view	relational	A subset of a database as defined by a query.
vocabulary	semantics	List of terms in a particular dialect, often with definitions.

Term	Context or Acronym Expansion	Definition
VRML	*virtual reality markup language*	Description of a three-dimensional space, in a tagged document.
W3C	*World Wide Web Consortium*	Nonprofit organization responsible for maintaining the standards on which the World Wide Web is based.
warehouse	database	A copy of the operational data of a firm, stored to optimize analytic retrieval instead of updates. Also organized to be robust in regard to changes in the structure of the operational databases or the hierarchic roll-ups of the dimensions.
Water	XML	A scripting language for building XML-based Web sites.
waterfall	methodology	A style of development that progresses sequentially through a series of tasks to develop a software product. As opposed to iterative or agile methods.
Web Services	architecture	RPC in which the request is in XML. Allows caller and receiver to be in different technologies as long as each can queue the message and process the XML request or response.
well formedness	XML/HTML	Property that a given tagged document adheres to the rules of documents of that type (e.g., all the tags match). Does not require a schema. See *validation*. Note that most HTML tools and browsers have become slack on well formedness, to the point where one cannot rely on HTML tags matching.
WordNet	ontology	Open-source English language repository of meaning of one-half million concepts. Many of the concepts have hypernymy, polysymy, and mereologic links.
work flow	process	A prespecified sequence of human and computer activities that should complete a business activity.

Term	Context or Acronym Expansion	Definition
WSCI	*Web Services choreography interface*	Describes the flow of messages exchanged by Web Services in choreographed exchange. Pronounced "whiskey."
WSDL	*Web Services description language*	A description of the XML needed to invoke a specific Web Service. Pronounced "whizdull."
WSFL	*Web Services flow language*	Predecessor to BPEL4WS.
WWW	*World Wide Web*	The layer on top of the Internet that most people now think of as the Internet. Includes Web servers that are reachable by URLs and DNS, that accept HTTP requests on port 80, and that serve up user interfaces in HTML.
XCBL	*XML common business library*	Language promoted by CommerceOne for use in B2B eMarketplaces.
XDR	*XML data reduced*	Earlier version of XSD.
XLANG	work flow	Earlier version of BPEL4WS, expressly for Biztalk orchestration.
XMI	*XML metadata interchange*	Standard for interchanging metadata.
XML	*extensible markup language*	Tagged markup language, to which the tag set can be added. Note: It is considered poor form to capitalize the x in extensible.
XP	*extreme programming*	First of the agile methods, focused on pair programming, test as you go, and refactoring.
XP	operating system	Recent version of Microsoft Windows.
XPath	XML	Declarative way to define a subset of an XML document that you are interested in. Robust to many structural changes to the document.
XQuery	XML	Query language for retrieving data from an XML document or XML database.

Term	Context or Acronym Expansion	Definition
XSD	XML schema	Schema language for XML, expressed in XML (as opposed to DTD, which was not in XML).
XSL	*XML style sheet language*	Declarative language creating a style sheet for XML documents.
XSLT	*extensible style sheet language transformation*	Extension to XSL that includes more structural changes to an XML document.
Y2K	*year 2000* "Armageddon"	Remediation spending on legacy systems that were not, or were not believed to be, capable of processing in the new millennium due to ambiguity about century years in dates.
ZLE	*zero-latency enterprise*	Result of integrating a firm's processes in such a way that all the latency (especially the human-caused and batch-caused latency) has been removed and end-to-end processing happened immediately.

Index

P

The Savvy Manager's Guides

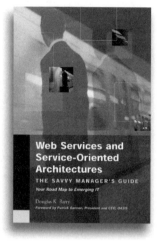

Web Services and Service-Oriented Architectures
THE SAVVY MANAGER'S GUIDE
Your Road Map to Emerging IT

Douglas K. Barry
Foreword by Patrick Gannon, President and CEO, OASIS

Business Intelligence
THE SAVVY MANAGER'S GUIDE
Getting Onboard with Emerging IT

David Loshin, Knowledge Integrity, Inc.
Foreword by Ronald J. Powell,
Publisher/Editorial Director of DM Review

Semantics in Business Systems
THE SAVVY MANAGER'S GUIDE
Your Road Map to Emerging IT

Dave McComb
Foreword by James Hendler, University of Maryland

SERIES EDITOR: DOUGLAS K. BARRY
WWW.SAVVYMANAGERSGUIDES.COM

Interesting, timely, and above all, useful, these books will give IT managers the information they need to effectively manage their technologists, as well as conscientiously inform business decision makers, in the midst of technological revolution.

Special Features

MORGAN KAUFMANN PUBLISHERS
AN IMPRINT OF ELSEVIER
WWW.MKP.COM

- Accessible descriptions of cutting-edge technologies, with increasing levels of technical depth
- Business justifications
- Advice on change management
- Back-of-book quick reference guide to buzz words and related technologies